A GOLDEN AGE OF CYCLING

A GOLDEN AGE OF CYCLING

A GENTLEMAN'S ADVENTURE ON TWO WHEELS, 1924-33

CHARLES JAMES POPE

EDITED BY SHAUN SEWELL

Published by 535
An imprint of Blink Publishing
3.08, The Plaza,
535 Kings Road,
Chelsea Harbour,
London, SW10 0SZ

www.blinkpublishing.co.uk

facebook.com/blinkpublishing
twitter.com/blinkpublishing

Hardback – 978-1-911-27430-8
Ebook – 978-1-911-27431-5

A CIP catalogue of this book is available from the British Library.

Typeset by Envy Design
Printed and bound by Clays Ltd, St. Ives Plc

1 3 5 7 9 10 8 6 4 2

Blink Publishing is an imprint of the Bonnier Publishing Group
www.bonnierpublishing.co.uk

CONTENTS

INTRODUCTION

THE 'GOLDEN AGE' OF CYCLING – THAT'S RIGHT NOW, ISN'T IT?

Cycling has certainly experienced a striking renaissance at all levels of riding in the last two decades. The unprecedented success at the Olympics and World Championships, and dominance of the Tour de France, has catapulted cycling to new heights of popularity and made household names of the cycling superstars of Hoy, Wiggins, Froome, Trott, Kenny and Boardman. Who would have thought 20 years ago that a cyclist would have the same marketing status as a Premier League footballer and would lift the coveted BBC Sports Personality award three times in the last decade?

This success has filtered down to all levels from the resurgent home Tours and an increase in amateur club cycling to a huge upturn in leisure and commuters cycling for the pure exhilaration of being on the open road or track. According to a British Cycling report over two million Britons cycle every week, a level never seen before. The Tour of Britain has really captured the imagination of the public who have given enormous support to a Tour which previously had been and gone through towns without much of a fuss. The Tour of Britain finishing in my home town of Blyth in Northumberland was the highlight of the year and brought the town to a standstill.

A GOLDEN AGE OF CYCLING

The only downside to modern day urban cycling in Britain is the perceived danger of cycling with the high level of motorised road users. Cycle paths have certainly helped but there's nothing like taking to the open road and cycling along the highways and byways of this beautiful nation. This was the utopia that Charles James Pope experienced in the years after the First World War to the middle of the 1930s. The perfect storm of more leisure time due to changes in the working week, improved and more reliable bicycles and an upsurge in the popularity of exploring the country alone or in a club creating the first golden age of cycling.

Charles returned from his service during World War One and fell in love with the ability to leave the stress of the working week in London behind and head out to adventures and exploration of the unspoilt beautiful towns and villages of rural England. The simple pleasure of cycling on a three gear bike with a Bartholomew map and the latest copy of the Cycling Tourist Club handbook to hand was all Charles needed to be happy and content. Charles' love of cycling was shared by the masses and the popularity of being part of the emerging cycling clubs made cycling the recreational craze of the time.

There was something quaint and romantic about the freedom of cycling from village to village only interrupted by a beer and a feed at a country pub at a pace you could appreciate the rustic rural life. The only horsepower Charles usually came across was the loyal Shire ploughing the fields or pulling the carts along the country lanes. However, the increased pace of life and 'advancement' is never far behind and Charles knew this life was changing with the advent of the increasing numbers of motor cars and the apparatus and support network the combustion engine needed.

Charles, throughout his diaries, made no secret that he greatly disliked the motor car and usually those who drove these vehicles. The need for new roads, stronger bridges, petrol stations was changing the land Charles knew so well and that it would change his cycling paradise forever. Looking back Charles was fortunate that he was the last generation of cyclists who could cycle without the noise and pollution the combustion engine brought upon the land. The freedom that cycling gave the working classes was soon to be taken over by the popularity of car ownership.

This interwar period was definitely the first golden age of cycling and Charles certainly made the most of it. Not only was it his route to freedom but it became his social life and would eventually be the catalyst to leave his bachelor days behind and married his beloved Doris.

INTRODUCTION

I am grateful that I managed to find Charles' diaries and photographic albums at an auction a few years ago and began the journey getting to know the man through his cycling tours of England and Wales in the 1920s and 1930s. I think anyone who has cycled will appreciate his writing and observations of life on two wheels. I am fortunate enough to live in an outstanding area of countryside and have cycled many thousands of miles through Northumberland on, at times, quiet and peaceful country lanes watching the change of seasons and vistas from my Raleigh Pioneer saddle. Although we are many years apart, I feel a certain kinship with Charles, and I hope after reading Charles' accounts of his cycling adventures you will too.

Shaun Sewell
Northumberland
April 2018

THE MAIN CHARACTERS

CHARLES JAMES POPE

Charles was born on 11th March 1879 in Bridge Road, Hammersmith, London. The Popes of Hammersmith were synonymous with the furniture and auction business for generations until the late 1960s. Charles' father, also named Charles James Pope, was a furniture warehouseman who sadly died in 1881 when Charles was only two years old.

It seemed that Charles spent most of his working career as a solicitor's clerk. His mother, Harriet, is recorded in the 1911 Census as living by her own means and his brother Edward Brownfield's occupation is listed as a clerk.

Charles enlisted in the First World War and served in the 5th London Rifles. During the summer of 1916 he trained at the Fovant Camp in Wiltshire. Prior to leaving for France, the Rifles carved their regimental badge into the chalk hillside. Other regiments followed the example of the London Rifles and carved their badges alongside. The hillside became a monument to those whose lives were lost in the Great War.

Charles' cycling diaries commence in 1924 at a time when cycling was beginning to be extremely popular and a means of escape and adventure from the working week. Charles became a member of the increasingly popular Cyclist's Touring Club in the early 1920s and later became a Life

Member. The CTC provided an opportunity for likeminded cyclists to meet and socialise. Indeed, after the untimely death of his brother Edward, Charles found companionship with Francis and Alphonsine Sissons and in 1933 Charles married his latest cycling partner Doris Willson. Charles, Doris and their children lived happily in Chearsley, Buckinghamshire until his death at the age of 72. Charles was killed in a road accident when cycling back home in May 1951 (see Postscript).

EDWARD BROWNFIELD POPE

Edward was born in 1877 and named after his grandfather and uncle. He worked as a clerk and served in WWI in the Royal West Sussex Regiment. The brothers shared their love of cycling and the early diaries record their adventures with Charles being the author. Edward died in 1930.

FRANK & 'FON' SISSONS

Francis Thomas and Alphonsine, Charles in his diaries affectionately shortened her name to 'Fon', Sissons (nee Vaillant) were Charles' cycling companions in the early 1930s. Although they were much younger (born in 1903 and 1905) than Charles and a tandem pair, they all became great cycling friends. The Sissons lived at No.8 Highview Gardens in Edgware. The ever dependable 'Fon' served in Women's Auxiliary Air Force in WWII.

A HALT ON THE GRAMPIANS.

1924 HOLIDAY TOUR JAMES CYCLOMETER 3774

SATURDAY 9TH AUGUST

...a miss is as good as a mile

TWICKENHAM – HENLEY – OXFORD – WITNEY – BURFORD

Got off soon after 7.30 a.m. after the usual shutting up stunts, the hurried breakfast with tinned 'Ideal' milk, leaving nothing behind except E.B.P.'s (Edward Brownfield Pope, my brother) wrist watch which, thank goodness, he did not discover until we had got well away. And marvels of marvels, for once we started our annual holidays in fine weather. For the third year in succession we took the now familiar road via Twickenham, Whitton, Hounslow, Colnbrook and Slough to Maidenhead. Here the first incident occurred, E.B.P. coming within three inches of being smashed up by an erratic lady motor driver. However, a miss is as good as a mile, and this incident was soon forgotten when the monotonous Bath road was left for the 'stumpy' stretch between Maidenhead and Henley, via Hurley and Medmenham. After a stroll through the home of regattas, we took it gently up the stiff climb to Nettlebed, walking some of the stiffer parts, not because we could not ride them, but because we were out for a holiday and not for hard work.

After passing Nettlebed the road to Oxford is all smiles, and after the first holiday midday meal of bread and cheese at the 'Three Horseshoes', Benson, resisting the appeals of the many comfortable little pubs at Dorchester, which, like Nuneham Courtenay was looking particularly alluring this bright August morning. We never find much to linger for in Oxford, and were soon through the 'City of Learning' only stopping at a wayside refreshment house just beyond the toll bridge at Eynsham. At Witney we had made such good going that we loafed on the grass at the top end of the town for quite a long time, smoking and contemplating the beauties of this old fashioned town. Our first stage soon came to an end in the ever delightful town of Burford where the 'Swan' as ever, gave us the usual warm welcome and excellent tea. Here we found a friend of Ing's by the name of Castell, who was just concluding a fortnight's holiday there. He was seeing a friend off by the Oxford bus, so after tea we strolled down the old High Street with the usual stop for contemplation of the beautiful garden, full of phlox and dahlias at this season which borders the fast flowing Windrush on the further side, before continuing our stroll up to Fulbrook, a quaint little agricultural village about a mile uphill from Burford. Then returning we came upon Castell reclining on the grass on the Lechlade road, we did ditto and much pleasant conversation ensued, which continued at the supper table so that the Tolsey clock chimed 11 o'clock some time before we finally turned in.

Distance ridden: 76 miles

SUNDAY 10TH AUGUST

...at a sedate pace as befitted the day of rest

BURFORD – LECHLADE – FAIRFORD – AMPNEY ST. PETER – CIRENCESTER – BIBURY – BURFORD

Woke up to sunshine again and to a late breakfast (9 o'clock) partaken with great gusto after the usual stroll down to the bridge and a cigarette. I have described a 'Swan' breakfast so often that nothing further need be said except that it was of its usual excellence. After parting with Castell, who had to go back home to Sheffield, we got out our James[1] and took the road to Lechlade via Filkins, at a sedate pace as befitted the day of rest, making a diversion to find Kelmscott, the home of William Morris

---

1 In referring to his 'James', Charles may be using a slang term for his bicycle, after inventor and 'father of the cycling industry', James Starley.

which we somehow missed, but struck upon a beautiful bridge, St. John's Lechlade, just where the Thames and Severn Canal commences. Here we lingered quite a long time before going into Lechlade, just outside of which we took our midday bread, cheese and beer at the 'Three Horseshoes'; the landlord, a small man of mighty sinew, entertained us meanwhile with stories of the doings in sport of the locals' athletes. A sharp shower took us up to a thick tree in the High Street of Fairford which led to an exploration of that picturesque town, we having on previous visits only passed through the outskirts, and we were well repaid, voting it as one of the pleasantest of the smaller Gloucestershire towns which we had come across.

Our next diversion off the main road was to examine the village of Ampney St. Peter, a perfect gem of grey stone and thatch, its natural beauty having been added to by some ingenious person who had scattered the seed of poppies of all colours and hollyhocks, wherever they could find a foothold. The next of the Ampneys, Ampney Crucis, is not as compact as St. Peter but is still a pleasant enough place to warrant more exploration than we were able to give it. Here at the 'Crown' we partook of some more refreshment before going on into stately Cirencester, and after sometime visiting the beauty spots of this miniature Bath, decided to return to Burford via Bibury, the only town of any size on that portion of the Icknield Way between Cirencester and Burford. The other two villages, Barnsley and Aldsworth presented no special features. Bibury is a place where anyone of a contemplative nature could spend a lifetime. Surrounded by hills it lies in a wooded valley with the river Coln cropping out beside and across practically every street, and one could hardly imagine what this beautiful town can be like when churched up[2] by the annual Bibury Races. And we returned to the 'Swan' with that satisfied feeling of the second day of our holiday well spent without any particular exertion, the whole distance covered only amounting to *43 miles*.

MONDAY 11TH AUGUST
...the ideal English village
BROADWAY – EVESHAM – WORCESTER – MARTLEY – LUDLOW

Up to another fine morning, undecided as to where we were going next, but on the principle that you can have too much of a good thing, took

---

2 Old expression meaning 'to make prettier than usual'.

the steep and stony road to Stow-on-the-Wold, the wind being kind to us so that we reached that bleak Cotswolds town in very little over an hour after saying goodbye to the hospitable 'Swan'. And so on to the still steeper road which culminates in Broadway Hill, the view from which was somewhat obscured by mist, walking down the steeper portions of the precipitous descent to the always lovely village of Broadway, (beloved by the American tourist as the ideal English village), the 'Coach and Horse' supplying our usual needs in the way of midday refreshment. When passing through Evesham last year we were not particularly struck with that ancient town, but farther investigation caused us to alter that opinion and we were well repaid for the hour we spent there, the ancient buildings in the vicinity of the twin churches, which share one tower standing by itself between them, especially calling for admiration, while the Warwickshire Avon, which is of considerable volume here, adds to the beauty of the scene.

The road continues to the 'Faithful City[3]'; in the spring time the flowering fruits trees must make it very lovely, for plums, apples and pears are the sole harvest of this district except for an occasional hop garden. The next town, a very ordinary looking one, was Pershore, which is famous for its plums. The cramped, tram lined streets of Worcester itself never appeal, even the Cathedral seems to have been put into an unsavoury corner, nor does the Severn present any features of attraction in this part of its course. We had a feeble apology for a tea (eggs nearly raw) at Tower's Restaurant, before tackling the very strenuous road, via Martley where we refreshed at the 'Crown', a pleasant enough little watering place but as time was getting on we were not disposed to linger there. From there the road led us to Clifton-upon-Teme, Upper Sapey and Tenbury Wells.

From here to Ludlow, via Little Hereford and Ashford Bowdler the road flattens out, of which fact we were glad as we had both had enough hill climbing and required some more refreshment at the 'Salwey Arms', before finally arriving in Ludlow about 8.30 p.m. where as usual we were taken in at the comfortable 'Blythwood House'. Now under new management, but as homelike as ever, we devoured an excellent cold meat supper and caught the last act of 'Midsummer Madness' transmitted from the 'Lyric' at Hammersmith (!), which put us on good terms with ourselves.

---

3 The nickname for the city of Worcester, translated from the City's Latin motto *Civitas Fidelis,* in reference to the city's support during the English Civil War for the Stuart (Royalist) cause.

It is worth mentioning that this is the first time we have arrived in Ludlow in fine weather. Is this an omen? If so what does it portend?

Distance covered: 73 miles.

TUESDAY 12TH AUGUST

We walked, and walked. And walked some more…

LUDLOW – LEINTWARDINE – KNIGHTON – CLUN – MONTGOMERY

Got up to sunshine once again and we said one unto another, "Now surely is our rain star set, and we may even venture on the Leintwardine road which we have never before traversed with dry skins."

Accordingly, after an exceedingly bountiful breakfast and the usual look from the castle ramparts over the wild Welsh borderlands, we set forth on the familiar road to Shrewsbury turning off to the left at Brownfield for the inviting mountains, still under a cloudless sky. We had just reached the top of the first ascent when a huge black cloud hurried up from somewhere and gave us a good drenching before we could reach the monastic ruins by the roadside where we have so often sheltered before. However, we hurriedly donned our new 'Pagets' and soon freewheeled into Leintwardine, only three miles down in the Teme Valley, where not a spot of rain had been seen. The 'Swan' at Leintwardine like another famous 'Swan' can never be passed, so here we regaled with bread, cheese and beer before pursuing our way across the border into Knighton via Brampton Bryan. At Knighton we met two elderly C.T.C.[4] optimists sunning themselves on the steps of the 'Dragon', both of whom were so convinced that summer had come that they were congratulating themselves on having posted home their capes to save carrying them.

After a long talk on subjects dear to the heart of the cyclists, we saw them off on the road to Rhayader and then considered our next move, finally deciding that Montgomery would suit us very well. Accordingly we took the shortest route to Clun though warned that it was very rough. It was. We walked, and walked. And walked some more until we reached the top. Then we walked down, it was far too rough to ride any part of it. But undoubtedly it was the shorter way, only 8 miles as against 16 miles by the ordinary road. Clun, said to be the quietest town in England, (we

---

4 Cyclists' Touring Club, a charitable membership organisation founded in 1878

had got into Salop[5] again), was full of poultry, live ducks and fowls tied up by the feet in pairs and stacked in piles all over the streets, it being market day. I don't know what the R.S.P.C.A. would say on the subject, but they all looked supremely unconcerned, especially the ducks, so I suppose they get used to the custom of the country like the eels.

Here we gorged on custard tarts and lemonade at a baker's shop, which after our long rough walk was not an unwelcome interlude as we had still some tough road to get over to Bishop's Castle. Montgomery was soon reached and as the genial and rotund Mrs Maddox informed us that we could have the rooms we had occupied last year, we decided to remain at the 'Old Bell' for a few days before seeking fresh fields and pastures new. After the usual excellent tea, we sought the castle ruins and wrote letters until dusk, using a velvety rabbit cropped bank as a writing desk.

Our very strenuous travelling this day only amounted to *39 miles.*

WEDNESDAY 13TH AUGUST

The sun disappearing behind Snowdonia…

MONTGOMERY – WESTBURY – SHREWSBURY – MONTGOMERY

We made up our minds to cycle to Shrewsbury for two pressing reasons, one being the urgent necessity of E.B.P. getting a wrist watch, (I objected to being woken up in the small hours to tell him the time), and the other the replacement of a nut and bolt lost from his left toe-clip. As it is not a great distance from Montgomery we started somewhat late via Chirbury, Marton, Brockton, Worthen, Westbury, Yockleton and Cruckton to Shrewsbury, having refreshed on the way at the 'Red Lion' at Westbury with a curious rustic company whose conversation was so entertaining that we spent upwards of an hour there. On our arrival at Shrewsbury we spent another two hours in that most picturesque of towns, feeding liberally on fruit and Plimmer's mixed pastries, not forgetting to despatch several boxes of the famous cakes from the successors of "Palin, Prince of cake compounders".

E.B.P. had obtained a watch to suit him, and we were looking for a cycle shop to supply the other requirements when I happened to find a nut and bolt of the very kind he wanted in the road. After he had fiddled with his

---

5 An old name for Shropshire, thought to derive from the Anglo-French 'Salopesberia'

toe-clip, I asked him how my find worked and he stated it was alright at a pinch but wanted a washer under the nut, so without a moment's hesitation I stooped down and picked up a washer of the very size he wanted. One would have thought it would have put him in good spirits getting these articles without having to pay for them, but he seemed preoccupied and on my asking the reason, said what was so worrying him was that he had been in such a hurry to buy that wrist watch!

We started on our return journey but we were not to get back dry this time, several sharp showers driving us to shelter beneath trees on the road. Plimmer's delicacies had rather affected my digestion, and the pain caused thereby was rather increased by a youth of great brawn who insisted on trying to prove his ability to ride up hills faster than we could, so that I was not in the best of form to tackle the enormous feed of chops, mushed turnips and potatoes, followed by Whortleberry tart with curds and whey, which the good Mrs Maddox had got ready for us. However we made a good clearance, E.B.P. eating practically the whole of an enormous bowl of mashed turnips, of which I, in my condition, was rather frightened. However, a sharp walk up to the top of Monument Hill (1600 feet), afterwards and a good feed of the wild raspberries growing on the top, coupled with the magnificent view and the sun disappearing behind Snowdonia, quite cured my indisposition.

Distance ridden: 44 miles

THURSDAY 14TH AUGUST

...shelter to contemplate nature under damp conditions

MONTGOMERY – WELSHPOOL – LLANFAIR CAEREINION – FORDEN – MONTGOMERY

A rather doubtful looking morning so we started out after breakfast with no definite intentions, making first for Welshpool, and from there up the steep road via Golfa and Heniarth to Llanfair Caereinion. The rain started in the steady Welsh fashion some time before we reached Llanfair, to which town vehicles of all descriptions were hurrying, it being that great event of country towns, the local Cattle and Flower Show, and we were saddened to see the crowds trying to make merry in the relentless rain. We turned in at the 'Goat' to lunch, hoping the rain would cease, but it seemed a fixture and we thought it useless going any further, donned our 'Pagets' and turned back, stopping frequently where there was any shelter to contemplate nature under damp conditions and envying the placid cows and sheep to whom the rain seemed to make no difference.

In Welshpool we had some more light refreshments, making our way back by the very hilly road via Forden, which put paid to my right knee on last year's tour. This time there was no bar to my enjoyment of the tea, dinner and supper rolled into one which awaited us at the 'Old Bell' and the rain having stopped, we again made for the summit of Monument Hill, and were rewarded by a magnificent stormy sunset.

Distance ridden: 34 miles

FRIDAY 15TH AUGUST

Off the beaten track...

MONTGOMERY – NEWTOWN – CAERSWS – MACHYNLLETH – ABERDOVEY

Up to now we had not departed from the beaten track of our last two tours, but now we decided to see some new country and make a thrust for the Welsh coast. There is always some reluctance in leaving comfortable quarters, and the 'Old Bell' is most comfortable. However, we set off about 10.30 a.m. making first of all for Newtown by way of Abermule and Llanmerewig. Newtown, about the largest town in Montgomeryshire is also one of the most difficult to find the way out of, as there are no sign-posts, and quite an appreciable time was spent in enquiring for the road to Machynlleth, considerably complicated by the difficulty in pronouncing the name of that interesting town. Apparently, the Welsh pronunciation is 'Mahoonthleth' delivered in the manner suggesting a combination of a bark and a sneeze, and we were finally directed to make first of all for 'Kassoose'. This we identified on the map as Caersws. The road we eventually took proved to be a very fine one, both as to the surface and the gradients.

At Caersws we had our first refreshment, the usual bread, cheese and beer, at the 'Unicorn' a very comfortable little pub, before continuing through Pontdolgoch and Clatter, both very ordinary villages, to Carno, a very pleasant spot. Beyond here through Talerddig, as far as Llanbrynmair, there is a continuous rise and henceforward an easy downward fall, following the course of the rapid running Dovey River, a very picturesque stream, with innumerable rapids and waterfalls, until Cemmes Road is reached, and the beautiful Dovey Valley opens out with a clear run down to Machynlleth. Before arriving at the last mentioned town we had got into a desperate state of hunger, the time being 2.45 p.m. and no house of refreshment having been passed for quite 1½ hours, but at Penegoes we spied a little public house called 'Talafarn'. Having effected an entrance into the bar, we found an elderly woman eating bread and butter there. I courteously enquired if the house was open, but the good lady replied "No Sassenachs[6]". Luckily just then the landlady came down from upstairs and supplied us with a large plate of bread and butter (she had no cheese!) and two pints of refreshing beer. Then the good lady who said "No Sassenachs", started conversing in good English in the most amiable manner and told us all about the fine fishing in the river. This suspicion seems to be the chief characteristic of the Welsh people, and though they are amiability itself when satisfied you have no designs on the spoons, it leaves an unpleasant feeling.

Machynlleth is a pleasant town enough and would be a grand centre in fine weather for exploration of the surrounding country, but after a short walk around we crossed the river into Merionethshire and took the road to Aberdovey, about the roughest and toughest road you could wish for, with nevertheless some very taking villages on the way, especially Penybont and Pennal. The road goes up as the estuary broadens, and after passing Gogarth the scenery is really magnificent. This inland sea with the mountains on either side reminds one somewhat of Exmouth, but on a far larger and wider scale. The road skirts this estuary and is of a rather strenuous, not to say rough, kind but the series of views is magnificent. The town of Aberdovey lies just inside the bar, and the front is rather marred by railway lines and mercantile buildings built on the beach, but otherwise it strikes one as being quite the ideal place for a quiet holiday, given fine weather. We put up at the 'Gwalia Temperance Hotel', which did not prove an unqualified success, but accommodation is always scarce in coastal towns.

After tea we took a walk along the magnificent sands towards Tywyn in a bitter wind and threatening thunderstorms, which however held off. We had taken the precaution to don our waistcoats, but were glad to supplement these with newspapers, so piercing was the wind blowing straight in from the Atlantic, and so that we were very soon glad to turn back and seek shelter in the town again. The company in the Hotel were too much of the seaside boarding house type, so we went to bed early making up our minds to strike inland again on the morrow.

Distance ridden: 49 miles

---

6 Derogatory term for an English person

A GOLDEN AGE OF CYCLING

SATURDAY 16TH AUGUST
Wild Wales...
ABERDOVEY – CAERSWS – CARNO – LLANGURIG – RHAYADER

We had ordered an early breakfast but the outlook when we got up was an appalling one, the drenching rain which had started about 10 o'clock last night looking as though it was a fixture forever. A soaking rain is always depressing, but never so much so as when the outlook comprises sea, river and mountains, and we decided to move off in spite of it. And so we left Aberdovey swathed in the invaluable Pagets retracing our wheelmarks, having no other alternative, right back to Caersws having a few periods when the rain gave us a short respite and enabled us to take a breather without our capes.

At Carno we took our first refreshment at the 'Aleppo Merchant' a very comfortable inn, but we were unable to obtain any information as to how it came by its curious sign, represented by a clipper ship in full sail. At Caersws we again visited the 'Unicorn' for a little more stoking before turning off on the Llanidloes road. The sun had at last conquered and the remainder of the day was for once quite bright and sunny. The Severn, that ubiquitous river, runs for some distance alongside the road via Llandinam and Dolwen, a very fine stretch. We found Llanidloes, a largish town with no very striking features, a very busy place indeed, it being market day. We soon took our departure after feeding up at a baker's shop, taking the road to Rhayader, that Mecca of the cycling tourist. Hereabouts one begins to realise the fascination of wild Wales and the realisation is in full blast when the pretty little town of Llangurig is past. The road here is nearly 1000 feet above sea-level and there is a gentle fall for over 10 miles down to Rhayader, between towering mountains on either side with the River Wye, now in its infancy, winding along the valley between the two ranges. We were entranced by the magnificence of this valley more especially as that rare visitor, the sun, still graced us with his presence. Rhayader is not a very striking town and might be described as of late Welsh architecture and cruciform in structure, its main streets being named North, South, East and West respectively. Its chief industry seems to be catering for visitors, so that we had quite a plethora of stopping places to choose from, finally deciding on the 'Glaumont Temperance' in North Street, a choice which was fully justified by its comfort and plentiful food supply.

After a hearty tea we traversed some of the road we had come, on foot and congratulated ourselves on having struck some fine weather at last. We had supper with some very nice people from Balham, who had just come from Ross and we stayed up quite late discussing things dear to the heart of the lover of the open road.

Distance ridden: 56 miles

SUNDAY 17TH AUGUST

... an awe-inspiring sight, like a young Niagara

RHAYADER – ELAN VALLEY RESERVOIRS – RHAYADER

Alas! Our self-congratulations as to the weather were premature! We got up to an absolutely drenching morning, not being consoled by our landlady's remark that it generally rains in Rhayader. However, our Balham friends were determined to push on, and after helping them to buckle themselves into their armour, (they had a motorcycle and sidecar outfit), we saw them on their way, and determined that the day should not be wasted.

Accordingly we set out to inspect the wonder of Rhayader, the Elan Valley Reservoirs. A very curious incident occurred on the way. We got off our machines to walk out on a footbridge to have a look at the stream running in flood, a most entrancing spectacle, which occupied our attention for some minutes. When we returned to the spot where we had left our machines, they had disappeared and it was quite an appreciable time before we found them at the foot of a steep bank, quite some 20 yards away. They must have caught a gust of wind and been run down the bank on their own wheels. Fortunately there was no damage done.

Shortly after this incident we came in sight of the first dam, quite an awe-inspiring sight, like a young Niagara, with fully a hundred foot drop, and here we met a most torrential rain and wind which practically drove us to the very inadequate shelter of some rocks, among which we squatted like huge black mushrooms, in our Paget capes, until its fury was spent. This operation was, at intervals of a few minutes, repeated during our tour of this wonderful engineering feat, the wonder of which no words can describe. Sufficient to say that the chain of artificial lakes extends for fully 10 miles, each of the three being linked by a dam similar to the one described above. The head lake, an immense sheet of water, quite two miles long, and anything up to a half a mile wide lies 1040 feet above sea-level. There is nothing except the dams to indicate that the lakes have been formed by human ingenuity and the scene is one of desolate grandeur, the surrounding mountains being mostly of the boulder strewn, rocky type and no sign of life anywhere except a few tough looking sheep on some of the lower slopes. We could not but be lost in admiration in spite of the intense hunger, coupled with extreme dampness of body which pervaded us.

With no hope of human habitation in sight since we had left Rhayader, we turned at the head lake for the return journey, fondly expecting we should have all the wind and rain against which we had been struggling for over four hours having accomplished a distance of just 10 miles on our backs. We were in error: both wind and rain seemed to beat against us in whatever direction we turned. In one spot I was caught by a gust which threw both my bicycle and myself into a bush at the side of the road. On other occasions we were forced to dismount by being blown backwards while the whirling rain storms, which came over up the valley like dense fogs, blotting out everything, transcend anything in the shape of rain which we had ever before experienced. Altogether we were not sorry when we at last struggled back into Rhayader about 4.30 p.m., our appetites were! We started on a few eggs, and then went on with bread, butter and jam and only ceased when we became ashamed to call for anymore!

The rain after tea came down to a mere drizzle, so we had another stroll along the wonderful Llangwig road, which heightened our regrets that we had not struck this wonderful country in fine weather. We took our supper in company with one of those wonderful people who have not only been everywhere and seen everything, but can talk about it in such an interesting manner that boredom is out of the question, and it was quite late before we finally went to bed, our companion remarking to the landlady that the late hour was our fault, as we had talked so much. This was only facetiousness on his part as he had confessed that talking was his one hobby in life.

One incident, as showing the curious Welsh character, is worth recording here. Our fellow guest was retelling one of his amusing anecdotes while the landlady, Miss Price, was in the room, and to illustrate a point he turned to her and said, "You know, Miss Price, how the Welsh people, especially in country districts, clip their English."

Miss Price bridled with indignation. "Oh no," said she, "It is no use asking me anything about the Welsh people or the Welsh language, I know nothing about them whatsoever." *Distance ridden: 20 miles*

MONDAY 18TH AUGUST

...the fairy-like Wye town in the golden evening sun

RHAYADER – LLANDRINDOD WELLS – PENYBONT – LLANFIHANGEL NANT MELAN – HEREFORD – MUCH BIRCH – ROSS-ON-WYE

With the rain still coming down in buckets we decided to clear out of Wales as quickly as we could, the wonderful country not compensating for the continuous rain. We accordingly emptied our oil cans on our chains, enveloped ourselves in our Pagets and set off in the direction of Hereford as far as we could judge, the entire lack of sign-posts making direction finding rather confusing. At any rate we left Rhayader by South Street, which, by its name should be our road. About 5 miles further on a curious incident occurred. A lad, apparently a farm apprentice, was coming towards us on a bicycle coasting down a hill when suddenly he collapsed all in a heap. When we got to him and sorted him out a bit we found his machine had broken off at the base of the steering pillar. Except for a few cuts he seemed none the worse after his lucky escape, merely remarking that he "was afraid it might do that", and we found on examining the fracture that it must have been hanging together by a miracle for some time. His chief concern was how to get to Rhayader by 11 o'clock – it was then 10.30 a.m. However, just then a charabanc[7] came into sight into which he got, after piling up the fragments of his bicycle by the side of the road, saying he would fetch them in the evening.

The road we had taken out of Rhayader, though in the right direction, was not the right one, and at the first village we came to, Llanyre, on enquiry we found ourselves close to Llandrindod Wells, so thought we might as well visit that popular watering place, especially as it was still raining! Llandrindod, a modern, clean town did not impress us much, but we found a clear direction at last via Penybont where a very snug pub in the Llanbadarn Hotel furnished us with our first refreshment. Here we ran across an elderly journeyman bricklayer from Fulham, who wished himself in the 'Greyhound' the very last place either I or E.B.P. would wish to be in at the moment.

After leaving Penybont there is a continuous rise to Llanfihangel Nant Melan. Here we could not pass the hospitable 'Red Lion' without calling

---

7 An early form of motorised bus, usually open-topped.

and had there been any fine weather in prospect, we should certainly have made arrangements to stay there the night, such is the atmosphere of homeliness and comfort about this charming little inn, the praises of which have been so often sung by 'Wayfarer'[8] and other cycling journalists. It was, however, still raining and we wanted to get out of Wales, so we proceeded onto New Radnor, surely the smallest county town in England and Wales, and so via Walton into Herefordshire. Here in England the sun came out, so that Kington struck us as being a very pleasant little town after nearly two whole days of continuous rain.

From Kington to Hereford, via Eardisley, Letton and Byford, the road is a splendid one, and we reached beautiful Hereford about 4.30 p.m., and after an extremely satisfying tea at the 'Hop Pole' spent more than an hour in the gardens overlooking the River Wye and round the Cathedral, looking extremely attractive in the sunshine which had continued since we crossed the border. We continued on our way via Kingsthorn, Much Birch (with a reviver at the 'Axe and Cleaver'), Llandinabo, Peterstow, to Ross-on-Wye stopping as usual on dear old Wilton Bridge to view the fairy-like Wye town in the golden evening sun which, from this spot, at this time, is surely one of the most beautiful sights in England.

At Ross-on-Wye we, as usual, received a warm welcome from Mr Pugh at the 'Gwalia' after surveying the setting sun from the Prospect and a beautiful supper; we went to bed satisfied that we had found the sun at last, after our easy and very pleasant stage of *67 miles*.

TUESDAY 19TH AUGUST

...the rain has lost its power to dampen our spirits.

ROSS-ON-WYE – MONMOUTH – LLANDOGO – TINTERN – CHEPSTOW – ROSS-ON-WYE

A brilliant morning with every outward sign of settled weather at last. We made up our minds to stay another night at Ross and run over to Chepstow for another look at the grand old Severn and Wye, Castle, not to mention the glorious Wyndcliff[9], taking the usual road to Monmouth via Wilton Bridge and Whitchurch. Monmouth for once was not full of cattle and pigs (our usual experience), and we made a tour of the not-too picturesque town before going on the road by the side of the Wye

---

8 The pen name of the famous cycling journalist WM Robinson (1877–1956).
9 A steep limestone cliff rising to a height of 771 feet above the River Wye.

through Reabrook to Llandogo. Before reaching the last named village we had had warnings of distant thunder, though the sky was still apparently cloudless. However, after crossing the river at Llandogo it was upon us and we were glad to take refuge (and refreshments) at the 'Sloop Inn' for about three quarters of an hour, until the storm had spent its fury. But the clearance was only temporary, for when we had passed Tintern (without visiting the Abbey as it was besieged with day trippers) and had reached the highest point of the Wyndcliff, it was on us again. We made for a very thick tree which was no protection from the phenomenal rain and hailstones which descended upon us for about half an hour, so that we had to put on our Pagets again. But the sun came out again as we got into Chepstow, making that picturesque town with its precipitous streets look at its best.

After a stroll around and some beer, bread and cheese at the 'White Lion', we spent a couple of hours in the Castle with a broiling sun shining and a heavy thunderstorm in progress, a few miles away. We left for the return journey at about 4 o'clock, riding the stiff climb out of the town and thoroughly enjoying the lovely coast down the Wyndcliff to Tintern where we turned in at 'Bay View' for a very excellent tea, but before we had finished the clouds closed in on every side. We knew it meant it this time and a relentless rain set in, so we set off at once enveloped in our trusty Pagets, and so back to Ross after some 2½ hours of rain plugging. However, the rain has lost its power to dampen our spirits, and as we heard from a very entertaining traveller at supper that the sun had been seen on the other side of the Bristol Channel, we made up our minds to wend our way southwards on the morrow. *Distance ridden: 53 miles*

WEDNESDAY 20TH AUGUST
A terrifying descent…
ROSS-ON-WYE – MITCHELDEAN – GLOUCESTER – STONEHOUSE – SWANSWICK – BATH

It was not raining when we got up but looked as though it might start at any moment as we made up our minds to make for Bath as our next stopping place, and accordingly after bidding goodbye to our old friend Mr Pugh and the pigs and chickens in the farmyard which makes 'The Gwalia' such a pleasant place to stop at, we took the road to Gloucester. After passing through Weston under Penyard and Lea, we somehow got off the main road and found ourselves at Mitcheldean, quite a nice little village and, as it only added a few miles to our journey, it did not worry us much.

We regained the main road after passing through Longhope, and Huntley and eventually reached the familiar tram-lined City of Gloucester, after some refreshments at the 'Dog Inn' at the foot of the ugly bridge over the ugly Severn, which always seems to become an unsavoury stream whenever it passes through a town. Our road out of Gloucester, via Quedgeley, Hardwick, through to the very picturesque little town of Stonehouse, where we refreshed at the 'Hayward's Field Inn', was not a very prepossessing one and the rain, which had kept off up to now, just caught us on the steepest part of the hill up from Nailsworth, where we took shelter for half an hour. From this point to the outskirts of Bath it would be difficult to find a bleaker and more desolate road in England, and it seemed more so than ever with a strong wind in our faces and heavy rainstorms at intervals of 10 minutes or so. The descent into Bath from this road through Swanswick is rather a terrifying one when your brakes are beginning to get a bit worn and we were glad to get safely down into the famous city which we found full-up owing to the races being on, and which, had we known, would have kept us away from Bath. On the last occasion we stayed here we put up at the Egremont Hotel and were not impressed with that establishment. Consequently, we tried every other place on the list, being told everywhere that they were full up owing to the races so that we were driven back to the Egremont after all, securing the last room there and finding new management and excellent cuisine. In fact nowhere on our tour had we had better quarters and grub. We spent the evening exploring the city in a gentle drizzle, which, with the steamy atmosphere that seems particular to Bath, helped us decide to quit it again on the morrow – rain or shine.

Distance ridden: 57 miles

THURSDAY 21ST AUGUST

...gleams of brilliant sunshine and rainbows

BATH – STANDERWICK – WARMINSTER – KNOOK – STAPLEFORD – SALISBURY

The gentle Bath drizzle had become a fairly heavy rain by breakfast time, and in the course of a very excellent breakfast we decided to make for Salisbury, a city we had frequently passed through but never explored.

1924 HOLIDAY TOUR

We were undecided at the start whether to don our Pagets or get wet, and decided on the latter course. We accordingly took the road between Bathampton and Claverton, the latter a sweet little grey stone and thatch village, and through to Beckington and Standerwick, where some Banbury cakes and Bass came very welcome at the 'Bell'. The road led us into the beautiful little town of Warminster, only a few years ago the centre of the Salisbury Plain Camping grounds, no trace of which now remain and onto the more charming little town of Heytesbury, on the outskirts of the ground covered in my army days. We repaired to the bar parlour of the 'George', where we used to foregather for tea on Sundays being painfully familiar, though eight years have passed since then, and so many of the carefree companions of those days sleep the last sleep on the battlefields of France and Flanders.

Dreaming over those old memories, I hardly noticed the excellence of the lunch we consumed there. The weather had cleared up and we basked for some time at Knook on the Wiltshire Downs, before ambling on our way via Upton Lovell, Codford St. Peters and Codford St. Marys, Deptford and Steeple Langford to Stapleford. The beauty of this last named village tempted us to explore the portions off the main road, and we were well repaid, for it is one of the most beautiful of the many lovely villages which abound in this comparatively unknown part of Wiltshire.

Our route now lay through Wishford and Fugglestone and Wilton, and Salisbury was reached about 4.30 p.m. after a very easy day's work. At Salisbury we had an indifferent tea at 'William's Temperance Hotel', which did not tempt us to stay the night there, so we finally came to rest at the 'Coach and Horses' in Winchester Street, which subsequently proved a very excellent stopping place. The evening was spent in the vicinity of the Cathedral which we admired from all points, chiefly from under trees to which we had to repair for shelter from thunderstorms, interspersed with gleams of brilliant sunshine and rainbows; these were hardly the worst conditions in which to view this magnificent edifice with its 400-foot spire, surrounded by velvety lawns, on the outskirts of which the residence of the host of dignitaries who cluster around a Cathedral make a scene which must turn the American tourists, who are always plentiful in Salisbury, green with envy. Altogether we rejoiced exceedingly that we had decided to explore this fine old city, and it has taken its place with Winchester in our affections.

Distance ridden: 43 miles

FRIDAY 22ND AUGUST

An unlikely tea...

SALISBURY – FOVANT – SHAFTESBURY – WINCANTON – SOUTH PETHERTON – ILMINSTER CHARD

A dull and ominous sky greeted us on rising, but we have become used to this, and it did not mar our enjoyment of the excellent breakfast that the 'Coach and Horses' put before us. E.B.P.'s time was drawing to a close, so we decided to part company, he to proceed on the homeward track by a devious route, while I determined to use my last week by making a lightning thrust into the far west.

We exchanged farewells at 10.30 a.m. and I turned in the direction from which we had come yesterday, but at Wilton took the road via Barford St. Martin, Compton Chamberlayne and Fovant, where I paused to view the spot where the L.R.B. (London Rifle Brigade) Camp in which I spent those merry weeks in the summer of 1916, once stood. No trace now remains of the city of wooden hutments which then stood there, nor of the host of galvanised iron shops, which disfigured the village, which now looks as though it could never have been infested with the seething crowds of khaki-clothed figures which then inhabited it. The regimental badge on the hillside is however still faintly visible, and in spite of the changed aspect the countryside – and there is no sweeter county in England – it was strangely familiar.

Of course, the hilly road via Ansty and Ludwell to Shaftesbury is also a very familiar stretch having previously undertaken it painfully, marching loaded up like baggage mules. The rain had started long before Shaftesbury was reached and continued at intervals for the rest of the day. Acting on local advice, instead of taking the more direct road, I turned off in a north westerly direction to Wincanton, via Gillingham and Bayford stopping at the 'Hunter's Lodge' Leigh Common, for some much needed bread and cheese supplemented by some juicy Williams pears in Wincanton, which is a plain ordinary town, like so many of those in this part of Somerset.

The road onward in the teeth of a strong headwind and driving rain seemed of a most strenuous character. The lack of anywhere to obtain refreshment is one of the drawbacks of this country, so that, having passed through Sparkford and Ilchester without finding anywhere to get some tea, I found myself strolling through the village of South Petherton and spotted a small cottage with an open door and a very attractive looking tea table laid.

There was a comfortable looking old dame at the door of whom I enquired how far it was to Ilminster and whether she knew if there was a chance of getting any tea there. She was doubtful about it but said she expected her husband in in a few minutes and would I care to have tea with them. Of course this was what I was fishing for, knowing the hospitality of the West Country folk, and I required little persuasion, with the consequence that I spent over an hour over that very delightful tea, telling the good dame and her husband all about the wonders of London and eventually persuaded her to accept double what she considered was reasonable for the two eggs, bread, butter, jam and cakes which I had consumed, which was about half of what I should have expected to have paid at a tea shop.

At Ilminster I looked around for a stopping place being a bit fagged by the hard pushing against the rain and the wind, but not being particularly impressed made for Chard, where I was pretty certain of comfortable quarters at the 'Crown'. I arrived about 8 o'clock and partook of an exceptionally good supper of cold beef and salad followed by apple tart and cream before turning in for the night.

Distance ridden: 63 miles

SATURDAY 23RD AUGUST

Lunatics in motors...

ILMINSTER – HONITON – FAIRMILE – EXETER – STARCROSS – DAWLISH – DAWLISH WARREN

It was raining as usual when I got up but gave promise of better things so that after breakfast, being eager to push on into Devonshire I got a move on about 9.30 a.m. walking up a considerable extent of the stiff ascent to Yarcombe. Here I met the first real blackberries while taking shelter from a particularly drenching shower and coasting down into Honiton in a misty drizzle. Honiton was full of livestock of every description, it being market day, and I was frustrated in my endeavours to obtain a bit of real Honiton lace [10] to adorn my only niece.

The rain ceased enough to allow me to discard my Paget at Fairmile and the 'Fairmile Inn' supplied me with some cider with bread and cheese about 12 o'clock before pushing onto Exeter via Rockbeare and Honiton

10 Famous lace from Honiton, Devon, usually featuring ornate patterns of flowers and leaves.

Clyst. The road from Honiton to Exeter was in a shocking condition and seemed teeming with lunatics in motors, one of which ripped off its near side mudguard on a tree, just close to where I happened to be standing having a chat with a farmer on the subject of pigs, without apparently noticing it.

Exeter on a Saturday morning wanted a little careful negotiation so that I only had just time to get some bread, cheese and beer at the 'New Inn' Alphington before closing time at 2 o'clock after which short work was made of the familiar road through Exminster and Kenton to Starcross, still the old sleepy Starcross that can scarcely have altered since the Great Western Railway first invaded it in the early years of Queen Victoria's reign. The light following wind made this hilly road quite easy and I don't remember ever going over it before without walking up some of the stiffer bits. I was not, however, destined to get to my destination (Dawlish) without a reminder of the 1924 summer in the shape of a torrential thunderstorm just past San Marino, but this was followed by genial sunshine such as I had not seen for over a week which lasted for the rest of the day[11]. I was just in time to secure the last room at Harris's Hotel, which decided me to stay a couple of days in dear old Dawlish, spending the rest of the afternoon around the old familiar haunts which have not changed since our childhood days and talking to the old inhabitants.

The evening was a lovely one and on the falling tide I strolled out to the Warren[12], on the way finding the breakwater under Langstone Cliff where E.B.P. and I cut out initials nearly 30 years ago, the initials being still clearly visible though the breakwater has been bathed by stormy seas for all that time.

After a heavy supper the inhabitants of the hotel (including myself) stopped up until past midnight being regaled by stories of early Victorian life in London from our worthy host. *Distance ridden: 44 miles*

---

11 Charles may be referring to a previous excursion across the mountains of northern Italy.
Weather records suggest that the summer of 1924 was a particularly wet one across continental Europe.
12 Dawlish Warren

SUNDAY 24TH AUGUST

A ramble full of memories...

DAWLISH – TEIGNMOUTH – TORQUAY – PAIGNTON – BRIXHAM – DAWLISH

A cloudless morning. It looks as though I have found the sun at last. The fascination which Dawlish always exercises is in full play and I am determined to spend the morning rambling around the old familiar spots starting off with the mill stream past the church; the banks of the stream are enveloped as usual in masses of sweet smelling meadowsweet; and the stream, with its usual tinkling note is running swiftly with crystal clearness over its stony bed and pouring like a glass wall over the mill dam to dissolve into a mass of snow white foam at the bottom.

Onto Greylands Bridge where the vegetation ever assumes a tropical aspect. Beneath the bridge in the deep pool formed by converging cataracts, apparently the same aged trout, who has been there for the last 30 years, was lurking around. And back through the Barton's, those mid-Victorian houses with the magnificent gardens, which have always excited our admiration and envy.

After this little ramble full of memories, a stroll to Teignmouth over Leigh Mount, out onto the main road and down the romantic Smuggler's Lane filled up the rest of the morning.

Having fed sumptuously off roast fowl and ham followed by plum tart and cream, I decided to have a quiet afternoon ride over to Torquay and strolled off in a leisurely manner up the steep ascent onto the Teignmouth road and over the straggly old toll-bridge to Shaldon not realising the toil that lay between that village and Torquay, suffice it to say that it was some ten miles of mostly rough walking.

Torquay is no doubt a very wonderful place and its natural advantages are made the most of but on this Sunday afternoon, with its crowded streets and parades, it presented few attractions to me, and I was soon on my way through Paignton over to Churston Ferrers Heath to Brixham, whereafter I partook of an excellent tea at the 'Globe'. I spent nearly 2 hours admiring this quaint picturesque and somewhat smelly fishing town, most of it down by the harbour where the fishing fleet, the largest on the South Coast, prepared to go out for the night. The sapphire sea and the golden evening sun made a picture which would delight the eye of any artist.

The return journey, with a slight wind behind, did not seem quite as strenuous as the outward one, which was as well considering the lateness of the hour. Darkness overtook me sometime before I got back to Dawlish, and after I spent about half an hour over a pint of cider and some biscuits, as it was too late to expect any supper at the hotel, at the Country House, I was glad to walk the last mile and a half of precipitous road rather than be run down by the many reckless motorists which seem to infest this part of the country. *Distance ridden: 40 miles*

MONDAY 25TH AUGUST

My old friend, the rain...

DAWLISH – TOTNES – AVONWICK – PLYMOUTH – TORPOINT – LOOE

A bright sun and balmy atmosphere made one very regretful at leaving fascinating Dawlish but I was anxious to see something of Cornwall before turning on the homeward track. So after a breakfast consisting of two eggs, five rashers of bacon and two sausages and posting off a parcel containing some of my dirty clothing, this considerably lightening my load, I paid my bill and took leave of the kindly Mr and Mrs Harris and set out once more on the Teignmouth road. This time I did not cross Shaldon Bridge but climbed the ever rising road overlooking the Teign through the somewhat spoilt village of Kingsteignton to the equally uninteresting town of Newton Abbot. But from there onwards the road is full of interest through Wolborough and Littlehempston along the banks of the fast flowing Dart to the lovely old town of Totnes, where I whiled away an hour and consumed an enormous quantity of stewed Victoria plums and cream. I proceeded on the Plymouth road which rises continuously to the fishermen's village of Avonwick, where at the 'Avon Inn' a pint of cider and a large chunk of bread and cheese put me in good fettle for the next stage. Ivybridge via Bittaford Bridge has no particularly picturesque features in itself but is in the centre of some of the loveliest country in South Devon, and the sight of the wonderful River Erme, the whole course of which is a series of cataracts, made me resolve to devote more time to it on the way back. Alas, I had only got a mile or two on our way when my old friend the rain again made his appearance and accompanied me on my travels for the remainder of the day.

The road has a downward trend from here to Plymouth through Lee

Mill Bridge, Smithaleigh and Plympton, where the unsavoury particulars of Plymouth commence. It was now raining nicely and my impressions of Plymouth with its narrow steep streets cobblestones and tram lines was a most unpleasant one. I found it most difficult to get any directions for the ferry at Devonport, it being quite an hour before I found the right spot for crossing the rain-swept water to Torpoint but eventually got across in a small tugboat which apparently officiates when there is not sufficient traffic to justify the ferry going across.

At Torpoint, which is quite a small town, a small refreshment shop supplied me with a most excellent tea with oceans of cream and delicious Cornish cutrounds[13]. I nearly decided to put up for the night in Torpoint but a temporary cessation of the rain lured me onto the road again and a very wonderful road it is, skirting the backwaters of the Sound and the St. German rivers via Antony and Sheviock, where a native advised me to keep to the main road to Menheniot Station before making down to Looe. This was my intention, but, as I found this would make it about 7 miles further, I decided to take the direct road across the hills turning left just pass Polbathic and consequently it was mostly a walk, the road being too steep up to Hessenford and too rough to ride down.

The rain had ceased when I finally got into Looe about 8 o'clock. I was charmed with the place but on making enquiries as to putting up it was not encouraging to be informed that I should not find a bed vacant in the town. However, I had heard that tale before and, being an optimist when on holiday, eventually succeeded in being accommodated in sections: that is to say by the help of two worthy dames, Mrs Butters and Mrs Hoskins, I got a bedroom in one house and a promise of food in another, and as it turned out both were excellent.

I just had time to explore the Banjo Pier and the tiny seafront before darkness set in and was filled with regret that I could only stay one night in this enchanting little town that goes to sleep apparently immediately as the sun sets, for I was bound to turn my face homewards on the morrow.

Distance ridden: 60 miles

---

13 A white bun rolled like pastry and cut into rounds; a traditional component of a North Devon cream tea

TUESDAY 26TH AUGUST

One of the loveliest corners of the show county of the West...

LOOE – POLPERRO – LOOE – TORPOINT – DEVONPORT – PLYMOUTH – IVYBRIDGE

My landlady roused me with a cup of tea, shaving water, bread and cheese at 6.45 a.m., an attention I am unaccustomed to, so that I had quite a nice time for admiring my surroundings before turning in to an excellent fish breakfast at 8.30 a.m. of which I partook in company with a Surrey Walking Club enthusiast who was tramping to Land's End. After another stroll around I set off for Polperro some 4½ miles away, of which quite 1½ miles was rideable.

Polperro struck me as a veritable wonderland, a gem of the first order, an unsophisticated Clovelly with many charms which Clovelly has not and the inhabitants, a dark-haired silent, meditative race, are almost as interesting as the place itself. No wonder that artists are to be found on every corner round the tiny harbour.

Here I spent a couple of hours, leaving it with great regret after some bread, cheese and Bass at the 'Three Pilchards', reaching Looe at 1.30p.m., where some of the inevitable stewed plums and cream put me into condition for the homeward track. This time I was determined to profit by the advice I had neglected yesterday and found the road to Menheniot, a splendid one, and from there easy work was made of the fine road back to Torpoint where tea time being due I indulged in more of those cutrounds and cream, as well as stewed plums and a variety of cakes while the sun was kind to me on the ferry crossing.

Going back, Devonport and Plymouth were more of a Chinese puzzle than they were the preceding day. I had been instructed to find George Street and that would take me onto the Exeter road. I did find George Street, a long narrow cobblestoned thoroughfare with double tramlines down the centre. I pursued it for, it seemed, miles and finally landed into the back end of Devonport. On enquiry I found that this was George Street Devonport and that it was George Street Plymouth I wanted, which was so far away that no one could direct me to it. However by enquiring of postmen, policeman, soldiers, sailors and civilians all of whom gave me different directions, I did at last find my way to Plympton and reached Ivybridge, where I proposed to stay the night about 5 o'clock.

A survey of inns decided me that the 'Kings Arms' was the one for me and I did not regret my choice. After tea the wonderful Erme river beguiled me into an extended exploration up stream and I was in no way disappointed. I walked about 3 miles all steadily uphill through fairy like woods, the river roaring and leaping in a tortuous course all the way with occasional deep dark pools which made one wish for a fishing rod. I could have wished for a little sunshine to enliven the scene but even without this it appealed to me as being one of the loveliest corners of the show county of the West.

I got back in time for supper of cold boiled leg of pork of a most delicious quality with tomatoes followed by apple tart and of course the inevitable cream, and I came to the conclusion that a month in Devonshire, the only county in which they really know how to feed, would make me a rather fat man! *Distance ridden: 43 miles*

WEDNESDAY 27TH AUGUST
Racing touts and reckless traffic
IVYBRIDGE – ASHBURTON – BICKINGTON – KENNFORD – CULLOMPTON – WELLINGTON – TAUNTON

Was wakened early by the sound of drenching rain of the real Dartmoor variety which, however, did not affect my appetite for breakfast. In spite of the protests of my host, I determined to proceed on my way, so wrapped myself in my Paget and set off. My optimism was justified, for the rain ceased before I reached Bittaford Bridge and there was even an occasional glimpse of a watery sun by the time I reached South Brent from whence there is a steady pull up for nearly 5 miles through Dean Prior to Buckfastleigh, a pleasant little Dartmoor village but rather infested by charabancs from Torquay and Newton Abbot.

The road runs down to Ashburton – one of the centres for the Dartmoor tourist and so a pleasant, clean town but one with no special features – and then there is a stiff climb to Bickington where at the 'Jolly Sailor' I had my midday bread and cheese. From here to Chudleigh is a lovely road through thickly wooded country and then commences the climb up to Great Haldon culminating in the racecourse, and I was disgusted to find Haldon Races on and this beautiful down desecrated by the hordes of riff raff who make country race meetings peculiarly their own. It is 8 miles from the racecourse down into Exeter and there was no alternative but to walk most of it in face of the reckless traffic and led horses which were streaming from the city.

I was compelled to stop at the 'Anchor' at Kennford for some bread and cheese, as it was near closing time, but this usually quiet little inn was full of a most vile collection of racing touts from every part of England. I was glad to get on the road again reaching Exeter which, it being early closing day, was nearly empty, by way of Alphington.

I did not tarry in Exeter but rode straight through the town on the Taunton Road via Pinhoe, Broad Clyst, Westcott to Cullompton, where 'Paul's Restaurant' provided an excellent tea before undertaking the tough climb from Willand with a fierce run down into Wellington where I further refreshed on bananas. From this town to Taunton is mostly downhill and as time was getting on I decided to stop the night at that clean, shoppy but uninteresting town. 'The Winchester Arms' in Castle Square, a quaint old ivy-covered inn, which was originally a wing of the ancient castle, attracted me and here I fared splendidly. A walk around Taunton before supper did not reveal anything particularly attractive and I rather regretted not having carried out my original intention of going on the other 22 miles to Glastonbury.

Distance ridden: 65 miles

THURSDAY 28TH AUGUST

Shower Bath...

TAUNTON – GLASTONBURY – WELLS – KINGWELL – MALMESBURY – CIRENCESTER

It was a watery looking morning when I set out from Taunton to encompass the monotonous level road over Sedgemoor through the agricultural villages of Cheddon Fitzpaine, Durston, Lyng, Othery, Walton and Street to Glastonbury. With the wind behind, the 23 miles occupied only one and a half hours, and nor did I linger in the romantic town of Glastonbury, which was very full up with a marketing crowd, but continued straight onto Wells, only stopping for some bread and cheese and beer at the 'Coxley Pound'. Here I was much entertained by the recital of the riotous doings at a fete held at the vicarage the preceding day and the grievance felt by the civilian population that the chief sporting event of guessing the number of grains of corns in a bottle had been won by the village policeman who had carried off the prize, a whole cheese, while the pig, which was the prize for the

Hopscotch match, had been won by the postman. At Wells I spent some time in and around the lovely Cathedral which, though one of the smallest in England, can have no rival for the beauty of architecture which is set off by its situation, surrounded by velvety towns and the hills in the background.

On leaving Wells, a steady drizzle set in which made the passage through the Mendip Hills via Chewton Mendip and Farrington Gurney, a particularly tough proposition and at Kingwell, about 6 miles from Bath, I was very glad of an excellent munch of lamb and peas and plum tart with cream at 'Anglesey House'. It was raining nicely when I got into Bath (I think this damp City should change its name to Shower Bath) so I took the London road, through Batheaston and Box to Chippenham where I had some idea of putting up for the night, but not caring for the look of the town, Malmesbury sounded more attractive.

Now, Malmesbury is a very picturesque place and would no doubt look a charming little town on a fine sunny day but here again there seemed rather a dearth of stopping places so I pushed on in the rain once again via Crudwell to Cirencester where I knew I should find comfortable quarters at the 'Swan'. And there in the Commercial room I spent a very pleasant evening with a bagman who had been travelling by motor in much of the same country as I had come through. This was so far the longest day's riding of the tour amounting to some *82 miles*.

FRIDAY 29TH AUGUST

Wet through and some miles from home...
CIRENCESTER – CRICKLADE – FARINGDON – WANTAGE – BURFORD

The Cirencester 'Swan' gave me a breakfast which almost rivalled the same meal at that other 'Swan' to which I was making for, and as my next stopping place was only 20 miles away, I spent an hour in the beautiful old Abbey Church before packing up and setting off for Burford by taking the Cricklade road which is exactly in the opposite direction!

This road is the Ermine Way and I found Cricklade an extremely pleasant little town from whence I proceeded via Highworth and Coleshill to Faringdon where a baker's shop supplied me with some milk and biscuits. From Faringdon it is a lovely road to Wantage, which is a beautiful town to which I did not do full justice as the rain made up its mind to set in soon after I arrived there, so that I soon took my departure taking a rather circuitous route via East Hanney, Kingston Bagpuize and Buckland to Bampton. It was here that my first casualty of the tour took place, one of my front spokes breaking with that musical "ping" which it is so objectionable to hear when you are wet through and some miles from home.

However, in this case a repair was soon effected at a cost of 6s and I continued (as one could rejoice in the rain) through Brize Norton arriving at Burford about 4 o'clock, establishing communication with the outside world by finding letters awaiting me at the 'Swan' and a large fire by the side of which I was glad to sit and dry my knees before tea.

The rain ceased after tea and the usual stroll round the most fascinating town in England took place after I had replied to my various correspondents in order to catch the post at 6.45 p.m.. For a wonder there were no other visitors at the 'Swan' so I retired early after the usual excellent supper which this doyen of inns always provides.

Distance ridden: 55 miles

SATURDAY 30TH AUGUST

Pure joy

BURFORD – WARWICK – BANBURY – SWERFORD – CHIPPING NORTON – BURFORD

For a change the sun was shining when I took my usual stroll down to the River Windrush before I decided to make a dash into Warwickshire as a last effort before the home run tomorrow. However, before setting off I took the precaution of getting my oilcan filled and dowsing my chain, which was beginning to get rather dry. And so for the second time I set off for Stow-on-the-Wold now becoming quite familiar with its immense square where the annual horse fair is held. Now Stow-on-the-Wold lies some 900 feet above sea-level while Moreton-in–Marsh is as its name implies at or below the sea-level and as they lay some 4½ miles apart it can be imagined that the run from Stow to Moreton is pure joy especially as the road is one of the finest in England[14].

And so I found it and the road onward to Warwick via Halford, Ettington, Wellesbourne and Barford is a magnificent one. I had nearly

---

14 Stow-on-the-Wold actually sits 800 feet above sea level while Morton is 423 feet above sea level.

reached Warwick before the rain really made up its mind to swamp out the glimpses of sun which had been appearing at intervals, so that after waiting under a thick tree for about half an hour, until the tree became waterlogged, I made up my mind to push on into Warwick and get something to eat. Which I did at the 'Woolsack', a very swank[15] place where as I was very wet and muddy, I did not feel particularly comfortable. The lunch consisted of innumerable courses and by the time I had got to the end of it I felt almost as hungry as at the start. However, the rain had ceased in the meantime so that I was able to spend a couple of hours strolling around this beautiful old town which is overshadowed by the magnificent castle. I came to the conclusion that Warwick can be put in the same class as Ludlow, Cirencester and Bridgnorth for beauty.

The weather turned fine, so I made up my mind to extend my run by going back to Burford via Banbury – a road which when I traversed it four years ago I stigmatised as being the worst surface I had ever come across. I was therefore arguably surprised to find it quite the reverse now and the greater part of the 20 miles to Banbury was covered at between 18 to 20 miles per hour, the whole distance including the walk up the steep and strong Warmington Hill occupying 1¼ hours, so that I was able to spend an hour in Banbury visiting the old familiar spots in that curious old town.

I was quite prepared to find the road back to Burford, though only 24 miles, hard work, and was not disappointed. I had not got very far on my way before the desire for tea became very pressing but the villages of Bloxham and South Newington both failed to provide for my wants which, however, were amply satisfied at the 'Mason's Arms' Swerford. Before I had reached the picturesque town of Chipping Norton the rain commenced again – at first a fine drizzle which became a thorough drencher by the time Shipton-under-Wychwood was reached, leaving me with 6 miles of the bleakest part of the Cotswold Hills to do in the teeth of a strong headwind and this torrential rain. Consequently I was pretty wet by the time I got back to the 'Swan' though the rain had toned down enough to allow of my discarding my Paget in Fulbrook. However, after I had changed as much clothing as I happened to have with me and dried my knees in front of the fire, I was quite in good form to tuck away

---

15 Early Victorian word meaning "showy" or "attention seeking"

an excellent supper in company with several more C.T.C. members who had arrived for the weekend and a very pleasant evening resulted.

Distance ridden: 82 miles

SUNDAY 31ST AUGUST

The last run home…

BURFORD – WITNEY – OXFORD – DORCHESTER – MAIDENHEAD – TWICKENHAM

There is always a certain dumpy feeling on starting for the last run home after a cycling holiday and especially when taking leave of Burford for another year. However we had a very cheery breakfast, our party being reinforced by a brisk young Belle Vue clubman who had been riding through the rain all night having started at midnight from Upper Tooting. One of the party, a Western Wheeler, was also on his way to London and suggested that we should chip in together, a suggestion I regarded with some diffidence as from his appearance and from the appearance of his machine, a new Grubb racer, I rather feared he would want to go faster than my old bones would care about. We loafed for a long time after breakfast reluctant to break away from the 'Swan' and consequently it was nearly 11.30 a.m. before my new friend and I finally set off after strolling up to the main road at the top of the town. My companion was keen to go at a fair lick from the start and the 8 miles to Witney was done in under half an hour and it was not 1 o'clock when we came into Oxford.

Of course I was not beginning to feel it yet being in very hard condition after three weeks buffeting in the wind and rain, but my companion suggested a walk after which I took the lead, and though I made no attempt to force the pace he did not seem very happy especially up the long slopes and at Nuneham Courtenay thought it was time we had something to eat. However, we went onto Dorchester and got an excellent feed at the 'Fleur de Lys' where we stopped for upwards of an hour. After this refreshment, short work was made of the stiff climb from Benson up to Nettlebed, part of which I generally walk, and he afterwards confessed that he would have preferred to do so too but was too proud to say so.

From Nettlebed down to Henley was a giddy march as he wanted to demonstrate the superiority of his fixed wheel over my free one. I let him go pedalling for dear life while I coasted about 20 yards in the rear with both brakes on most of the time so I still remain unconverted. We walked up the steep hill out of Henley and some of the other stiff rises between Henley and Maidenhead.

At Maidenhead my friend felt in need of more sustenance so we had tea at a place he knew of but which did not particularly impress me. It is hardly necessary to describe the remaining 25 miles of the Bath road except at beyond Colnbrook I sustained my first puncture of the tour which delayed us about a quarter of an hour, shortly after which I took leave of my companion who took the new West road as he had to make for Notting Hill and announced his intention of going to bed as soon as he got home. Meanwhile I speeded up and made for home by the usual way via Whitton, Twickenham, reaching home about 6.30 p.m. The day had been a remarkable one as we had encountered no rain all the way.

Thus ended the wettest holiday we have ever experienced but it had taught us that rain is no bar to cycling when you get used to it and for myself I can truly say that there was no part of it I did not enjoy.

Distance ridden: 76 miles

GENERAL REMARKS ON 1924

The past year has been one of the wettest on record yet the percentage of fine Sundays was above the average and some riding was possible on every one throughout the year, the average working out at 41.88 miles – the longest Sunday ride was 96 miles and the shortest 20 miles. The August holiday tour may be counted a success as it reached a record mileage.

This was more because of, than in spite of, the wretched weather (only three days out of the 23 being free from rain) so that one was constantly moving on to try and find finer weather.

A GOLDEN AGE OF CYCLING

CYCLING STATISTICS FOR 1924 BY MILES AND NUMBER OF RIDES PER MONTH

MONTH	NUMBER OF RIDES			MILES RIDDEN				AVERAGE MILES PER RIDE			
	SUNDAY	TOURING	OTHER RIDES	SUNDAYS	TOURING	OTHER RIDES	TOTAL	SUNDAYS	TOURING	OTHER RIDES	ALL RIDES
Jan	4	-	-	126	-	-	126	31.50	-	-	31.50
Feb	4	-	-	158	-	-	158	39.50	-	-	39.50
Mar	5	-	-	181	-	-	181	36.05	-	-	36.05
Apr	4	-	2	144	-	133	277	36.00	-	66.50	46.16
May	4	-	4	193	-	72	265	48.25	-	18.00	33.12
June	5	-	7	262	-	261	523	52.40	-	37.29	43.58
July	4	-	7	223	-	194	417	55.75	-	27.71	37.90
Aug	5	19	2	226	1087	105	1418	45.20	57.21	52.50	54.53
Sept	4	-	-	183	-	-	183	45.75	-	-	45.75
Oct	4	-	-	145	-	-	145	36.25	-	-	36.25
Nov	5	-	-	207	-	-	207	41.60	-	-	41.60
Dec	4	-	2	130	-	57	187	32.50	-	28.50	31.16
Totals	52	19	24	2178	1087	822	4087	41.88	57.21	34.25	43.02

Burford. Swan Inn

1925 HOLIDAY TOUR – CHATER-LEA – CYCLOMETER 1625

SATURDAY 15TH AUGUST

Queen Elizabeth's bedstead...

TWICKENHAM – MAIDENHEAD – HENLEY – BENSON – OXFORD – EYNSHAM – MINSTER LOVELL – BURFORD

After a great rush the previous evening and working late at the office I got started about 7.45 a.m. taking the usual road to the end of the first stage which seems to be the inevitable first day's trip on these holiday tours. The flat, uninteresting stretch to Maidenhead was soon covered though broken by sundry stops to adjust luggage which had presented some difficulties owing to the position of the Chater-Lea brakes.

Henley, past the long pull up to Nettlebed was taken easily and some of the steepest parts walked. Then we made up speed to our first stopping place 'The Three Horseshoes' at Benson, which, as usual, supplied us with extremely excellent bread and cheese and ale. We walked through Oxford which, it just being 1 o'clock, was crowded with the usual heterogeneous collection of cyclists, since it is not term time, business people leaving the city for their Saturday half holiday. A few cakes in Oxford supplemented the midday bread and cheese and another stop was made near Eynsham for some fizzy liquid of unknown manufacture to wash down the solids. There was tons of time for half an hour's rest and reflection on the grass close by Witney Church and also to explore once again the village of Minster Lovell and the adjacent ruins, and we arrived at Burford in time for an early tea after which a long walk down the old Cirencester Road gave us a good appetite for supper.

The 'Swan' was invaded by a large contingent of the Manchester District Association of the C.T.C. North West Section. Consequently for this night we had to sleep out at 'Smith's' a few doors away in an ancient four post bedstead in one of the most ancient houses in Burford, the very house and bedstead Queen Elizabeth would have slept in had she ever come to Burford, but we slept nonetheless sound for that after the exertions of the day, the cycling part of which amounted to 76 *miles*.

SUNDAY 16TH AUGUST

To the Slaughters...

BURFORD – BOURTON-ON-THE-WATER – UPPER AND LOWER SLAUGHTER – LOWER SWELL – SHERBORNE – BURFORD

Another brilliant day during which the sun shone continuously. There was plenty of grub to satisfy the crowd of 16 who sat down to breakfast at the 'Swan' and we spent some time afterwards wandering around before starting out for the day.

We were determined to take things easy and set out up the Stow road turning off about a mile past the 'Merry Mouth' through Little Rissington to Bourton-on-the-Water, one of the most charming little towns in Gloucestershire. From there we made our way to Upper and Lower Slaughter, both of which are perfect gems in their way but as time was getting on we began to get nervous about our midday sustenance and were horrified at being informed that the nearest house of call was at Lower Swell about three miles away. Thence we departed without delay and had a satisfying repast of the usual bread and cheese and beer at the 'Golden Ball' with a company of village worthies all engaged in the discussion of the approaching football season.

Having done full justice to the bread and cheese we made our way back to Lower Slaughter once more and on by a very rough and hilly route to Sherborne getting back to the 'Swan' along the valley of the Windrush through the village of that name and Little Barrington to the main road. The evening was spent wandering around the town and discussing cycling topics with the sporting cyclists who had arrived at the 'Swan' for the night.

Distance ridden: 29 miles

MONDAY 17TH AUGUST

The wasp sting…

BURFORD – STOW-ON-THE-WOLD – MORETON-IN-MARSH – STRETTON-ON-FOSSE – WELLESBOURNE – WARWICK – STRATFORD-UPON-AVON – LONG COMPTON – SHIPTON – BURFORD

The weather still holds good and both of us being in need of a quiet time had decided overnight to stay one more night in Burford in the sure comfort of the 'Swan'. E.B.P. fell in with my suggestion of visiting the ancient town of Warwick, familiar to and well esteemed by me but erstwhile unvisited by him.

Hence the Stow road was again our start, taking the usual hour for the 10 miles to the bleak town of Stow-on-the-Wold. The 4½ miles down into Moreton-in-Marsh was a trifle rougher than I traversed it last year but was nevertheless very enjoyable as was also the refreshment of which we partook at the 'Golden Cross', Stretton-on-Fosse, a curious little village with a very sleepy railway station where the station master, ticket clerk, head porter etc. seemed to amuse themselves by propelling themselves along the line by a species of hand cycle. And so on that superb surfaced road through Halford and Ettington to Wellesbourne, where we struck a most comfortable rest house for our midday bread and cheese and beer, the 'Old Stag's Head', the only thing which marred my enjoyment was a wasp sting on my neck which worried me for days afterwards.

A few more miles passing through Barford brought us to Warwick where we spent a couple of hours exploring the quaint old streets and the picturesque Avon and then onto Stratford which did not impress me any more than it did on my last visit five years ago.

Here we had an indifferent tea at the 'Shakespeare Restaurant' before making our way back to Burford by way of Alderminster, Tredington, Shipston-on-Stour and Long Compton, a straggling but picturesque village much frequented by the Birmingham Cyclist as evidenced by the numerous tea places showing the C.T.C. sign. However we had tea and wanted something more sustaining which we obtained in a tiny bar parlour of the 'Red Lion'. The stiff road through Chipping Norton and Shipton gave us a further thirst which was satisfied at the 'Red House' at the latter place, and it was about 8.30 p.m. before we finally arrived back to the 'Swan' for supper and after a run of some 79 *miles*.

TUESDAY 18TH AUGUST

A precipitous descent…

FILKINS – LECHLADE – FAIRFORD – CIRENCESTER – BIRDLIP – GLOUCESTER – HUCCLECOTE – CHURCHAM – HUNTLEY – ROSS-ON-WYE

Having made up our minds to move on, after the usual heavy breakfast we decided to proceed no further than Ross. We took a circuitous route on the old Cirencester road, the misty and damp morning showing signs that the weather would further deteriorate.

E.B.P.'s back brake gave way soon after the start and neither Filkins nor Lechlade seemed to possess a likely looking repair shop but the job was finally done at Fairford. However, too much time had been lost to allow us to spend much time at the Ampneys. I had a little light refreshment at the 'Bull' at Fairford while E.B.P's repairs were made.

Cirencester was looking as attractive as usual, but there was a lack of sun and we went straight on the long pull up to Birdlip where we had a very excellent tea at the 'Golden Heart' before undertaking the precipitous descent into Gloucester through the insalubrious suburb of Hucclecote with its five miles of bad tramlines. Then for the toughish bit of road through Churcham and Huntley to Ross stopping on the way at the 'King's Head' about 6 miles on the way for light refreshments. The good woman who managed the establishment also went in extensively for poultry and fruit farming, and insisted on our filling our pockets with freshly picked plums before we left, which were very useful on the way.

At Ross we, as usual, made for the 'Gwalia' and also, as usual were made welcome and comfortable by Mrs Pugh and so, after supper and a stroll out to the prospect, to bed after a very satisfactory day's riding amounting to 54 *miles*.

WEDNESDAY 19TH AUGUST

Purring like young tea kettles...

ROSS – PETERSTOW – MUCH BIRCH – HEREFORD – BRIDGE SOLLERS – STAUNTON – WELLERSLEY – KINGTON – LLANFIHANGEL NANT MELAN

Ross, like Ludlow, is rarely kind to us in the way of weather and the outlook in the morning was a far from cheerful one – a cloudy dull sky being accompanied by drizzling rain; but we have learned long ago to take no account of the weather, so after breakfast we prepared to continue our pilgrimage, taking the familiar road in relentless rain to Hereford via Peterstow and Much Birch where the 'Axe and Cleaver' supplied us with our first refreshment and a breather without our capes.

Hereford was looking dull and cheerless in the rain and we continued straight on our way through Bridge Sollers, Staunton and Wellersley to Kington, that pleasant little town just this side of the Welsh border, just beyond which we had a very pleasant feed of bread and cheese and beer at the 'Three Horseshoes', a very ancient little pub which has recently been very badly restored by the proprietors.

Soon after this the rain eased off enough to allow of our discarding our capes permanently and we took it gently up the long slopes to New Radnor and finally arrived at the 'Red Lion' at Llanfihangel Nant Melan. After the usual mediation, which seems inseparable from obtaining accommodation in Wales, on the part of Mrs Williams, the landlady, she finally decided that we might stay there for a day or two and we were soon sitting down to an excellent tea befitting the reputation which this beautifully situated little inn has gained among cycling folk.

The evening turned out fine and sunny and we set out for a stroll along this wondrous mountain road accompanied by the two dogs belonging to the 'Red Lion', Skip and Rover, a very lively pair. And we returned to our inn as dusk was falling with that deep feeling of satisfaction of having struck a lovely district and a comfortable billet. Skip had in the meantime gone hunting on her own and captured a nice young rabbit, which was duly taken home for tomorrow's dinner. We were dossing in a double bedded room and after expelling one small tortoiseshell kitten who came in at the window, were invaded by a large cat and two more kittens all purring like young tea kettles. As it seemed impossible to keep entirely cat free we had to put up with them and they gave us no trouble.

Distance ridden: 43 miles

THURSDAY 20TH AUGUST

A mere 21 miles...

LLANFIHANGEL NANT MELAN – NEW RADNOR – KINGTON – KINNERTON – LLANFIHANGEL NANT MELAN

Got up feeling lazy and content with our surroundings and after a very excellent breakfast and inspection of the garden and livestock (cows, pigs, rabbits, chickens and ducks), we set out for a short exploration leaving word that we should be back to lunch. Retracing yesterday's route as far as New Radnor for the purpose of photographing the curious ruin used as the local branch of Barclays Bank, we turned off to the left on a road to Kington, which was mostly hill climbing and very rough, so that by the time we had got to the village of Kinnerton it was time to think of returning for lunch.

Lunch was an event, the first course consisting of Skip's kill of yesterday evening marvellously dished up with other things followed by plum tart and cream. We cleared everything up so as to get into form for the tramp we had planned for the afternoon. We had not gone far on our way (accompanied by Skip) before a very high hill attracted us, and, encouraged by the bounding Skip, we started to climb it. It was quite easy at first, but half way up E.B.P. had had enough of it. I went on progressing mostly on all fours until it got very difficult being mostly loose shale. Then I turned round and was appalled at what I had to descend, and having made up my mind that I was going to roll down and make a splash on the tiny strip which represented the road below, took two hasty photos and commenced the return journey.

This was a very trying experience but was accomplished at last without any broken bones. We then walked on across country trying to find the famous waterfall 'Water Breaks-Its-Neck' but with rain coming on we were compelled to return. After tea we took another walk round and I had a short run up the Llandrindod road to try a new position for my handlebars but the whole day's riding only totalled a mere *21 miles*.

FRIDAY 21ST AUGUST

A wash out in Llandovery

LLANFIHANGEL NANT MELAN – BUILTH WELLS – CILMERY – BEULAH SPA – LLANWRTYD WELLS –LLANDOVERY – LLANDILO

We made preparations for leaving the pleasant 'Red Lion' with much regret promising ourselves another visit there some day but we wanted to get on into new country. We accordingly took the road to Builth Wells and a pleasant enough road too. Builth, quite a popular Spa, did not strike us as a particularly attractive town but the River Wye is very pretty about here and is spanned by a very picturesque bridge. The weather was getting rather doubtful as we proceeded through rather plain country after some very excellent bread and cheese and Bass at the 'Prince Llewellyn Inn', Cilmery, to Beulah Spa and Llanwrtyd Wells. The latter is a very popular Welsh pleasure resort and was full of provincial holidaymakers, but we heard no word of English in the town. We could not fathom where its attractions lie though the surrounding country is extremely picturesque.

After leaving Llanwrtyd there is a long climb of some miles up to the top of the Sugar Loaf. The view from the top of this hill is of the wildest description and its terrifying aspect was enhanced by an approaching storm, which soon began to dampen us. The descent of this hill was one of the roughest and most tricky we have come across.

When we got into Llandovery the steady rain became a perfect deluge and soon the streets of this not too interesting town were flooded. We took refuge beneath a thick chestnut tree for about an hour, but with the deluge showing no signs of abating, we thought we should get no wetter by continuing onto Llangadog where we had had good reports of the 'Red Lion' and proposed having tea there. However, when Llangadog was reached we decided not to stop for tea in our drenched condition but to make for Llandilo, 11 miles further on, the storm still continuing in full force. Llandilo proved to be quite a nice little town so we decided to put up there for the night, the 'Castle Hotel' supplying us with a very satisfactory tea and quite good accommodation. The rain ceased enough to enable us to have a walk round the town about 8 o'clock before supper and bed.

Distance ridden: 47 miles

SATURDAY 22ND AUGUST

Queen of the Welsh Watering Places

LLANDILO – CARMARTHEN – BANCYFELIN – ST. CLEARS – TENBY

Got up to a fine day after our damp experiences of yesterday and after having a look round Llandilo, which was very busy it being market day, set off for Carmarthen via Abergwili – a very good and pleasant road, though the country hereabouts has more of an English aspect than any other part of Wales we have visited.

Carmarthen is a long, straggling town which was also very busy for market day and we walked through most of it before continuing on our way via Bancyfelin where at the 'Wheatsheaf' we were regaled with excellent bread and cheese and beer and excellently entertained by conversation with a very intelligent cattle drover, a much travelled man who had even been as far afield as 'England', that is to say 'Ross'. He expressed surprise at seeing us on bicycles as they are very rare in these parts which rather surprised us seeing how excellent were the roads and pleasant the country.

St. Clears is the next big town but it did not impress us and then, after passing through the smaller village of Llanddowror, there commences a 3-mile climb up to the village of Red Roses. With the sun being rather powerful we were not particularly sorry to get to the top since from here onwards the road is a strenuous one. We came on an isolated coal mine at Kilgetty where we turned off to the left down to Tenby, which is quite justly termed the 'Queen of the Welsh Watering Places'. Situated on a promontory it seems to have the sea all round it, and with the rocky coast and Caldey Island looming up on the south, it has a diversified character not to be found in many other seaside resorts we have visited. We found fairly comfortable quarters at the 'South Wales Hotel' and after tea and a wash and exploration of the town, walked out to the Waterwynch – a very picturesque bit of coast about 2 miles out of the town. Here we basked in the sun for about an hour and incidentally I got soaked by a wave that came over a rock upon which I was sitting. We then returned to the town and after a very good supper went to bed praying for fine weather on the morrow.

Distance ridden: 42 miles

SUNDAY 23RD AUGUST

Blessing on the name of Jenkins!
TENBY – MANORBIER – PEMBROKE – TENBY

I learned that four motorcyclists, who arrived late last night and 'kept it up' until about 3 in the morning, had rather disturbed the hotel, but needless to say had not kept me awake. With the weather looking promising we set off after breakfast by the coast road to Pembroke making a detour after passing Lydstep to visit Manorbier, and it was well worth going out of our way for the village, the castle (inhabited) and the coast were most picturesque.

We regained the road near Jameston and reached Pembroke via Hodgeston and Lamphey, the latter quite a pleasant little village. Pembroke is the usual type of Welsh town but the castle (from what we saw of its outside) should be well worth investigation but it was closed to visitors on Sundays. We had forgotten that we were in Wales and came out unprovided with grub of any description and on my enquiring of a milkman – the only sign of life in the town – what time the pubs opened, he put me right by telling me they don't in Wales, nor is any form of refreshment whatsoever allowed to be sold. To add to the discomfort this caused us, the storm that had long been threatening suddenly descended on us in full force, driving us to seek shelter under the castle entrance.

After about half an hour standing up we were spied by the local coal merchant Mr Jenkins who runs a refreshment business on a weekday, and he ushered us into his back kitchen where we were excellently regaled on roast lamb and mint sauce washed down by dry ginger – blessing on the name of Jenkins!

The rain ceased down after this repast[1] so we made our way to Pembroke Dock – a scene of desolation now there is no war to keep it busy, and not picturesque, though there is a wide view over Milford Haven and so we returned taking a rough, more inland road back to Tenby via Penally. The evening being fine was spent loafing around in Tenby mostly around the harbour, and as dusk was coming down E.B.P. suddenly made up his mind he would like to see Salisbury – some 200 miles away. So we decided to turn our noses in that direction – wet or fine – on the morrow and so to bed with no noisy motorcyclists to disturb our repose this time.

Distance ridden: 29 miles

---

1 Formal word for a meal.

MONDAY 24TH AUGUST

Destination Brecon

TENBY – BANCYFELIN – LLANDEILO – LLANDOVERY – TRECASTLE – BRECON

After a final walk round the pleasant town of Tenby we started back the road we had come on Saturday – there being no alternative if we wished to get into Wiltshire, and the first part of it is, if anything, tougher than going the other way. My back tyre expired just outside the 'Commercial Inn' and, before repairing, we entered and though it was not yet opening time the landlady made no bones about supplying our needs in the way of bottled Bass. The main midday meal was, however, taken at the 'Wheatsheaf', Bancyfelin, and our visit brought luck to that quaint little hostelry for a lordly motor party drove up and partook of Bass and bread and cheese which so excited the landlady that she hurried within and changed her pattens[2] for a pair of high heeled shoes.

We were badly in need of tea by the time we reached Llandeilo only to find that there was a great fair on at this exciting town and all eatables had been demolished. So we continued onto Llandovery where the 'Wajfrin Restaurant' provided us with a very excellent tea. We now started over new ground, our destination being Brecon, with the prospect of a continually rising road for about 10 miles but the rise was so gradual that it was hardly noticeable and the scenery on this road is so magnificent that had the gradient been four times as stiff we would have still rejoiced in the splendid views.

The limit of the upgrade is reached at Trecastle where at the 'Black Horse' we had some much needed refreshment before the long, and to tell the truth, rather cold descent into the picturesque town of Brecon where we found accommodation at the 'Angel' after a somewhat strenuous *trip of some 75 miles.*

---

2 a wooden clog or sandal on a raised wooden platform or metal ring

TUESDAY 25TH AUGUST

A break in Monmouth

BRECON – ABERGAVENNY – RAGLAN – MONMOUTH – NEWENT

We were in no hurry to depart from the pleasant town of Brecon and spent an hour or two on the banks of the picturesque Usk before thinking of going on our way on the Abergavenny road – a lovely road with the Brecknock[3] Beacons on either side. There is a long pull up to Bwlch onwards through Crickhowell is a good and easy road and Abergavenny is more prepossessing than the majority of the larger towns in this part of the world.

About a mile beyond Abergavenny we struck a very comfortable 'Three Horseshoes' for our midday bread and cheese, and then went on to Raglan where about 1½ hours was spent in the castle (one of our favourite castles). Just as we were leaving, curiously enough three friends – Mabel and Guy Paice and Mrs Wilton – arrived per motor, and extracted a promise from me to spend a day or two at Barry next week.[4]

At Monmouth we had an indifferent tea at the 'Rising Sun' over which we decided to make Newent our next stopping place, but the road we took after leaving Ross was both rough and hilly. However, we got there in good order and found at the 'George' as good entertainment as we had met anywhere, an extremely good supper putting a finish to a fairly easy *59 mile run*.

WEDNESDAY 26TH AUGUST

A glorious run into Cirencester

NEWENT – GLOUCESTER – BROCKWORTH – CIRENCESTER – MALMESBURY – CHIPPENHAM – TROWBRIDGE – FROME

Newent had struck us two years ago as an extremely pleasant little town and this impression was confirmed on our morning survey. It is quite a large place but on a road that leads to nowhere in particular. Hence it

---

3 Another name for the Brecon Beacons
4 According to the 1939 census Guy and Mabel Paice lived at No.12 Cambridge Street, Barry, Glamorganshire. Guy was born in Kensington on 5th November 1888 and in 1939 was a railway clerk in charge of wages. Mabel Paice nee Rivers was born on 3rd January 1893. They married on 4th June 1917. Guy served in the RAF during WWI as a clerk.

remains unspoiled and the 'George' is a stopping place which will well bear revisiting.

As we had to get to the other side of the Severn it was, of course, necessary to go through Gloucester, a pleasant bye-road of some 8 miles taking us to that extensive city; and as we proposed ascending Birdlip Hill from this side, we had the 4 miles of bad tramlines to Hucclecote to negotiate first, stopping for a refresher at the 'Crossed Hands' Brockworth before the long steep climb.

But once at the top it is a glorious run into Cirencester, though it was broken by midday bread and cheese at the 'Five Mile House' on the Ermin Way. From Cirencester we took the road to Malmesbury through Crudwell. Malmesbury looks a different place in fine weather to what it did in the pouring rain when I was through there last year. The Abbey is very fine too and we spent some time exploring before going on through Corston to Chippenham badly in want of our tea, which we obtained of excellent quality at the 'Central Café' in that up-to-date town which was very empty (it being early-closing day).

We decided on Frome as our next stopping place, reaching it through the thriving towns of Melksham and Trowbridge, the latter giving us our evening refreshment at 'The Ring O' Bells'. It was latish when we arrived in Frome so we put up at the first C.T.C. place we came to – the 'Bridge Hotel' – which though of an unprepossessing exterior, proved both cheap and comfortable. *Distance ridden: 68 miles*

THURSDAY 27TH AUGUST

...a glorious evening for our walk around the city
FROME – WARMINSTER – HINDON – SALISBURY

Pigs being loaded into lorries outside our bedroom window woke us up early to a rather unpromising morning with a gentle rain falling, which looked as though it might last for 24 hours. However, this did not check our progress towards Salisbury. Before making a start we explored Frome, which must be about the hilliest town in England – there not being a level street in it. The church is a remarkable one but it was too early to penetrate into its interior and what took our fancy most was Cheap Street with a stream running in a deep stone channel down the centre of it.

Our way took us first to the picturesque town of Warminster where the 'Fox and Hounds' refreshed us with cider and biscuits. The rain had left off, and as we had only a short journey to do, we made up our minds to loaf on a roundabout route, but nevertheless the bye road we took to Hindon through the lovely village of Longbridge Deverill was both steep and rough. It was past 1 o'clock before we reached the picturesque and ancient town of Hindon for our midday bread and cheese at the 'Grosvenor Arms', a very comfortable pub.

From Hindon we made our way to Fonthill Bishop and through Fonthill Park eventually arriving at the (to me) very familiar village of Dinton, which was the station for Fovant Camp; from here we continued through Barford St. Martin (where E.B.P.'s back tyre required repairs), Fugglestone and Wilton into Salisbury where we made at once for the 'Coach and Horses' in Winchester Street, a stopping place which we had last year decided was one of the best. After tea it was a glorious evening for our walk around the city and we confirmed our impression of last year that Salisbury's is the most impressive cathedral.

At supper, we were entertained by two elderly motoring ex-cyclists in general road talk and agreed perfectly with them except on the subject of rear lights!

Distance ridden: 36 miles

FRIDAY 28TH AUGUST

A steep and twisty descent

SALISBURY – FOVANT – SHAFTESBURY – WINCANTON – SOUTH PETHERTON – ILMINSTER – CHARD – YARCOMBE – HONITON

As per our tour last year, Salisbury was the parting place for E.B.P. and myself – he to proceed to Winchester on the homeward way while I proposed trying to make Honiton on another thrust into the West Country.

A fine sunny morning made us loath to leave Salisbury and after mending a punctured back tyre it was noon before we parted company. I retraced my way as far as Barford St. Martin and then took the very familiar road to Fovant where a good hour was spent at the old 'Cross Keys' in converse with sundry local worthies on the theme of old army days.

Consequently, by the time I had negotiated the strenuous road through Swallow Cliff and Donhead to Shaftesbury my prospects of reaching Honiton seemed somewhat remote. However, in fine weather and with a favouring wind, the road onwards from Shaftesbury is a fast one and I decided to stick to the road I knew through Gillingham, Wincanton (custard tarts and lemonade purchased) Sparkford, Ilchester and South Petherton (where a new refreshment house provided me with an excellent tea after a badly needed wash) to Ilminster. Here I thought it advisable to take the road through Chard as time was going on and walked up most of the steep main street of that not very interesting town and of course up the impossible hill leading out of it.

By the time I reached Yarcombe, dusk was already approaching and after a Bass and biscuits at the 'Yarcombe Inn' I was nearly persuaded by the landlord of that comfortable hostelry to put up for the night as there was a good mile and a half walk before me before the run down into Honiton. However, I resisted the temptation and by the time the mile and a half uphill walk was finished it was quite dark enough to light up – the first time I had done so since the start of the tour.

The steep and twisty descent into Honiton was a bit terrifying and I was not sorry to see the lights of the town at last putting up at 'Scotts' in the West High Street where the remainder of the evening was spent in company with two of Lyon's motor engineers from Cadby Hall, along with a four valve set radio and loud speaker transmitting Daventry[5] rottenly. *Distance ridden: 75 miles*

SATURDAY 29TH AUGUST

Footballs and footballers

HONITON – EXETER – COPPLESTONE – SAMPFORD COURTENAY – HATHERLEIGH – HIGHAMPTON – HOLSWORTHY

I had ordered an early breakfast and was almost sorry I had done so as the morning started distinctly unpromising; the gentle drizzle, however, ceased after breakfast and I strolled for some time in the streets of the town preparing for Saturday market and got the bit of lace which I omitted to get when last I was here which I duly despatched to the proper quarter.

Even with these delays I got on my way soon after 9.30 a.m., arriving in Exeter at half past eleven. Here I spent a considerable time trying to get a fresh stock of films, only succeeding at the sixth attempt and then having a

---

5 Daventry 5XX was a BBC radio station that opened on 27th July 1925

blow out of pastries and ginger ale before proceeding on my way through Newton St. Cyres to Crediton and onto Copplestone, where it being near closing time I thought it as well to stock up with bread, cheese and of course some Bass at the 'Cross Hotel'. And of course it being the first day of the football season the hotel was full of footballs and footballers.

Being mapless I had to trust my memory to find the road turning off just past Bow on the right to North Tawton, quite a large village I had never visited before. However, I was able to obtain sailing directions to Hatherleigh through the very Devonian village of Sampford Courtenay where the weather, which up to now had been dull and gloomy, cleared. The road past Exbourne onto Hatherleigh was very familiar and roused many old memories, and Hatherleigh provided me with a real Devonshire tea at 'Walter's' in Bridge Street.

I spent quite a lot of time in Hatherleigh and prepared to go in a very leisurely manner along the road, which five years ago we had to scorch over to get to the same destination. I had designed to have a Bass at the 'Golden Sun' Highampton but had to be content with taking a photograph of it as it was not open. However, I found a very comfortable Inn – 'The Bickford Arms' – further on where the local postman gave me much interesting information on such diverse subjects as the cause of the failure of the fruit crop, which he attributed to the decline in the bee-keeping industry, and the glories of fox-hunting which is the great sport of these parts so that the winter is eagerly looked forward to by all and sundry.

The unpicturesque town of Holsworthy, the scene of pleasant memories to me, was reached about 8 o'clock and I was warmly welcomed by the Misses Jollows at the 'South Western Hotel'. After a walk around, I had a proper Holsworthy supper of cold fowl and ham followed by blackberry tart and cream in the company of some very nice people from Surbiton who had been staying in the hotel since February waiting for vacant possession of a house they had purchased at Bude. And much pleasant converse with the Jollow family before going to bed convinced that there is no other part of England like Devon after all.

Distance ridden: 58 miles

A GOLDEN AGE OF CYCLING

SUNDAY 30TH AUGUST
A young balloon
HOLSWORTHY – BOSCASTLE – BUDE – HOLSWORTHY

A fine bright morning caused me to decide on having a fleeting glimpse of Cornwall, and after an ample and leisurely breakfast I set off fortified with a huge parcel of sandwiches which Evelyn Jollow insisted on my taking with me, on the Bude road, not forgetting to sample the blackberries at the boundary bridge which I found as luscious as ever.

With Stratton looking very enticing in the morning sun I turned off on what used to be the very rough road pointing to Camelford, but in the five years since last I traversed it, it has been made like a track and a beautiful road it is, with frequent views of the blue Atlantic on the right and the picturesque Cornish villages on the left. I was curious to see if the quaint cottage where we had such a wonderful tea once still catered for the traveller and was gratified to find it between Poundstock and Wainhouse Corner. Though it was rather early I could not resist the temptation to fill up with milk and good Cornish cake before going over the wild country to Boscastle, stopping at the top of Penally Hill to devour the greater part of Evelyn's sandwiches.

In Boscastle my first business was to visit the 'Wellington Hotel' where a bottle of Bass washed down the sandwiches, after which a couple of hours was agreeably spent in wandering around this picturesque place taking numerous photographs and basking in the sun on the cliffs. I then returned to the aforesaid cottage to tea which consisted of so many different items that I felt like a young balloon when I had finished, for it was impossible to refuse to sample any of them.

I had hoped to get back to Bude in time to get some photographs but was foiled by the sea mist that arose suddenly. Bude was full of people and I walked out on the sands before returning through Stratton to Holsworthy for supper and more talk of the doings of the day. And so to bed wishing I had more time to spend a week in this delightful district with these pleasant people.
Distance ridden: 49 miles

MONDAY 31ST AUGUST

Ready for the regatta

HOLSWORTHY – MONKLEIGH – BIDEFORD – APPLEDORE – INSTOW – BARNSTAPLE – ILFRACOMBE

The sea mist, which had risen overnight, still persisted in the form of a light drizzle. I was entertained while getting up watching the evolutions of three flocks of sheep which had got mixed up and were finally sorted out in an amazing way by their respective sheepdogs urged on by the shepherds by signs and inextricable sounds.

After breakfast I was very loath to make a start but I eventually bade them all farewell promising to come again if possible next year and bring E.B.P. I departed, the sun having driven the sea mist away, taking the Bideford Road.

Having only a short stage to do there was no need for hurry and stops were made frequently to partake of the blackberries, which are such a feature of this part of the country. Frithelstock, a previously pretty village, is rather spoilt by a new large motor garage with its attendant hideous petrol advertisements, but Monkleigh is as of yore and having passed the 'Bell' before I did not do so on this occasion, cider and biscuits being my fare.

Of course the River Torridge, beside which the road now ran, was at low tide and as usual exhibiting much mud and seagulls. Bideford, however, was looking very attractive in the sunshine – the farther end of the quay being littered with accessories ready for the regatta which was due to take place in a few days.

I did not spend much time in Bideford as I wished to visit quaint old Appledore which I reached through Northam. Just outside Appledore I was 'attacked' by a boatman who wanted to ferry me across to Instow; the suggestion struck me as a good one but I explained that I wanted to spend an hour in Appledore first and he cheerfully agreed to wait. Unfortunately the sea mist had arrived again but nevertheless I exposed several films on this picturesque old place and fared sumptuously on cold pork sandwiches and Bass at the 'Champion of Wales' in company with a curious collection of natives who, in spite of their piratical appearance, were most courteous and told many curious yarns for the benefit of the stranger in their midst.

After this interlude I found my boatman and had a pleasant journey across to Instow, the fare being just 1/-[6] for self and machine. Instow is a pleasant, but not extremely lively little pleasure resort and the road from there to Barnstaple is a good and level one. Barnstaple strikes one as a very fine town but I did not stay long there as the sea mist had turned to a gentle drizzle and after taking the opportunity of getting a local dairy to take some post orders for cream, I set off on the Ilfracombe road which, for a considerable distance, is dead level.

At Bittadon, a largish village, I obtained a very satisfying tea; the remainder of the road to Ilfracombe (until the top of Woollacot Hill is reached) is of a strenuous nature and the run down into the town rather steeper than is pleasant especially as there is plenty of heavy traffic in the way of charabancs and buses. I put up at the first C.T.C. place I came to – 'Delves' in the High Street – which was as good a billet as one could expect to get in a place like Ilfracombe and, after a stroll round in the growing dusk and supper, went to bed.

Distance ridden: 43 miles

TUESDAY 1ST SEPTEMBER
An ancient mariner
ILFRACOMBE – BARRY

Got up to a most dismal prospect, the town being enveloped in a misty rain, which I was assured would last all day. I had also ascertained last night that the only steamer across to Barry did not leave until 5.30 in the evening, and so it looked as though I was not going to have a very lively day. However, after a hearty breakfast I set out on an exploration tramp and am bound to say that even in fine weather I could not imagine caring to make a lengthy stay here. The only thing that struck me as useful was the Winter Garden where I spent most of the morning writing letters and mended my back tyre, which had been requiring attention for some days.

After dinner I could not stick it indoors, so paid my bill and thought I would try and beat the rain to Mortehoe. However, by the time I had got to the top of the hill the rain was so solid that I returned to the comparative shelter of the town. Here I loafed around the harbour spending an hour over tea consisting mostly of apricots and cream at a

---

6 1 shilling

refreshment house on the Quay until it was time to go on the boat the 'Lady Moyra'. Not finding any shelter on deck, I used my Paget to cover my machine but having no relish for below-deck, finally left the machine to look after itself and donned the Paget myself. Long before we left the pier, sundry of passengers were looking a bit green, and one mother with a baby and two small children was glad to turn over the two latter to me to look after. I think I gave them quite a good time and neither of them showed the least inclination to be ill, though their mother was sure they would be, having never been on the sea before.

As it was much too rough to call at Minehead and Lynton on the way, the journey only took about 2½ hours and I was quite sorry when the Welsh coast came in sight wonderfully bathed in sunshine. It was here that the rain stopped so that I was able to turn myself from an ancient mariner into a cyclist once more. Having turned over my two charges to their mother (both in first class health and spirits) I disembarked at Barry pier and eventually found my way up to Barry where much talk, after not having seen one another (except that brief encounter at Raglan) for nearly a year, kept us up until nearly midnight. This was the shortest day's *riding being a mere 11 miles.*

WEDNESDAY 2ND SEPTEMBER

Mushrooming!
BARRY – ABERTHAW – LLANTWIT MAJOR – ST. DONAT'S CASTLE – MARCROSS – BRIDGEND – WICK – BARRY

A different prospect from my yesterday morning's awaking – a brilliant day and after breakfast I made up my mind to visit the very interesting village of Llantwit Major. Again I took the usual road through Aberthaw, where I posed with shepherd and dog for a photographs, then made for St. Athan and Boverton where the castle is now enclosed so could not get a photograph of it. Half an hour in Llantwit sufficed and after a perilous climb to get a photograph of the church, I took the coast road to St. Donat's Castle – quite a wonderful old residence said to be the oldest inhabited house in the British Isles with moat and drawbridge surrounded by thick woods.

After there I went on to Marcross where the 'Horseshoe' supplied me with bread, cheese and Bass and then on through St. Brides Major to

Bridgend, the road between these two places being a beautiful one. Bridgend is always associated on one's mind with coal and is quite a nice little country town. Here I turned back, making a descent into Southerndown, a bijou seaside resort consisting for the most part of a sandy bay with Lord Dunraven's Castle perched on the cliff overlooking it.

The return to Barry was made by a slightly different route via Wick. After tea, Guy and I spent the evening mushrooming and we collected enough for breakfast, though the evening was rather a chilly one.

Distance ridden: 43 miles

THURSDAY 3RD SEPTEMBER
BARRY – CAERPHILLY CASTLE – CARDIFF – NEWPORT – CHEPSTOW

Another fine morning. I prepared to take leave of my kind friends and turn my nose towards home but I was determined to make a detour first to visit Caerphilly Castle, having first to make for Cardiff via Wenvoe and the mean streets of Canton. I was wiser than on my last visit in going by the left hand road at Whitchurch via Taff's Well and the ugly mining village of Nantgarw though this means about a mile walk uphill before the run down into Caerphilly. I was unlucky at the Castle as far as photography was concerned as the light was very poor and it finally started to rain heavily before I took my departure, this time going straight up the hill which is, of course, quite unrideable. I stopped at the 'Traveller's Rest' at the top for much needed bread, cheese and beer.

It is a rundown all the way into Cardiff by this road and I did not linger long in that handsome city but continued straight on by the excellent road via Rumney, St. Mellons and Castleton to Newport – the state of the tramlines in that town making it necessary to walk the greater part of it. From here to Chepstow is a lovely road and at about five miles on the way the 'New Inn' supplied me with a very excellent tea (the route was via Llanbeder, Llanvaches, Caerwent and Crick).

A beefy local on a dreadnought took me on over the last seven or eight miles and I did not shake him off until the steep rise just outside Chepstow which otherwise I would rather have walked; he hung onto me about half way up and then started pushing his machine but I was able to put on enough steam to leave him.

At Chepstow I put up at 'Skrymes Café', a very comfortable quarters and spent the evening mostly by the river, which was swirling around the castle at high tide, making a splendid picture. I finished up in very pleasant company at the 'Bridge Inn' with Bass and biscuits before supper and bed, hoping for a fine morning so that I could get some photographs of the castle.

Distance ridden: 57 miles

FRIDAY 4TH SEPTEMBER

A favourable day for photography

CHEPSTOW – TINTERN ABBEY – LLANDOGO – WHITCHURCH – ROSS-ON-WYE – GLOUCESTER – CHELTENHAM – PUESDOWN – NORTHLEACH – BURFORD

A stormy sky and frequent showers did not make my prospects very hopeful but after an early (8 o'clock) breakfast (the best breakfast I had met outside the 'Swan', starting with porridge) things improved and the sun made momentary efforts to break through. I took full advantage with the river once again at high tide and by the time I had done the interior of the castle it was noon. I had a longish stage before me, as I wanted to take the magnificent Wyndcliff road instead of the easier one via Lydney. More time was spent in obtaining photographs of Tintern Abbey – rather a difficult subject, necessitating climbing onto the top of a narrow wall with a 40-foot drop in front.

The 'Sloop Inn' at Llandogo supplied me with midday refreshment and the familiar road via Redbrook, Monmouth and Whitchurch (refreshments at 'The Crown') to Ross was negotiated without incident and at good speed. This was the third visit to Ross on the present tour and at last I was able to get Wilton Bridge in a favourable light for photography. Ross to Gloucester is also a familiar road and outside the City I obtained a very good tea at a wayside cottage and also shelter from a passing storm.

Gloucester was all beflagged in honour of the Three Choirs Festival but I had no time to linger and went straight through and onto Cheltenham, then the heavy pull up through Charlton Kings and Andoversford to the top of Puesdown. I was very glad of some refreshment at the 'Puesdown Inn' before the run down to Northleach. It was getting late and a very nipping wind made me unpack my luggage and get out my waistcoat outside Northleach after which very short work was made of the nine miles to the 'Swan' in Burford. Here an excellent supper in good company sent me to bed as happy as could be expected having regard to the fact that my holiday was coming to an end.

Distance ridden: 73 miles

SATURDAY 5TH SEPTEMBER

A goodly company

BURFORD – STOW-ON-THE-WOLD – BROADWAY – EVESHAM – BURFORD

A fine morning made me resolve to make northward with a view to 'picturising' Broadway and Chipping Campden. Hence I took the Stow road and from Stow to Broadway stopping only at the 'Coach and Horses' at Stow for refreshments. By that time rain had come on the scene and it looked like continuing for the rest of the day, so I put up temporarily at the 'Swan' Broadway and had a very excellent lunch of cold fowl and ham followed by apple tart and cream.

The rain showed no sign of abatement so I decided to push on to Evesham, spending about half an hour in that pleasant town, pleasant even in the rain. I then took the road through Bretforton and the pretty village of Weston-sub-Edge to Aston-sub-Edge being anxious to see what the 'Cottage' beloved of 'Wayfarer'[7] was like; I must say that it seems a most comfortable crib and gave me a very good tea. Just as I was leaving a young man named Cash of Birmingham came up and on my telling him I was going back to Burford asked me to tell Miss Lomas he was on his way there in the hope of being put up.

The road onwards to Chipping Campden is only a short (but very steep) one and I was unable to take in all the beauties of that lovely village owing to the rain which still continued and the road on to Stow is a very stiff one. However, I got back to Burford by 8 o'clock in advance of Cash and secured him his quarters. A goodly company had gathered at the 'Swan' including C.A. Sewell, the North Road[8] man I had met on Whit Saturday and a very nice old chap named Vickers from Birmingham with whom I had a long stroll after a very heavy supper along the Lechlade road before turning in.

Distance ridden: 60 miles

---

7 The pen name of the famous cycling journalist WM Robinson (1877–1956)
8 North Road is a cycling club, founded in 1885 in Hertfordshire

1925 HOLIDAY TOUR

SUNDAY 6TH SEPTEMBER
The final leg
BURFORD – DORCHESTER – MAIDENHEAD – TWICKENHAM

As usual I meant to make an early start for any last day's run home and also as usual found myself very reluctant to leave Burford, so it was 12 o'clock before I started on the last stage by strolling up the High Street with Vickers who was going to Cirencester. Nevertheless, I put on so much steam that the 'Fleur de Lis' at Dorchester was reached by 1.30 p.m. and I was able to spend an hour over lunch at that comfortable hostelry. After some refreshments in Maidenhead I reached home in good order at 6 o'clock in time for tea, finding all in order and starting developing the photographs straight away after the *75 miles run* which made the total of the three weeks' *tour exactly 1200 miles.*

1925 ANNUAL REVIEW

A very successful year's cycling which produced a record mileage. This was mainly due to the early part of the summer being so fine as to give opportunities for a long ride every Sunday and good evening runs during the week.

The century was exceeded on three occasions, two of them on Saturday holidays, (the Saturday before Whitsun and August Bank Holiday) and a weekend at Burford in July was also obtained.

The annual holiday was taken rather later than usual in the same general direction as in 1923 and 1924. The weather though by no means perfect was better than we had experienced in the two preceding years. A welcome revisitation was made to North Devon with just a snatched dive into Cornwall, a trip across the Bristol Channel taking me for a short visit to Barry.

A new feature was the combination of photography with cycling and many good pictures were obtained, no less than 130 exposures being made on the holiday trip.

Both 'James' and 'Chater-Lea' machines gave admirable service and except for tyres gave no trouble. Consequently, they will both be retained for the next year.

A GOLDEN AGE OF CYCLING

CYCLING STATISTICS FOR 1925 BY MILES AND NUMBER OF RIDES PER MONTH

MONTH	NUMBER OF RIDES			MILES RIDDEN				AVERAGE MILES PER RIDE			
	SUNDAY	TOURING	OTHER RIDES	SUNDAYS	TOURING	OTHER RIDES	TOTAL	SUNDAYS	TOURING	OTHER RIDES	ALL RIDES
Jan	3	-	-	119	-	-	119	39.66	-	-	39.66
Feb	4	-	-	149	-	-	149	37.25	-	-	37.25
Mar	5	-	1	219	-	7	226	43.80	-	7.00	37.66
Apr	4	-	3	212	-	174	386	53.00	-	58.00	55.14
May	5	-	6	264	-	230	494	52.80	-	38.33	44.90
June	4	-	7	306	-	218	524	76.50	-	31.14	47.63
July	4	1	6	260	76	144	480	65.00	76.00	24.00	43.63
Aug	5	14	3	208	774	134	1116	41.60	55.28	44.66	50.72
Sept	4	5	-	253	244	-	497	63.25	48.80	-	55.02
Oct	4	-	-	178	-	-	178	44.50	-	-	44.50
Nov	5	-	-	209	-	-	209	41.80	-	-	41.80
Dec	4	-	1	151	-	50	201	37.77	-	50.00	40.25
Totals	51	20	27	2528	1094	957	4579	49.56	54.70	35.44	46.72

1925 HOLIDAY TOUR

5 of the Sunday rides having been done on tour have been deducted from the touring figures. Consequently the actual touring figures are: 25 rides, 1351 miles, Average miles per ride: 54.04

1926 SUMMER WEEKEND RIDES

SATURDAY 3RD JULY – CHATER-LEA

A True Cotswold Road

HAMMERSMITH – WINDSOR – CAVERSHAM – GORING – WANTAGE – STANFORD-IN-THE-VALE – FARRINGDON – FAIRFORD – COLN ST. ALDWYNS – BIBURY – BURFORD

Started off in a gentle drizzle at 7.30 a.m., which soon gave way to brilliant sunshine that thankfully lasted all day. Reached Windsor, which had only just awoken, soon after 9 o'clock and then went off the rails[1] to Winkfield, from which village the newly tarred cross track to Waltham St. Lawrence was too much for my back tyre, which I had to repair. At Caversham the 'Prince of Wales' supplied me with my first refreshment at 11.30 a.m. and the road to Goring required some finding. By the time I arrived it was time for bread and cheese at the 'Queen's Arms'.

From Goring it is out over the Berkshire Downs very soon after leaving Streatley and these same Berkshire Downs require some beating; although it is all up and down, there were no banks steep enough to require walking between Streatley and Wantage. Wantage was very busy this Saturday afternoon and after some light refreshments I passed on my way through the

---

1 This could be referring to an 'off road' route.

Vale of the White Horse. At Stanford-in-the-Vale, a water splash provided a very welcome sluice before going onto Farringdon where the 'White Hart' provided an extremely excellent tea about 4 o'clock. After tea, the six miles across the tail end of Wiltshire into Gloucestershire, and across St. Johns Bridge where the Thames and Severn Canal starts, to Lechlade, did not take long, nor the few more miles to Fairford from which picturesque little town a road was taken (rather a rough one) through Quenington to Coln St. Aldwyns – a beautiful village. Then onto beautiful Bibury, which was looking particularly entrancing in the late afternoon sun. After wandering around by the banks of the Coln and enjoying a Bass with some biscuits at the 'Catherine Wheel', I took a true Cotswold road to Burford via Aldsworth and I took it at speed. After all the Cotswold country is an exhilaration all of its own. The Tolsey Clock was just striking 8 o'clock as I entered the delectable town where the 'Swan' gave me its usual welcome. A wash and a small drink and then a walk round, supper of cold beef and salad, gooseberry tart and cream and blancmange with five other C.T.C. members, an hour's chin-wagging and then bed at 11 o'clock rounded off a glorious day with a cyclometer record of *102 miles.*

SUNDAY 4TH JULY

A somewhat damp ramble

BURFORD – WITNEY – DUCKINGTON – NEWBRIDGE – ABINGDON – SOTWELL – HENLEY – WALTHAM – HORTON – HAMMERSMITH

It was nearly 8 o'clock when I awoke to a brilliant sunshine morning notwithstanding the arrival to breakfast at 7.30 a.m. of the noisy party of 33 members of the Western Section of the C.T.C. who had been doing a night ride. It was hard to leave Burford after breakfast and I sat with a young Birmingham man just finishing a holiday tour until nearly 12 o'clock before thinking of making a move for home. Then I set out on the old road as far as Witney turning off past the church on the Abingdon Road. About two miles on I came across one of the prettiest villages even in this part of the world, Duckington, of which I took a photograph before going on my way.

At Newbridge the 'Rose Revived' attracted me and here I had my midday bread, cheese and beer only to find when I had finished it that my back tyre had collapsed. However, this was soon mended, but after about half a mile the same thing happened again. While I was repairing it an elderly cyclist came along in whose company I went to Abingdon via Kingston Bagpuize and Marcham.

From Abingdon, where it started to rain, it was a little difficult to find the road to Wallingford, which I did through Sutton Courtenay and Appleford, stopping at 'The Bell' at Sotwell for one of the finest 1/- teas I had ever met with. As the rain still continued I thought it as well to take the shortest route so made for Nettlebed, having the stiff climb up to Huntercombe Golf links to do first. As I entered Henley the rain came on in earnest so that I traversed the road through Wargrave and Twyford to Waltham St. Lawrence enveloped in my trusty Paget.

The 'Star' at Waltham provided Bass and Banbury cakes before I headed back into the rain, which mercifully died down to a drizzle until nearly into Windsor when a cloudburst occurred that drove me to shelter for half an hour. I then took the usual road from Windsor, stopping for more refreshment at the 'Five Bells', Horton, where the rain having ceased I shed my cape. The only other incident was that I shed my lamp in Twickenham so that it required tying together with string and I had to light up before reaching home about 10.30 p.m. after a pleasant but somewhat damp ramble of *84 miles.*

SUNDAY IITH JULY

A hungry cyclist

HAMMERSMITH – HORTON – BILLINGSHURST – PULBOROUGH – FITTLEWORTH – CHIDDINGFOLD – NEWARK – STOKE D'ABERNON – HAMMERSMITH

Got off about 9.30 a.m. in hopes of escaping the traffic. Was grievously disappointed as the road from Leatherhead to Beare Green was like a railroad[2] and beyond to Pulborough was little better. From there, however, the roads were moderately quiet.

A dull watery outlook first greeted me but it was very warm and as the sun broke through the heat became intense. I arrived in Billingshurst just in time for bread, cheese and beer at the 'Six Bells'. Pulborough was full of charabancs and nosebaggers![3] I had further refreshments at the picturesque 'Swan' at Fittleworth with a curious company.

---

2 Charles' metaphor isn't completely clear here, but it's likely he's referring to the bustle of the road to Beare Green.

3 A mid 19th century slang term for tourists who visit a place for the day but bring their own provisions

It being too early for tea at Petworth I went onto the 'Old Forge' Tea Rooms at Chiddingfold – a very swank little place but not suitable for a hungry cyclist. Made a detour from Ripley for a very welcome wash in the River Wey at Newark and had two Worthingtons and Banbury cakes at 'The Plough', Stoke D'Abernon.

Arrived back home at 9.30 p.m. just after E.B.P. who had been weekending at Burford. A pleasant but somewhat hot and strenuous *108 miles*[4].

SUNDAY 18TH JULY

A very pleasant ramble

HAMMERSMITH – CHOBHAM – PIRBRIGHT – ELSTEAD – EASHING – STOKE D'ABERNON – SURBITON – HAMMERSMITH

With the weather being hot and sultry, I set out for a loafing day. Made first of all for Chobham via Esher, Hersham, Weybridge, Chertsey, and Ottershaw. Then onto Knaphill turning off along Brookwood Cemetery walls to Pirbright, a pleasant but rather over civilised Surrey village. We were rather at a loss regarding which way to proceed but decided to get the other side of Hog's Back[5] through Normandy and Ash – a fairly easy climb except the last few hundred yards.

A mile across the sticky tarred Hog's Back took us to an off road pointing to Seale where we hoped to find a pub to refresh but were disappointed, so had to make full speed through three mile of glorious country to Elstead where the 'Star' supplied us with 1½ pints of ale each and some cheese of quite remarkable strength. After that the whole afternoon was loafed away in the woods, and a short roundabout way via Mousehill and Milford to Eashing, where a very satisfactory light tea was obtained at the 'Stag'. This meant taking the main Portsmouth road back as far as Ripley via Godalming and Guildford. There we took the usual Ockham and Cobham bye-pass with a long rest on Cobham Bridge and a pint of ale at 'The Plough' Stoke D'Abernon and a Bass at 'The Oaks' Surbiton.

The weather was extremely hot and sweltering all day with threats of

---

4 It appears Charles broke his previous cyclometer record, set on 3rd July (102 miles), but fails to acknowledge it here.

5 A section of the North Downs in Surrey lying between Farnham and Guildford

thunder, which culminated in a heavy storm after we had got home. A very pleasant ramble of some *84 miles*.

SUNDAY 25TH JULY

Two young bucks and three ill-favoured damsels

HAMMERSMITH – EALING – RADLETT – ST. ALBANS – MARKYATE – DUNSTABLE – HOCKLIFFE – FENNY STRATFORD – LEIGHTON BUZZARD – BILLINGTON – DAGNALL – EALING

A desire for something new led us to adopt a northern route – a last minute decision. So we made for Ealing over Hanger Hill through Wembley and Wealdstone on the Watford road, turning off some three miles short of that unlovely town by a bye-way, rough but countrified which brought us out on the Birmingham road at Radlett.

This narrow main road was rather trafficky through Frogmore and Park Street to St. Albans in which city E.B.P.'s front tyre required attention. We then decided to go ahead to Dunstable through Redbourn, Markyate Street and Kensworth. At the 'Chequers' near Markyate we took our midday refreshment of bread, cheese and ale both of the most excellent quality.

Dunstable is not a particularly attractive town even on a weekday and we did not linger there in search of any of its hidden features but kept straight on the road, cutting through the chalk over the Downs stopping for another refresher at the 'Bell' at Hockliffe as closing time was drawing near. This is a lovely desolate stretch of up and down road but the surface is all that could be desired and notwithstanding a strong headwind, Fenny Stratford was reached at 2.30 p.m. the only other village passed being Little Brickhill.

Fenny Stratford presents no attractions but the road we took to Leighton Buzzard via Stoke Hammond is quite a diversified and attractive one though we were driven to shelter by rain for about half an hour on the way. The rain resumed at the not unpicturesque town of Leighton Buzzard but did not last long and the wind being now behind us made it easy work up the long Chiltern slopes through Northall and the beautiful village of Billington, with its prominent church on a hill by the side of the road.

However, the 'Red Lion' at Dagnall displaying a sign "Teas" was too attractive to pass so here we stopped having a moderate tea in company with two young bucks and three ill-favoured damsels before making our way via Great Saddlesden, Water End and Piggott's End to Hemel Hempstead.

A GOLDEN AGE OF CYCLING

From here we found the main road rather crowded but there was no escape but to continue through Boxmoor and Kings Langley to Watford where we took the sharp right turn to Rickmansworth after seeking refuge from a perfect drencher at the foot of Scots Hill.

From Rickmansworth a bye-pass road took us up to Moore Park (ridden all the way) – an improvement on the usual precipitous climb – and from there through Northwood and Ruislip to Northolt and Greenford to Ealing is easy work although the Uxbridge Road is not a pleasant finishing stretch. However we arrived home at 9.30 p.m. after a pleasant spin of some *102 miles* rendered more pleasant than otherwise by the heavy showers which laid down the dust and made the air fresh and clean.

SATURDAY 31ST JULY

What more can a man want?

HAMMERSMITH – GUILDFORD – GODALMING – LIPHOOK – PETERSFIELD – SOUTH HARTING – MIDHURST – HASLEMERE – BROOK – GODALMING – COBHAM – HAMMERSMITH

Having the Saturday before the Bank Holiday off as usual left me rather in a quandary as to how to make the best of it.

However, a fine morning and a light North West wind decided me on a jaunt down the main Portsmouth road. Consequently I set off on the old James machine about 9 o'clock through the Park[6], Kingston, Esher, Wisley and Ripley to Guildford where the Saturday morning traffic compelled me to walk the greater part of the High Street. I got away from Guildford about 11 o'clock and soon fell in with a young C.T.C.-ite bound for Portsmouth for the Isle of Wight. In his company, we soon got through Godalming and Milford and the gruelling grind up to Hindhead with its compensating four mile run down into Liphook.

We did not stop in Liphook but continued straight on the glorious road through Rake and Sheet to Petersfield and, to tell the truth, I was feeling rather peckish. All the pubs in Petersfield, however, seemed infested with charabanc parties so I set out on an off-road pointing to South Harting in search of some quiet refreshment. Some four miles of stiffish country brought me to this pretty village where I found the 'White Hart' – an inn

---

6 Presumably Richmond Park.

to my liking which provided me with some excellent bread, cheese and 1½ pints of good beer. What more can a man want? After a stroll round the village I made up my mind to make for Midhurst, which I eventually reached via Rogate, Terwick and Trotton – all pretty little places.

Midhurst supplied me with two bananas and an orange, which were very welcome with the sun being somewhat powerful. It is only eight miles from Midhurst to Haslemere but I doubt if there is a tougher eight miles in the South of England: I was glad of a walk in some parts – especially the rise out of Fernhurst. I was nearly 1½ hours doing this stretch of the journey. It is easier work from Haslemere to Godalming and about midway between these towns, at Brook, struck a snug little inn the 'Dog and Pheasant' which gave me a most excellent 1/3 tea[7].

Godalming to Ripley was very trafficky and I was glad to take the usual bye-pass via Ockham, Cobham and Oxshott with another refresher at 'The Plough' Cobham. I reached home just after 9 o'clock after an exhilarating wind up to the record month of July totalling *113 miles*.

SATURDAY 11TH SEPTEMBER

A last dash

HAMMERSMITH – MAIDENHEAD – HENLEY-ON-THAMES – NETTLEBED – BENSON – DORCHESTER-ON-THAMES – ABINGDON – KINGSTON BAGPUIZE – WITNEY – BURFORD

Had made up our minds overnight to have a last dash for Burford, so got home from the office as quickly as possible and on the road by 1 o'clock, taking the shortest route. The roads were rather trafficky as far as Hounslow, but after that we opened our throttles and made the old James machine jump through Colnbrook and Slough so that we arrived at Maidenhead a good twenty minutes ahead of schedule and were able to take the difficult stretch to Henley at easy speed. Thus we had done very well considering the gale of wind in our faces.

We did not stop in Henley but went straight ahead riding all the way up to Nettlebed, the first time I remember to have done so, and not stopping until Benson where E.B.P. badly wanted some ginger beer[8]. The 'Fleur de Lys' at Dorchester gave us a very excellent tea and here we met some

---

7 Costing 1 shilling and threepence.
8 Indeed Charles had visited Nettlebed before – in 1925 – but he had never ridden all the way up without walking some of the way.

old Burford acquaintances so we lingered for over an hour. The six miles from Dorchester to Abingdon was done at a speed approaching evens (20 mph) warranting a stroll through the busy streets before going on through Marcham to Kingston Bagpuize where at the 'Hind's Head' a Bass came very welcome.

Here a shower overtook us and onwards through Newbridge and Standlake to Witney. It became rather thunderous, the heavy clouds bringing on darkness before its proper time and we were obliged to light our lamps before reaching the welcome 'Swan' about 8.15 p.m. Here the usual kind of supper and good company kept us well occupied until nearly midnight.
Distance covered: 76 miles

SUNDAY 12TH SEPTEMBER
A last farewell to 1926
HAMMERSMITH – CUMNOR – ABINGDON – DORCHESTER-ON-THAMES – GORING HEATH – CAVERSHAM – HAMMERSMITH

After breakfast we lingered until the other wayfarers had all gone their ways before preparing for our last farewell of 1926 to Burford, taking the Oxford road to within a few miles of that city to the right. This let us in for some stiff climbing which eventually brought us to the pretty village of Cumnor which has been noted for further exploration next year.

Here at the 'Vine Inn', a beautiful little hostelry, covered as it name implies by a vine, we had a most satisfactory lunch before dropping down into Abingdon. From Abingdon we took some more new country going by way of Culham to Dorchester, from thence over Shillingford Bridge to Wallingford and from thence by way of Cholsey and Moulsford to Streatley and to Goring Heath. This took us to teatime and we had an excellent tea at 'The King Charles' Head' before descending to Caversham and on the usual road via Sonning, Twyford, Waltham St. Lawrence and Windsor. We took the Datchet–Bedfont way back calling in for a Bass at the 'Albany' at Twickenham, and arrived home at 8 o'clock – quite good going considering that it was 11.15 a.m. when we left Burford and we had loitered on the way making *86 miles* of it.

This weekend was a truly joyful event and made us regard the old James machines with renewed affection, the new handlebars seeming to give them a new lease of life.

1926 HOLIDAY TOUR – CHATER-LEA – CYCLOMETER 3361

SATURDAY 7TH AUGUST

Buns and tons of time to spare

HAMMERSMITH – WINDSOR – CAVERSHAM – PEPPARD – NETTLEBED – BENSON – ABINGDON – DUCKLINGTON – WITNEY – BURFORD

For the fifth year in succession we were making for the same destination for our first day's holiday. We did not take the well-worn route of our previous tours, however, and for once we were under way at 7 o'clock facing a strong west wind. The new route encountered Windsor (via Bedfont, Horton and Datchet) Waltham St. Lawrence, Twyford, Sonning (where we stopped for the first breather and witnessed the Kingston–Oxford boat pass under the bridge), to Caversham from whence we took a rather strenuous road via Rotherfield and Peppard. Here, the 'Bird in Hand' not only supplied us with some Bass and biscuits but also some amusing company – notably a hearty looking individual who declared he never got a wink of sleep unless he had seven or eight Guinnesses beforehand!!

From Peppard there is a long but picturesque pull up to Nettlebed, from whence we hastened onto Benson for our midday bread, cheese and beer at the 'Three Horseshoes' – a pub we never pass if it is open. Continuing on the Henley–Oxford main road to Dorchester we took the left hand road to

Abingdon, where we walked through a considerable part of that pleasant old town and also indulged in some buns as we had tons of time to spare.

From Abingdon there is a good road through Marcham to Kingston Bagpuize, but from thence onward it is at present only highly recommended for those suffering from a sluggish liver. However, there is only about nine miles of this potholey road over Newbridge, Standlake and Ducklington to Witney. At Ducklington, we tried to get tea at the 'Bell' but we were fobbed off with the excuse that there was no fire to boil the kettle and so we were thrown back to 'Puringburnes' at Witney, which provided its usual indifferent tea. However, we had not far to go now so we made the best of it and speeded on the last familiar eight miles to Burford where the 'Swan' provided us with a proper tea. After a stroll around the never changing village and a bountiful and long drawn out supper we went to bed mightily content with our first day's journey which ran us into *84 miles.*

SUNDAY 8TH AUGUST

One thing we all agree on

BURFORD – ALDSWORTH – BIBURY – CIRENCESTER – KELMSCOTT – LECHLADE – BURFORD

Yesterday was a perfect day as to weather and today promised to be as good but we did not intend to make it too strenuous and it was 11.30 a.m. before we took the road via Aldsworth to the ever delightful watery village of Bibury.

At Bibury we spent a meditative hour including bread, cheese and beer at the 'Catherine Wheel' before setting out to find the villages of Coln St. Denis and Coln Roger – both perfect in their way – and from the latter we emerged onto the rolling Fosse Way near Foss Cross which eventually took us to Cirencester. While contemplating this dear old town, now quite familiar, rain clouds began to gather and soon it was pelting down. After standing up for about 20 minutes under a chestnut tree in the station yard, we decided it had come to stay, donned our Pagets and prepared to make a dash for our base. However, though it continued through Ampney Crucis and Fairford, before we got into Lechlade it had ceased. Pagets were tucked away and the sun was shining once more so we basked for some time on the bridge looking towards the picturesque mill at Kelmscott, before journeying back to the 'Swan' via Filkins over the now perfectly surfaced road that used to be so rough and potholey.

The evening was spent mostly in converse with the Sunday evening gathering as usual from all parts of England – discussion of roads, inns and above all of cycles and components. It is a remarkable thing that every cycle maker and every special accessory is bound to be condemned by someone among the crowd but there is one thing upon which all are agreed every time and that is of the excellence of everything at the Burford 'Swan'.

Distance covered: 43 miles

MONDAY 9TH AUGUST

The finest ten miles in England

BURFORD – STOW-ON-THE-WOLD – EVESHAM – ASTON-SUB-EDGE – CHIPPING CAMPDEN – BURFORD

Again the day dawned bright and sunny, finding us still at the 'Swan' as a base though we had made up our minds to start touring in earnest on the morrow. However, it would be possible to spend a week or longer at Burford as a base, and find new and delightful country each day.

This time the Stow road called us – the road which has been described by the great Wayfarer as the finest ten miles in England. In truth, this stretch, with the rolling Cotswolds on each side, the range of vision only limited by the ridge of the Chilterns on one side, and the ragged Malvern Beacons on the other, is always a wonderful experience even to those who have traversed it as many times as we have.

Arriving in Stow we decided to follow the usual way to Broadway, calling in as is our usual custom at the 'Coach and Horse', about four miles on the road, trusting we might at last get a clear view from the famous Fish Hill but it was as usual somewhat murky. We had already viewed the rather artificial charms of Broadway often so did not linger there, but proceeded on our way to Evesham, stopping on the way at the comfortable 'Sandys Arms' for our midday bread, cheese and beer.

Evesham as usual was full of bundling old women. Why they should always flock to this charming old town passes comprehension. From Evesham we made our way in very leisurely fashion via Bretforton and Weston-sub-Edge to the famous 'Cottage' at Aston-sub-Edge for tea, and from there up the stiffish three miles to the quaint old town of Chipping

Campden where we did not linger too long as a thunderstorm appeared in the offing and we had scarcely got a mile on our way before it was upon us. However, it was of short duration and soon after we fell in with a walking tourist (who had been at the 'Swan' on Saturday night) with whom we strolled for about a mile, and while doing so two lively young cyclists passed us who, we surmised, were making for the 'Swan'. We mounted at length and on arrival at the 'Coach and Horses' saw two cycles outside and curiosity (and some thirst) made us go in to investigate. Within we found the said two young cyclists who were as we expected making for Burford in the hope of being put up at the 'Swan'. While conversing with them our old friend the walker arrived and seeing our machines outside the 'Coach and Horses' he also joined the conclave and remained for some time after the two cyclists (who hailed from Stockport) had proceeded on their way. Another member of the supper party was a stocky lad from Manchester who was requested to cut some bread. He steadily set to work and sliced up the whole loaf but there were only two or three slices required by the rest of the party so it was suggested that as he had cut up the whole loaf he ought to eat it. He seemed to see the justice of the suggestion, got off the mark straight away and the fascinated watchers saw the last of that loaf disappear exactly 13½ minutes later.

Distance covered: 56 miles

TUESDAY 10TH AUGUST

Magnificent views and a tea of extreme excellence

BURFORD – PUESDOWN – CHELTENHAM – TEWKESBURY – EASTNOR – LEDBURY – DYMOCK – NEWENT

We had not decided last night where our next move was to be. We wanted to try the famous 'Stowe Inn' at Whitney-on-Wye but on the map it looked too far for a day's run on a leisurely holiday so we left our stopping place to chance. So after taking leave of the 'Swan', and making arrangements to call there on the way back, we strolled up to the top of the High Street and took the Gloucester road, making short work of the long grind through Northleach to Puesdown, where at the 'Puesdown Inn' we loitered for the greater part of an hour – the bread and cheese and beer being excellent and the company amusing.

So bleak is Puesdown even in summer that we could well believe the statement by a farmer that whenever there is two inches of snow elsewhere, there is two foot on Puesdown. However, we could not stay there all day so we continued on the easier way via Charlton Kings to Cheltenham, that spacious, bright and prosperous looking town. However, towns – especially new built shoppy ones – are not our object and so we made our way through this one as quickly as the traffic would allow on the road to Tewkesbury via Uckington, having to bustle up Coombe Hill to shake off a fast steam lorry burning some of the abominable foreign coal that has invaded this country since the coal strike[9] has been on. However, he was no hill climber and we left him.

A shower drove us to shelter just outside Tewkesbury for about 15 minutes but the sun speedily shone out again. From Tewkesbury we decided to make for Ledbury with some idea of putting up at or in the vicinity of that picturesque town. The road from Tewkesbury is of a particularly strenuous character with many stiff hills but a very pleasant one with a magnificent view from the summit of the hill at Hollybush, and when we came to Eastnor we were quite ready for tea at the 'Somer's Arms'. Tea was of such extreme excellence that we made enquiries as to putting up for the night there but alas! – it was full up and so we went on into Ledbury.

At Ledbury, looking very attractive in the evening sun, we could find nowhere suitable as a stopping place and as we had really come quite a short distance and there was plenty of daylight left we made up our minds to go on another dozen miles to the excellent 'George' at Newent stopping on the way for light refreshment at the picturesque and comfortable 'Beauchamp Arms' at Dymock. We were lucky at the 'George' which gave us the usual excellent feeding and accommodation and we had an hour to stroll around this quaint old world town before supper and bed feeling quite satisfied with our day's work, the actual mileage of which only amounted to *54 miles.*

---

9 The General Strike of 1926 lasted nine days from 3–12th May in protest at deteriorating conditions for Britain's miners and the government's plans to reduce their wages. The miners maintained resistance for several months afterwards.

WEDNESDAY 11TH AUGUST

The famous Stowe Inn

NEWENT – DYMOCK – LUGWARDINE – HEREFORD – WHITNEY-ON-WYE – HAY – GLASBURY – WHITNEY-ON-WYE

After a chat with an old ex-policeman full of humorous local anecdotes, a very first class breakfast and a stroll around the wonderful garden which is one of the features of this hotel, we retraced our way first of all to Dymock, then taking the road to Hereford through Tarrington and Stoke Edith. This is a hop growing district and the usual kind of hop pickers were winding their way to the gardens. Here the malt houses are in the midst of the hop gardens, which seems a very sensible arrangement in these days of heavy freights.

We stopped at the 'Crown and Anchor' at Lugwardine, one of the snuggish inns it would be possible to imagine, for bread and cheese and beer, before going into Hereford where we spent about an hour before going on our way on the Hay road and having another helping of bread, cheese and beer at the 'Bay Horse'. This gave us shelter from a sharp shower which only lasted some twenty minutes, leaving nice dustless roads and a much fresher atmosphere so that we sped on the beautiful highway through Bridge Sollers, Byford, Staunton and Winforton, with the Wye on our left. We speedily reached our destination, the famous 'Stowe Inn' at Whitney, which is kept by two old dames whose one idea in life seems to take in wandering cyclists and make them fat and happy.

Here we were lucky in finding accommodation and after a wash and an exceptionally hearty tea we set off to explore the road onward to Hay, crossing the Wye over a toll bridge where you pay ½d for the first crossing and are then allowed to come back free of charge. As no ticket is issued it must sometimes be rather difficult for the tollgate keeper to remember who has paid and who has not! Hay has no particularly picturesque features except a restored castle of which it is somewhat difficult to get a view. We went a few miles further on to Glasbury where we stayed some time on the bridge over the broad but shallow Wye watching the last rays of the sun lighting up the Brecknock Beacon, a truly beautiful view. We were not to get back without a wetting, a heavy storm overtaking us about a mile from home which we weathered under our Pagets and some thick leafed bushes. We found our house party reinforced by a mixed tandem

pair from Islington – a curious couple but quite decent and talkative.
Distance covered: 54 miles

THURSDAY 12TH AUGUST
A sudden apparition
WHITNEY-ON-WYE – LLYSWEN – ERWOOD – BUILTH WELLS – WHITNEY-ON-WYE

Got up to a pleasant breakfast in the bar of the 'Stowe Inn' starting with porridge then fishcakes and other things, and ending with marmalade as an Englishman's breakfast should. We did not feel like quitting this pleasant hostelry in a hurry so made up our minds to stay another night and spend the day in an exploration trip.

Having seen the mixed tandem pair off on their homeward way, who were in need of a little joy on the road for their four tyres were leaking, we, on our hostess's recommendation, took the road to Builth Wells keeping to the right bank of the Wye through Clyro and Llowes to Glasbury Bridge, which we crossed after the road runs alongside the Wye practically the whole way to Builth. We stopped for some time on the bridge at Pipton which crosses the Afon Llywfi[10], a small but pretty tributary of the Wye.

At Llyswen, the sudden apparition of a suspension bridge caught me by such surprise that I inadvertently steered into a bank at the side of the road and collapsed in a heap, to the great surprise of the oldest inhabitant who was digging 'tatties' in his front garden. Of course, I picked myself up as though this was my usual method of dismounting and strolled out onto the bridge from which there was a lovely view over the river both ways. In fact, all along this road one has to be constantly dismounting to admire the view, with the Wye changing its character in every mile – sometimes a placid albeit swift, deep stream and a little further on rushing in a series of cataracts over its rocky bed and flecked with foam.

At Erwood we stopped for our midday refreshment at the 'Erwood Inn' an ancient hostelry with a mounting block outside which is still very much in use, it being the custom of this part of the world for housewives to do their marketing on horseback. I should like to have obtained a photograph of one of these good dames in the act of dismounting, of goodly girth and laden with baskets and parcels, one hand clutching a stout umbrella. And

---

10 Welsh for the River Tywi

so we eventually arrived at Builth Wells, a "seasidey" kind of town with no particular features of interest. We were quite content to retrace our steps back by the beautiful road by which we had come finding new beauties in it at every mile and we were in fine fettle for enjoying the bounteous tea or dinner that awaited us at the 'Stowe Inn'.

The evening was spent loafing around on foot including an interesting conversation with an old dame on the subject of the manufacture of ensilage, an article of which we had never heard before. Apparently, it is a winter cattle food made by compassing all kinds of green vegetation into a tower called a silo.

Distance covered: 50 miles

FRIDAY 13TH AUGUST

Four enormous mutton chops

WHITNEY-ON-WYE – KINGTON – TITLEY – PRESTEIGNE – KNIGHTON – CLUN – MONTGOMERY

Much as we should have liked to stay on another day at the 'Stowe Inn' we thought it time to be seeking fresh fields. The morning was not a very prepossessing one, it being dull and rainy, but we have learnt not to let this sort of thing interfere with our plans, and during the course of breakfast, which was interrupted by a badling[11] of ducks from a neighbouring farm who would keep walking in at the front and had to be expelled each time, we decided to visit another of our old haunts – Montgomery.

And so after taking leave of our two kind old hostesses and promising another visit someday we took the road to Kington through Eardisley and Willersley – a long climb with a corresponding downhill rush into Kington. From that town we took rather a roundabout but picturesque route to Presteigne, stopping via Titley, which necessitated plenty of collar work.

At Presteigne the 'Radnorshire Arms', a wonderful old house, provided us with our midday refreshment and fortified us for the long ascent (some 1200 feet) which lay between Presteigne and Knighton. At the 'Radnorshire Arms' we met the oldest inhabitant, a brisk young fellow of 90 with a roguish eye. Knighton provided an excellent lunch of bread, cheese and butter at the 'Dragon' and we discussed at length our route to Clun, which

---

11 Archaic term for a group of ducks

was our next point. We finally decided to ride the 16 odd miles round to that village in preference to the steep and thorny path via New Invention[12], which we had traversed before. Even so the road took a little finding. Bucknell, however, was on the way and as there was a show on there we only had to follow the crowd.

This road via Bucknell, Bedstone, Twitchen, Purslow and Clunton proved quite a soft one and we arrived in Clun about 3 o'clock. We lingered in this peaceful town until 3.30 p.m. when we felt like tea, which we obtained at the 'Buffalo', a famous C.T.C. house the visitors, book of which records visits by all the great ones of the cycling world. Naturally the tea was a good one. And then comes more climbing on the road to Bishop's Castle but once up the hill to Bishop's Castle the "strenuosity" calms down and the road rises at a high level for the remainder of the way to Montgomery with magnificent views on both sides which caused us to loiter. At the 'Bluebell', where we enjoyed a Bass, we met a lumberman who was endeavouring to dispose of a motor lorry load of "sticks" – in other words logs for burning purposes – with the best offer from the Landlord being 30/-. Those "sticks", however, would have been worth four times as much in London during the present coal strike!

Nevertheless we finally ambled into the familiar and restful town of Montgomery, being received with open arms by the genial and rotund Mrs Maddox at the 'Old Bell' who informed us our usual rooms were vacant. Late though it was she insisted on knocking up the local butcher and when we came back from a stroll up to the castle there were four enormous mutton chops ready for us to which, we did full justice before retiring to roost after a fairly strenuous day of *52 miles.*

SATURDAY 14TH AUGUST

The town band
MONTGOMERY – CRUCKTON – SHREWSBURY – BROCKTON – MONTGOMERY

The restful atmosphere of Montgomery pervaded us this morning so we decided not to venture further afield than Shrewsbury. After loitering until nearly 11.30 a.m. we took the road to Chirbury, Marton, Brockton, Worthen, Westbury, Yockleton and Cruckton, stopping at the 'Red Lion' at

---

12 A hamlet in Shropshire; the origin of the name is unclear but 'Vention' could have its origins in 'Fenton' meaning 'settlement in a marshy place'.

the last mentioned village for beer and biscuits where two years ago we had met with curious and interesting company who, however, were not present on this occasion.

Shrewsbury, as usual at this time of year, was getting ready for the Flower Show and it being Saturday was very crowded. We failed not to visit 'Plimmers', as usual, and regaled on some of delicacies before having a Bass at the 'Plough' in the Market Place where some sandwiches also helped to fill up. In order to spin out the miles we took a road back through Hanwood – a veritable speedway – and then cut across from Flaxgreen to Brockton, a pleasant bye-way. A sharp shower drove us to shelter beneath a tree close to Chirbury but did not last many minutes.

We arrived back punctually at 6 o'clock to devour a very large steak with plenty of onions, marrow and potatoes and some way delectable apple charlotte and rice pudding, which necessitated a sharp walk to the top of the Monument Hill to shake it down. Unfortunately, it was too misty to see much from this point, 1500 feet up, and very cold. Strains of music greeted us from the town as we descended, which we ascertained were coming from the town hall, the town band having its first practice of the season. *Distance covered: 51 miles*

SUNDAY 15TH AUGUST

A section of war-stricken France

MONTGOMERY – CORNDON HILL – GRAVELS – MONTGOMERY

A Sunday morning in Wales is quiet, very quiet. I took a stroll around the town after breakfast and the only living thing to be seen were dogs. These seemed surprised to see anyone so sinful as to be walking around before it was time to go to chapel but I suppose recognising that I was only a poor ignorant foreigner they were all very friendly and I soon had the whole pack at my heels.

Remembering last year's experience at Pembroke (where we were informed that pubs were not open in Wales on Sundays) we made up our minds to take a route that would enable us to get into England about lunchtime, and so we set off through Chirbury and Church Stoke to find a road parallel with the Long Mynd. We were greatly surprised when it landed us out by Corndon Hill by lunchtime near Shelve. Here we spied a cosy looking little pub lying off the road and after wading through much mud and carrying our machines through a watersplash to get to it, we were informed that we were in fact still in Wales and so the pub would be closed. Fortunately, there was another a mile further on, back in England.

And so we proceeded on our way to recognise a weird piece of country, which seemed familiar in appearance like a section of war stricken France. It turned out to be Gravels and we remembered the comfortable 'Sun Inn' lying coyly behind the slag heaps to which we made tracks. The landlord, a man of varied experiences and obviously an ex-sergeant major, recognised us as having visited his house before. It was actually three years ago so the inference is that strangers are rare in those parts. However, the bread and cheese and beer was of the best quality.

After leaving Gravels we sped down the lovely Hope Valley and through Pontesbury and Minsterley nearly into Shrewsbury and then we took the road to Welshpool arriving back for our mutton and other things via Berriew and Garthmyl.

Feeling rather heavy after our mutton etc. it was latish when we went out for our evening stroll up to the castle where we spent an hour in perfect solitude looking down on the sleeping town and tracing the various roads, and when we did start down to the 'Old Bell' we were astonished at the difficulty of the descent in the dark.

Distance covered: 49 miles

MONDAY 16TH AUGUST

A most beautiful voice

MONTGOMERY – CRAVEN ARMS – CORFTON – BRIDGNORTH – BROWN CLEE – BURWARTON – LUDLOW

After our quiet weekend we made up our minds to move on today but were undecided as to our direction and it was my suggestion that we should have a run round Shropshire and spend the night at Ludlow as we did not visit that fascinating town last year.

Accordingly, after bidding farewell to the hospitable Maddox family we took the road through Chirbury and Church Stoke, Snead and Lydham when the road took some little finding to Craven Arms via Plowden. A late start made some refreshment desirable at the unlovely hamlet, which takes its name from the principle pub 'Craven Arms', but we inspected the Arms and did not fancy it. We also had a look at the 'Stokesay Castle Hotel' and liked this still less and so we decided to go on our way and chance finding a quiet little pub where we could obtain our bread and cheese and beer in comfort.

As time was going on this meant putting the pot on but we found one, 'The Sun', at Corfton, which fulfilled all our wants. We went joyfully on the easy and delightful road through Diddlebury, Munslow and the Corve Dale via Monkhopton and Morville until we reached the picturesque town of Bridgnorth where our first thought was tea, which we obtained at the 'Commercial Inn'.

After a walk round the ancient town we made up our minds to take the shorter but very strenuous road to Ludlow over Brown Clee[13]. Besides its many unrideable slopes this road was also in a most deplorable condition as to its surface, as far as Cleobury North after which it began to improve. Feeling distinctly thirsty after the strenuous uphill work we called in at the 'Boyne Arms' Burwarton for a Bass. While there a most beautiful voice – whether human, gramophone or wireless loud speaker we were not able to decide – sang Dell'Acquas' "Villanelle", [14]and such was the impression it made upon me that I shall never hear this lovely song again without associating it with 'Boyne Arms', Burwarton.

The run down from Brown Clee to Ludlow was all pure joy and we made straight for our old quarters 'Blythwood House' where, for the first time, we found there was no room for us, but they recommended us to the 'Bull' where we had an excellent supper and good quarters.

Distance covered: 62 miles

TUESDAY 17TH AUGUST

A day with the Tudors

LUDLOW – LEINTWARDINE – BROAD HEATH – NEW RADNOR – LLANFIHANGEL NANT MELAN

Our plan was next to make for Llanfihangel Nant Melan next, so we took the familiar road via Bromfield over the Fiddlers Elbow to Leintwardine where we had our first refreshment at the 'Swan'. After our stop we took a road which was new to us through Lingen and Newton – a beautiful rural road where all the adult male inhabitants were exactly like Henry VIII

---

13 The highest hill in the county of Shropshire, at 1,770 feet
14 Eva Dell'Acqua (1856–1930) was a Belgian singer and composer; her most famous piece – 'Villanelle' – was first performed in 1893.

– young Henry VIII, old Henry VIII and ancient decrepit Henry VIII. The climax was reached when we came upon a very fine specimen of one asleep in a wheelbarrow. I shall always regret I did not obtain a photograph of him.

We then came upon a most enticing inn 'The Cricketer's Arms' at Broad Heath, which it was impossible to pass. We entered and found an aged Henry VIII sitting in the bar parlour, a most laconic individual. Just after our arrival, a cyclist in a bowler hat and trousers who was on his way to Coventry arrived – a very talkative man, in consequence of which we each consumed two small Worthington's and many biscuits.

We proceeded on our way on the pleasant road by way of Knill and Walton to New Radnor from which town it is only a few steep miles to the 'Red Lion' at Llanfihangel Nant Melan. Here the beaming Mrs Williams was able to take us into our great content and though the afternoon was early, we did not stir until we had tea of the usual hearty kind which this inn provides.

After tea we wandered off accompanied by Rover to Llyn (Lake) Heilyn and climbed the heights above that picturesque piece of water, feasting on the wild raspberries which abound in this neighbourhood and rejoicing in the perfect solitude of our surroundings. And so home to supper and bed after only *30 miles of riding.*

WEDNESDAY 18TH AUGUST

A downhill dream of bliss

LLANFIHANGEL NANT MELAN – RADNOR FOREST – RHAYADER – LLANGIWG – LLANGURIG – RHAYADER

A fine cloudless morning gave us the desire to go and have a look at Rhayader with some intention of visiting the Elan Valley lakes albeit under less favourable conditions than prevailed on our last visit two years ago. This necessitated a climb of some miles up to the roof of the Radnor Forest with magnificent views on both sides and a boundless prospect when the top is reached, after which there is a gentle run down into Penybont (one of many Penybonts in Wales). Henceforward, the road is of a very varied character through many small villages until the very plain and unvarnished town of Rhayader is reached. We were hereabouts feeling badly in need of nourishment, no inns having been met with on the way, and the pubs of Rhayader were not very attractive. However, about half a mile outside the town we found the inn of our desires, the 'Eagle Inn', which gave us all that we wanted, the landlord also presenting us each with one of his bill heads[15] apprising us that he also dealt in coal, timber and small groceries. However our lunch was of the best and the problem of where to feed when in Rhayader is solved.

Here we debated our next move. I was not keen on the Elan Valley which I feared might be disappointing in the present placid weather conditions and we finally decided to make for Llangiwg, a road of which I had vivid memories and which seemed to me to possess great photographic possibilities. This road is surely the loveliest ten mile stretch in the kingdom running as it does between rugged mountains with the infant Wye in many cascades on the left hand side.

Half an hour was spent in the lovely dell where the Afon Marteg makes its junction with the Wye and it was difficult to leave this beautiful spot. However, we continued up the valley, the road rising all the way until the pretty village of Llangurig is reached. The all downhill return to Rhayader is a dream of bliss though we were not to escape one of the drenching showers which are always on tap in this region before we got there, calling in at 'Webber's' for a good and rapid tea before making our way back to the very special dinner which was awaiting us at the 'Red Lion'.

A good part of the evening was spent in the bar parlour listening to the talk of the local worthies and a discussion as to whether there were not still wolves in the Radnor Forest. And then a delightful family of three rejoicing in the name of Codd arrived with whom we had much pleasant conversation until bed time.

Distance covered: 53 miles

THURSDAY 19TH AUGUST

Refreshment in the wireless parlour

RHAYADER – NEW RADNOR – LYONSHALL – WEOBLEY – HEREFORD – LUGWARDINE – TARRINGTON – MUCH MARCLE – ROSS-ON-WYE

We would have liked another day amid the Radnor Forest but E.B.P.'s time was drawing to a close. A wet morning somewhat delayed our start and conversation with the Codds still further delayed us before we started for

---

15 A sheet of paper with a business name and address printed at the top

England. We made first of all for New Radnor, where the rain cleared off, and we had got no further than Lyonshall before it was time to think about refreshment, which we duly obtained in the wireless parlour of the 'Royal George', where the landlord told us of the great attraction of the loud speaker for the inhabitants of the district, especially on Sunday evenings.

After satisfying our needs we took the road onwards for Hereford via Woonton, turning off to visit the beautiful little town of Weobley, where we had a little more rain and a long stretch of very offensive tarry road to get out of it again. The road onward to Hereford is somewhat strenuous. We hurried out of Hereford with the idea of tea at the 'Crown and Anchor' at Lugwardine only to be turned down. We saw very little prospect of getting fed for many miles ahead – Donnington and Stoke Edith drew blanks – but at the 'Foley Arms' Tarrington we succeeded in getting an excellent tea, after which we made hay of the remainder of the road to Ledbury where a small thunderstorm over took us. It was, however, soon over and we decided to make for Ross for the night.

It was somewhat late but we knew we should be quite safe at Ross so we lingered some time at the 'Walwyn Arms' in the village of Much Marcle, where a curious company had gathered. This charming inn – an old favourite of ours – is now disfigured by a huge galvanized iron garage close by. At Ross we put up as usual at the 'Gwalia', one of the stopping places you can always rely on. And after a stroll as far as Wilton Bridge, supper then bed followed.

Distance covered: 58 miles

FRIDAY 20TH AUGUST

The wettest ride of my cycling career

ROSS-ON-WYE – MONMOUTH – DINGESTOW – RAGLAN – USK – NEWPORT – CARDIFF

Ross greeted us with its usual watery outlook when we got up this morning and it was the general opinion that we were in for a wet day. E.B.P. had decided to start homeways, while I intended to make for Cardiff and get a boat across to Devon.

However, E.B.P. having time to spare, decided to come on part of the way with me, so we took the usual road to Monmouth via Whitchurch. Monmouth as usual was not looking particularly attractive so we rode straight through over the Monnow Bridge and on to Raglan, but before reaching that village the rain made up its mind to set in for good. Having refreshed on the way at the 'Somerset Arms' Dingestow we waited for a short time to see if the rain would stop, but this was time thrown away.

At Raglan we somehow took the wrong road to Usk and a very steep and rough one it was, so that we only just got to the 'George' at Usk in time to get the bread and cheese and beer of which we then stood in dire need. At Usk I parted with E.B.P. to continue my lonely and rainy way via Llanbadoc, Llangybi and Caerleon to the unlovely town of Newport, which with its narrow, tram-lined streets is especially unpleasant in pouring rain. However, I stopped here for tea – an indifferent tea – and then donned my Paget again for the last stage to Cardiff.

This road is all under reconstruction and should be, when finished, one of the finest roads in the Kingdom. At present it is a mass of obstructions with sculptural warning signs erected by the authorities for the instruction of motorists. It continued to rain as far as Castleton but at St. Mellons it had left off sufficiently for me to remove my garment for a breather. However, a few miles outside Cardiff a cloudburst happened before I could get my cape on so that I was very and completely drenched.

My chief fear was I should find no boat running across on the morrow. So I went straight down to the Bute Docks to find out and was relieved to find a boat going to Ilfracombe at 8.45 a.m. next morning.

My next consideration was to find somewhere for the night. A dock policeman, who I consulted, strongly advised me to make back for the city as it was not safe anywhere in the docks neighbourhood. However, I consulted the C.T.C. handbook and found a billet within five minutes of the Pier Head, the 'Merthyr Café' on St. James's Street, which was quite comfortable and cheap, and they did their best to dry some of my clothes. This was one of wettest rides of my cycling career, yet it having a satisfactory ending leaves no bitter memories.

Distance covered: 51 miles

SATURDAY 21ST AUGUST

Wind, rain and spew

CARDIFF – ILFRACOMBE – MUDDIFORD – BARNSTAPLE – APPLEDORE– NORTHAM – BIDEFORD – STIBB CROSS – HOLSWORTHY

Got up to find it still raining and had an early breakfast to enable me to get on the boat which left at 8.45 a.m. Boarded the "Glen Usk" about 8.30

a.m. and got my machine safely stowed away on the lower deck under cover. It being Saturday, there were a fair number of passengers bound for Ilfracombe.

We got off to time and as soon as we were clear of the docks it was apparent that the water was none too smooth, so I at once fortified myself with a Guinness and some fat beef sandwiches to supplement my somewhat hasty breakfast. It was impossible owing to wind, rain and spew to remain on the upper deck; however, with newspaper to read and further refreshment, the three hours shake up was soon over and I landed at Ilfracombe only to find the rain still in full swing.

I made straight up through the town on that road to Barnstaple surprising myself by riding up Two Potts Hill in spite of the rain and wind in my face. Once at the top of the hill the rain began to abate somewhat and I was glad to remove my Paget and get a breather the remainder of the road to Barnstaple through Bittadon, Muddiford and Pilton being fairly soft.

At Muddiford I was able to get an excellent refreshment at the 'New Inn' it being close to closing time. The rain finally ceased at Barnstaple where I spent about half an hour, then took the road through Bickington, Freminton and Yelland to Instow, where the sun having appeared roused a desire to ferry across to Appledore instead of taking the direct road to Bideford.

It is rather an undertaking getting a cycle encumbered with luggage across this bit of the Torridge but it was safely accomplished and Appledore with its quaint inhabitants and fishy smells was so attractive in the sunshine that I spent over an hour there before making my way via Northam to Bideford where I obtained an excellent tea at the 'Kingsley Hotel'. From what I remembered I was under the impression that the road from Bideford to Holsworthy was an easy one. However, here my memory played me false for not only is it a constant succession of steep hills but the surface like most of the Devon roads is vile so that after toiling up through Monkleigh and Frithelstock a drink came in very handy at Stibb Cross at the 'Union Inn'.

The landlord cheered me up by telling me that I had got all the worst of the road to come. However this did not prove to be the case for though there were plenty of hills the road surface was much better and I got into Holsworthy about 8 o'clock being as usual received with open arms by the Misses Jollow at the 'South Western Hotel'. After an excellent supper and much talk, I was glad to get to bed after a very varied and somewhat strenuous day though the mileage only amounted to *42 miles.*

SUNDAY 22ND AUGUST

Sharp twists and breakneck descents

HOLSWORTHY – STRATTON – BUDE – KILKHAMPTON – MORWENSTOW – STRATTON – HOLSWORTHY

Made up my mind to have a quiet day and so, after a very excellent breakfast, I set off on the once very familiar road to spend the morning in Bude, lingering for a short time in the pretty village of Stratton on the way. Bude was as usual in August very full up with a somewhat swank crowd and except for its coast there is not very much attraction for the ordinary visitor who does not play golf. As I could find nowhere to get lunch in Bude I made my way up to 'Bay Tree House' where for 2/- I had a splendid feed of fowl and ham, peas and potatoes, followed by plum tart and cream. Feeling rather heavy after this feed, I set off on the road to Kilkhampton, which is rather a long grind after a heavy lunch.

However, Kilkhampton was looking as beautiful as ever and has not been so much spoilt by the motor curse as most of the villages in the West. Continuing on by Taylors Cross I took a very rough road to the left, which promised to lead to Morwenstow. Taking several sharp twists and breakneck descents I did eventually reach that rugged spot which I found in possession of several motor parties and it rather puzzled me to know how they got there. I inspected the church before turning to make my way back to Holsworthy.

I had intended having tea in Holsworthy but seeing a tea house indicated in Morwenstow I made for that instead. It proved to be a private house kept by a parson and I had a very good tea there with plenty of cream. I was directed by the parson on a new route back to Stratton, which proved to be very rough one with a long steep walk up Cleave Hill and the descent the other side too steep to be ridden. However it eventually led me to Stratton where I called in at the 'King's Arms' for a Bass before making my way back to the 'South Western Hotel', supper and bed.

Distance covered: 40 miles

MONDAY 23RD AUGUST
Saffron cake and ginger beer
HOLSWORTHY – CLAWTON – LAUNCESTON – SOUTH PETHERWIN – LISKEARD – LOOE

It was a damp and unpropitious looking morning for the cross country trip which I had in mind. However I got off about 10.30 a.m. on the steep and thorny road to Launceston via Clawton and I was unable to resist the open door of the 'Arscott Arms' – that quaint little hostelry which we visited so often in 1921. I found the interior had been renovated and the inn under new management but as enticing as ever.

By the time I got to Launceston a good steady drencher had set in. I did not linger to admire the beauties of this old town (one of the few picturesque towns in Cornwall) but took what I was advised was the shortest road in the direction of Liskeard. On reaching South Petherwin I realised that I was in for a rough journey and that I should have taken the road to Callington, which though considerably longer was a road and not a succession of cart tracks.

However I did not feel like turning back so decided to stick it out hoping to find a pub for some bread and cheese somewhere before closing time. However I speedily gave up hope of any such thing in the wild uncivilised country I got into and was thankful to obtain some Cornish saffron cake and ginger beer at a small hamlet rejoicing under the name Congdon's Shop.

And so I toiled on with the wind and fine rain in my eyes, sometimes finding half a mile or so of rideable road but mostly on foot. This was about the most desolate stretch of country I have ever struck, the only signs of human habitation for miles being a few dilapidated cottages clustering round a long unworked tin mine near Pensilva. Then the road makes a savage and rough descent into Liskeard, which is a grey stone town of the usual Cornish type. Here my first business was tea, which I obtained at 'Stone's' where, so wet and weary was I that I had half a mind to put up. My plan was to make for Fowey but the rain having ceased I decide to try my luck in Looe and come back to Liskeard if I was not successful. However as on a previous occasion, Mr Hoskin at 'Archway House' was able to put me up and I had just time to have a look around before supper and bed.

Distance covered: 29 miles

TUESDAY 24TH AUGUST

It might not look like a road…

LOOE – POLPERRO – FOWEY – PAR – LOSTWITHIEL – WEST TAPHOUSE – EAST TAPHOUSE – LISKEARD – ST. GERMANS

I was up early to find a distinct improvement in the weather and the indications were that it was going to be very warm.

A fish breakfast was very welcome after the interminable eggs and bacon. After a final look round I took the road over the bridge to Polperro riding quite two of the four and a half miles. A subdued sun had made its appearance, which made quaint old Polperro particularly attractive in spite of the strong odour of decaying fish, which might not suit everyone with a particular nose. After two hours exploration of Polperro and refreshments at the 'Ship' I was informed that I could get a short cut to Fowey via Lansallos and the ferry from Polruan by taking the "road" opposite the school. My informant was careful to add: "it does not look like a road but it is one". Without this warning I should most certainly have missed it. My further instructions were to follow the telegraph wire whenever it went. It was as well I had been told that it was a road for I should never have recognised it as such having in many parts to push my way through brambles. But the blackberries were the best I have ever met and I gorged! This remarkable road ended in what must surely be the steepest street in England, running sheer down to the broad Fowey river like the side of a house.

Needless to say I walked down it onto the quay from which a constant service of motor ferries runs across to Troy Town on the other side. It was rather a tricky job getting my heavily laden cycle down the seaweed covered steps into the ferry boat but it was safely accomplished. The outlook from Fowey struck me as one of the prize views of this enchanting coast and well worthy of the eulogies bestowed upon it by "Q" in his many "Troy Town" stories.

However I had not much time to linger and so toiled up the steep steps till I found the road to Liskeard, which meant going further west through Par and St. Blazey. At Par I had a wonderful shilling tea at a small general shop where the good lady tried her best to stuff me with various dainties until I could not move, after which I found it necessary to walk the stiff hill named I think Tywardreath Highway. The road onward through Penpillick and Crewel Cross to Lostwithiel is all uncommonly stiff especially with a strong headwind as I had against me.

Lostwithiel struck me as being a pleasant town but it was too late for me to give it much attention and there was still plenty of hard shoving to do over Druid's Hill, a wild moor of which the saving grace was the blackberries. Being rather in need of a drink I welcomed the dames of West Taphouse and East Taphouse but in spite of their names neither of these villages contained a pub, and it was not until I got into Liskeard that I was able to assuage my thirst at the 'Fountain Hotel'.

I was beginning to get a trifle anxious about putting up for the night as it was getting late but I did not care to stay in Liskeard and though I was assured there was no chance of getting taken in at St. Germans I determined to chance my luck being naturally of an optimistic nature. The Plymouth road is plain sailing until the side turning to St. Germans and it was a lovely run down to that village in the semi darkness though I was nearly overset by a fox which ran across in front of me missing my front wheel by about eight inches. In spite of the forebodings of the people at Liskeard I was welcomed at the 'Eliot Arms', a most comfortable inn where I fared as well as anywhere on the road. The cyclometer only showed *41 miles* but having regard to the amount of that walked it was quite sufficient for the day.

WEDNESDAY 25TH AUGUST

A proud old man

ST. GERMANS – TORPOINT – DEVONPORT – PLYMOUTH – IVYBRIDGE – TOTNES – NEWTON ABBOT – DAWLISH

It was another hot, steamy, misty morning, which greeted me. I had a look round St. Germans after breakfast, before lumbering up preparatory to pushing further on my homeward way. I then made my way up to Polbathic, Sheviock and Antony to Torpoint taking the cumbrous ferry across the Hamoaze[16] to Devonport. Here I was rather more successful in finding my way across to the amazing town of Plymouth, taking the road via Plympton, Smithaleigh and Mill Bridge to Ivybridge, in preference to crossing the Laira Bridge and going via Yealmpton as had been my intention as I was informed that the latter road was very bad.

---

16 The estuarine stretch of the tidal River Tamar

I took my bread, cheese and beer at the 'Julian Arms' at Ivybridge. The River Erme at this village was merely a trickle between the boulders, which form the bed of the river instead of the roaring torrent which it was when last I was here. It is an easy road through Wrangaton, Avonwick and Shorter Cross to Totnes where I was very glad of tea at 'Clarke's Restaurant'. As I was leaving the town a train of heavy circus tractors was climbing the steep and narrow High Street and I was amazed to see the shopkeepers watching with smiling faces with the road crumbling under these huge engines.

On the road between Totnes and Newton Abbot I met an aged man who was tramping his way from London to his native town of St. Ives to claim his old age pension, a proud old man who was doing the journey by stages sleeping each night at casual wards[17], doing his day's work after each rest and going on once more.

From Newton I took the road by the side of the Teign via Kingsteignton to Teignmouth and then that strenuous three miles to Dawlish stopping on the way at the 'Country House' for some bottled Ferris Ellis cider and the latest news of Dawlish worthies from the landlady. 'Harris's Hotel' was unable to take me in at Dawlish but I got a comfortable billet at the old 'Mill House' and after early supper at the 'Yorke Restaurant', I spent the remainder of the evening in the Strand[18] listening to a small but excellent orchestra and meditating on the many happy holidays in Dawlish in the past. And so to bed.

Distance covered: 52 miles.

THURSDAY 26TH AUGUST

The threepenny sandwich

DAWLISH – EXETER – BROADCLYST – TAUNTON – BATHPOOL – GLASTONBURY – WELLS

A most brilliant morning for some days, with a pleasant crispness in the air, made me wish time would have allowed me another day in this pleasant town. However, after posting off some of my used up underclothes and doing some necessary shopping I reluctantly took my leave of the friendly little town over the very familiar road through sleepy old Starcross, Kenton and Alphington to Exeter. I walked the busy lower part of the city but got out of it as soon as possible on the Taunton Road, through Pinhoe and Broadclyst

---

17 Purpose-built basic accommodation for vagrants in or adjoining a workhouse
18 The main street in the town of Dawlish

where, at the 'Merry Harriers', I took my midday bread and cheese with two bottles of Younger's Scotch Ale. Whilst enjoying my refreshing ale, a lady motorist came into the inn and demanded the services of a mechanic as her car had broken down. On learning there was no such thing on the premises she enquired if she could have a sandwich and if so how much would it cost. On being told 3d she then demanded to know how large it would be. This information being given she took her departure with her threepenny sandwich, after expressing her disgust at there being such a thing as an inn which had not got a skilled motor mechanic attached to it.

The long climb up to the 'White Ball Inn' is a familiar road: after passing through Cullompton and the run down to Wellington, I arrived at Taunton. At Bathpool, just beyond Taunton, I had an excellent tea in the garden of the 'Bathpool Inn' before attacking the long monotonous level stretch across King's Sedgemoor via Durston, Lyng, Othery and Burrowbridge, Greinton, Walton and Street to Glastonbury and then Wells stopping for light refreshment at the 'Coxley Pound Inn', where I indulged in some home brewed beer – queer stuff but very thirst quenching.

As time was going on I made up my mind to stay in Wells for the night. I obtained very comfortable quarters at the 'Crown' and had time before supper to have a look round and mark out any likely photographic spots around this charming little city before supper.

Distance covered: 73 miles

FRIDAY 27TH AUGUST

A local speed merchant

WELLS – CHEWTON MENDIP – BATH – BOX – CASTLE COMBE – MALMESBURY – FAIRFORD – LECHLADE – BURFORD

Had not much time for further exploration of Wells as a longish stage (I had to reach Burford tonight) necessitated an early start. However, after breakfast I visited the Cathedral and its precincts so that it was nearly 11 o'clock before I set off on the long rise up into the Mendips Hills that lie between Wells and Bath. Fortunately the wind was in my favour and I soon reached the highest ground at the pleasant little village of Chewton Mendip from which it is fairly easy going through Farrington Gurney, High Littleton, Kingwell and Corston into Bath.

For a wonder it was not raining in Bath and I lingered for about an hour there being able to lecture two youths, who were on tour and had been badly stung at some of the hotels they had stayed, on the advantage of joining the C.T.C.. I handed them the two membership application forms out of my handbook which I hope they used.

The uphill road to Box through Batheaston was fairly easy and just past Pickwick I turned left to try and find Castle Combe. This road took me through Biddestone, St. Peters, Yatton Keynell and much pleasant country to Castle Combe, which lies at the bottom of a precipitous hill and is worth going out of one's way to see. Consequently in spite of the necessity of "getting on with it" I spent more than an hour there, including tea, before making efforts to regain the road to Malmesbury.

I eventually reached Malmesbury by a circuitous route via Grittleton and Hullavington refreshing there with some milk and cake at a dairy. As it was now nearly 7 o'clock and there was nearly 40 miles between me and Burford it meant putting the pot on. I took the road to Cirencester via Crudwell, and as darkness was rapidly coming on I rode straight through Cirencester on the usual road through Ampney Crucis, where I had intended to refresh at the 'Crown'. A local speed merchant took me on just outside the town and I did not shake him off until just outside Fairford where 'The Red Lion' satisfied my wants. After this the familiar road through Lechlade and Filkins was taken at something like evens (20 mph) and I rather begrudged having to stop to light my lamp at Lechlade (the first time I had it on this tour). However, I arrived at the 'Swan' about 10.15 p.m. and was soon enjoying the usual kind of supper in company with the usual evening visitors and wayfaring tourists and was glad to get to bed at 11.30 p.m. after some *79 miles* of none too easy country.

SATURDAY 28TH AUGUST

A cheery supper party

BURFORD – CHIPPING NORTON – BANBURY – DEDDINGTON – OXFORD – BURFORD

Today I had a long-standing engagement to visit Mr and Mrs Ing at Oxford but as I was not due there until 4 o'clock I decided to make a long round of it.

So I set out after breakfast with one of the other home-going tourists, bound for Birmingham way, over the Cotswolds via Shipton-under-Wychwood to Chipping Norton where we spent some time at the 'Blue

Boar' over cider and biscuits before we parted – he for the road to Stow-on-the-Wold while I proposed to make for Banbury, a town which has many old associations for me. This is a very pleasant bit of country through Swerford and South Newington and Bloxham, and I arrived in Banbury about 1.30 p.m. doing a tour of the town before remembering that I had not had my midday refreshment. Consequently I had to hasten over my bread, cheese and beer at the 'Brown Bear' on the Oxford road, the closing hour being 2 o'clock.

It is a fairly modern road from Banbury to Oxford and today being exceptionally hot the tar surface through Adderbury as far as Deddington was like pudding which made it very hard work. After Deddington, however, it improved so that I was only a few minutes late in arriving at Oxford to keep my appointment, right at the far end of the city very nearly into Cowley. Here I spent some very pleasant hours, before starting back to Burford about 7.30 p.m. with the wind astern via Swinford Bridge, Eynsham and Witney.

The 'Swan' was full up tonight including Weller of the Western Section and his fiancée Miss Baker, who had arrived on a 'new' second hand Granby tandem with two punctured tyres, and young Sam Scott (the son of old Sam Scott who won the 50 mile Championship a few years ago). Altogether, it was a cheery supper party and it took the utmost persuasion of Miss Lomas to get us all off to bed somewhere about midnight. *Distance covered: 68 miles*

SUNDAY 29TH AUGUST

My fourth four-figure tour

BURFORD – GORING HEATH – CAVERSHAM – MARCHAM – SONNING – WINDSOR – RICHMOND – DATCHET – HAMMERSMITH

The end of a – well if not a perfect holiday – at any rate a very enjoyable one, such as it is only possible to get upon a cycle.

After breakfast, most of us at once had thought of moving as early as possible. The first thing was an inspection of the Weller tandem, which we found in a truly deplorable state. He and his 'donah[19]' were going for a week in North Wales with two punctured tyres, brakes that would not hold

---

19 Slang term for a lady, usually used to mean 'sweetheart'.

on the mildest of slopes and the front handlebar with only about a quarter of an inch of the stem in the head. Scott was properly scandalised and soon had his coat off and putting things in a more healthy condition, so that they were the first to get away. Eventually I was last (about 11 o'clock) to take the road, the same old road as far as Witney and then Ducklington, Newbridge and Marcham and Abingdon, from where I took a new road through Steventon and Blewbury to Streatley over Goring Bridge and over the top of Goring Heath to Caversham, having refreshed at the 'White Hart' Marcham.

At Sonning I was driven to an expensive indifferent and notorious tea house, the 'Kennet', which I do not wish to visit again. And so speedily through Twyford, Waltham St. Lawrence to Windsor, from where by the usual road to Datchet (with a Bass at the 'Royal Stag') Horton, Stanwell, Bedfont, Feltham, Twickenham, Richmond and home about 8 o'clock, making *84 miles* for the day's run. And so ended my fourth four figure tour, the total being *1265 miles*.

1926 ANNUAL REVIEW

This has been one of the best years for cycling for though the summer made a very late start, it was far above the average especially in June and July; the latter month produced a record mileage for any month except August and it included four century runs. Holiday weather, while not being by any means perfect, was better than usual and a good bit of new ground was covered though the general direction was the same as in previous years.

Another first class stopping place was found, the 'Stowe Inn' at Whitney-on-Wye, which we hope to visit many times again. I again made a dash across from North Devon into South Cornwall stopping for a weekend at the 'South Western Hotel', Holsworthy, on the way.

One of the most exhilarating runs was a short weekend at Burford in late autumn starting on a Saturday afternoon and coming back on the Sunday. On each of the many visits to Burford, a different route was taken and we hope to have several more weekends there next season.

The 'Chater-Lea' and 'James' machines again proved equal to all demands made on them. The latter fitted with a new handlebar came into great favour in the latter part of the season so much so that it will be retained as 'second string' for next year.

1925 HOLIDAY TOUR

The sequence of fine Sundays was remarkable, with only one in January being impossible on account of deep snow.

CYCLOMETERS AS OF DECEMBER 31ST 1926:-

Chater-Lea – 6895 miles

James – 7539 miles

A GOLDEN AGE OF CYCLING

CYCLING STATISTICS FOR 1926 BY MILES AND NUMBER OF RIDES PER MONTH

MONTH	NUMBER OF RIDES			MILES RIDDEN				AVERAGE MILES PER RIDE			
	SUNDAY	TOURING	OTHER RIDES	SUNDAYS	TOURING	OTHER RIDES	TOTAL	SUNDAYS	TOURING	OTHER RIDES	ALL RIDES
Jan	3	-	-	119	-	-	119	39.66	-	-	39.66
Feb	4	-	-	149	-	-	149	37.25	-	-	37.25
Mar	5	-	1	219	-	7	226	43.80	-	7.00	37.66
Apr	4	-	3	212	-	174	386	53.00	-	58.00	55.14
May	5	-	6	264	-	230	494	52.80	-	38.33	44.90
June	4	-	7	306	-	218	524	76.50	-	31.14	47.63
July	4	1	6	260	76	144	480	65.00	76.00	24.00	43.63
Aug	5	14	3	208	774	134	1116	41.60	55.28	44.66	50.72
Sept	4	5	-	253	244	-	497	63.25	48.80	-	55.02
Oct	4	-	-	178	-	-	178	44.50	-	-	44.50
Nov	5	-	-	209	-	-	209	41.80	-	-	41.80
Dec	4	-	1	151	-	50	201	37.77	-	50.00	40.25
Totals	51	20	27	2528	1094	957	4579	49.56	54.70	35.44	46.72

1925 HOLIDAY TOUR

5 of the Sunday rides having been done on tour have been deducted from the touring figures. Consequently the actual touring figures are: 25 rides, 1351 miles, Average 54.04 miles per ride

Arthur Street   Montgomery

1927 SUMMER WEEKEND RIDES

TUESDAY 19TH APRIL – MERLIN EASTER RIDE

A sojourn in Sussex

HAMMERSMITH – WIMBLEDON – CRAWLEY – BOLNEY – BRIGHTON – HOVE – PORTSLADE – SOUTHWICK – SHOREHAM – WORTHING – DIAL POST – HORSHAM – RUSPER – BROCKHAM GREEN – EPSOM – WIMBLEDON – HAMMERSMITH

I took the map of Sussex and started out at precisely 8.30 a.m. on the Brighton road via Wimbledon, Morden, Sutton, Banstead Downs, Burgh Heath, Kingswood, Reigate, Crawley, Pease Pottage, Bolney (where the 'Queen's Head' supplied me with a Bass and a wonderful meat pie) Patcham, Preston and into Brighton, making exactly 51 miles to the Aquarium (time 1 o'clock).

I was overcome with a desire for bread and cheese about this time, and so continued straight along the Parade to Hove and the insalubrious suburb of Portslade. At Southwick a little pub entitled 'The Sea House Inn' attracted me and in the bar parlour of that pleasant little hostelry a large chuck of bread and cheese and two bottles of Bass put me on good terms with myself. After exploring the picturesque town of Old Shoreham, I paid my 1^d to cross the toll bridge and struggled through the breezy stretch at the back of New Shoreham (the bungalow town) and Lancing to Worthing, spending about ½ an hour on the front before making up my mind for the return journey.

I eventually took the main road via Broadwater, Findon, Washington and Ashington. At Dial Post I made for a tea house, which is always a good billet, kept by a Miss Philpott, where two eggs, a large plate of bread and butter, strawberry jam and cake *ad lib* with a large pot of tea ditto, hot water and milk ran me into ½d. This fortified the remaining miles through Southwater to Horsham, which were soon ticked off, and I was feeling so fierce that I decided to forsake the main road and proceed by way of Faygate and Rusper, promising myself a Bass at the 'Star'. I was foiled, however, for it was twenty minutes to opening time, so I sprinted on through Newdigate to Brockham Green before having that Bass at the 'Duke's Head' at 7.15 p.m.. Brockham looked exceptionally peaceful in the evening sun.

From Brockham, except for the pull up to the top of Pebblecombe, it is an easy road via Headley, Epsom, Ewell, New Malden and Wimbledon and I reached home at 9.30 p.m. The day had been a perfect one for April – cloudless after 10 a.m. The strong South West wind, though rather bothering outward on the Brighton road, made it easy work on the return leg so that I was quite fresh after a run of *121 miles.*

SATURDAY 14TH MAY - WEEKEND TOUR

New mounts

HAMMERSMITH – HENLEY-ON-THAMES – DORCHESTER – KINGSTON BAGPUIZE – BURFORD

Set off on our weekend adventure about 1 o'clock, travelling via Richmond, Twickenham, Whitton, Hounslow, Cranford, Colnbrook, Slough, Maidenhead, Henley, Nettlebed, Huntercombe, Benson, Dorchester, Abingdon, Marcham, Kingston Bagpuize, Newbridge, Ducklington, Witney and finally arriving at Burford.

A strong headwind rather bothered us all the way but the new mounts were superior to this drawback. The first stop was for the usual and excellent tea at the 'Fleur de Lis' at Dorchester and a Bass at the 'Druid's Head' at Kingston Bagpuize. We had supper at our final resting place 'The Swan', where we arrived as the Tolsey Clock was striking 9 o'clock. *Distance covered: 76 miles*

1927 SUMMER WEEKEND RIDES

SUNDAY 15TH MAY
A chance encounter
BURFORD – WYTHAM – CUMNOR – ABINGDON – WALLINGFORD – GORING HEATH – STANWELL – HAMMERSMITH

It had rained all night up to about 6.30 a.m. making the air fresh and laying the dust. As usual much time was spent over the 'Swan' breakfast and it was 11.30 a.m. before we got back on the road for our homeward track. We decided to take the old road via Witney, Eynsham and Swinford Bridge to Wytham, about three miles northwest of Oxford and then climb upon the Downs to Cumnor – the beautiful village we had discovered last September. Here at the 'Vine' we regaled ourselves on beer and cheese while the local worthies were discussing the art of bell ringing.

The six miles from Cumnor to Abingdon is all along the crest of the Berkshire Downs and is rather lovely. From Abingdon we took the road to Culham and then turned off right to Appleford and Sutton Courtenay, a glorious bit of country new to us. At Wallingford we fell in with Basil Barham who writes such entertaining articles in 'Cycling' and the C.T.C. Gazette. He was pottering around getting photographs for his next lecture on the Thames Valley. We parted from him at Streatley where he went to photograph the church; I had ascertained from him that his oft-mentioned son and daughter Jack and Jill, did really exist but alas, they have now forsaken cycling for other pursuits!

From Goring we took the steep and stony road over Goring Heath to Caversham stopping for tea at the 'King Charles' Head'. We then travelled from Caversham via Sonning, Twyford, Waltham St. Lawrence, Dedworth Green, Windsor, Datchet, Horton and Stanwell where we had a Bass at the 'Wheatsheaf'. Then home via Bedfont, Feltham and Twickenham after a very enjoyable weekend, the day's run amounting to *85 miles.*

SATURDAY 11TH JUNE - WEEKEND TOUR
Tobacco and talk
HAMMERSMITH – HENLEY-ON-THAMES – DORCHESTER – NEWBRIDGE – BURFORD

The usual outward journey to Burford for the third time this year. Tea was taken at the 'Fleur de Lis' at Dorchester and a couple of Bass were partaken

at the 'Rose Revived' at Newbridge. We left home at 1 o'clock and rolled
into Burford and the 'Swan' at 8.30 p.m. precisely. Here there was a goodly
company to supper, gathered from all parts of the country – including
Birmingham, Manchester, Portsmouth, as well as parts of London – and
most of whom we had met before. Shaw of Birmingham was going on
through the night to Weston Super Mare while the Portsmouth lad meant
to make Cambridge by the morning. We finally got to roost about 11.45
p.m. after an enormous supper and much tobacco and talk.

Distance covered: 75 miles

SUNDAY 12TH JUNE

A most perfect weekend

BURFORD – BUCKLAND – KINGSTON BAGPUIZE – TUBNEY – GORING HEATH – WINDSOR – KINGSTON

Many arrivals and departures including a party of night riders from Barnet
C.C. (13 in total) to breakfast at 8 o'clock. We (the house party of eight)
had ours at 9 o'clock after the usual stroll and then at 9.30 a.m. eight
Southgate C.C. night riders turned up including Ballantyne and Myers –
the latter on three wheels.

We saw everyone off before we made a start at 11.30 a.m., making first
for Brize Norton and Bampton and then crossing the Thames at Tadpole
Bridge to Buckland – a perfect sample of the grey stone Oxfordshire
village and onto Kingston Bagpuize. From here instead of the usual road we
proceeded on to Fyfield and Tubney at which village the curiously named
'Dog House' supplied us with excellent beer, bread and cheese (the last
good powerful stuff). Then on via Shippon to Abingdon and then Culham,
Sutton Courtenay and Appleford turning aside up to the summit of Sires
Hill to Wallingford and the usual route to Windsor with tea at the 'King
Charles Head' at Goring Heath.

From Windsor via Wraysbury, Staines, Laleham, Shepperton, Walton,
Molesey, Ditton and Kingston. A most perfect weekend with light breezes,
cool and delightful air and a cloudless sky. A last Bass at the 'George'
Wraysbury.

Distance covered: 94 miles

SATURDAY 25TH JUNE – WEEKEND TOUR

Refuge in Petworth

HAMMERSMITH – RUSPER – HORSHAM – DIAL POST – PULBOROUGH – PETWORTH

We started in doubtful weather at 1.45 p.m. travelling via Wimbledon, New Malden, Ewell, Epsom, Headley, Pebblecombe, Brockham Green, Newdigate, Rusper (tea at the 'Star') Faygate, Horsham, Southwater, West Grinstead, Dial Post, Ashington, Thakeham, Storrington, Pulborough, Stopham, Fittleworth and Petworth.

We wanted to stay at Thakeham but the 'White Lion' was full up. We had a look at Storrington and did not like it that much. Pulborough was full of day trippers – the 'White Hart' at Stopham Bridge was also full up. As the headwind was now laden with a fine rain things began to look desperate and we were thinking of turning our backs to the south west gale and running home. However, we eventually found a comfortable billet at the 'Wheatsheaf' in Petworth and were soon filled with a decent supper and more than content. *We covered 63 miles of hard pushing against the wind.*

SUNDAY 26TH JUNE

A day of all seasons

PETWORTH – CHICHESTER – FISHBOURNE – LAVANT – MIDHURST – BROOK – GUILDFORD – CHOBHAM – HAMMERSMITH

A bleak looking morning greeted us and we were nearly frozen on a short stroll before breakfast. We set off about 10.30 a.m. once more against the wind from Duncton over the Downs via Upper Waltham to Chichester through Fishbourne, to the quaint village of Bosham, where we had a short spell of sunshine. We then returned to Chichester and then cycled due north to cross the Downs once more.

At Lavant the 'Earl of Marsh' provided some excellent bread and cheese and beer, and then through the glorious country via West Dean, Singleton and Cocking to Midhurst the sun being now in evidence for long periods at a time. That strenuous eight miles that consists of Midhurst, Easebourne, Fernhurst and Haslemere was taken at an easy pace but once out of Haslemere it was a rapid run to Brook where the 'Dog & Partridge' gave us a truly excellent tea.

Heavy rain accompanied us from Milford to Godalming but this soon stopped. From Guildford we took the now customary way through Woking, making a detour to Chobham where we had to take refuge under a chestnut tree from a perfect drencher of a storm. Thereafter, all was serene for the home run and a supper of bacon and tomatoes – a very enjoyable weekend in spite of meteorological challenges.

Today's run 90 miles.

SATURDAY 2ND JULY – WEEKEND TOUR

A glorious supper

HAMMERSMITH – HENLEY-ON-THAMES – DORCHESTER – NEWBRIDGE – BURFORD

We decided at the last moment to chance our luck in the face of a stormy sky and an appalling weather forecast but it was nearly 2 o'clock before we got on our way taking the usual Maidenhead, Henley, Abingdon route to Burford with tea at 'Fleur de Lis' and further refreshment at the 'Rose Revived'. There was a further delay caused by a puncture in E.B.P.'s front tyre, so it was 9.30 p.m. when we rolled into supper at the 'Swan' where a goodly company was assembled. The weather cleared at Henley and the remainder of the day was glorious as also was the supper. *75 miles.*

SUNDAY 3RD JULY

Back in the dog house

BURFORD – BRIZE NORTON – TUBNEY – GORING HEATH – WINDSOR – WRAYSBURY – HAMMERSMITH

Woke up to a bright and sunny morning which became overcast at times later. Having seen the last of the other wayfarers off we left the 'Swan' about 11.45 a.m. taking the same road as last time via Brize Norton, Bampton, Buckland, Fyfield and Tubney to Abingdon with some more of that bread and strong cheese at the 'Dog House' in Tubney. The wind, which we had against us yesterday, was again in our faces as far as Goring.

Tea, as usual, was taken at the 'King Charles' Head', and from Windsor to Staines, Laleham, Shepperton, Walton, Molesey and Ditton. A final Bass at the 'George' Wraysbury and home about 10 o'clock. The only rain we had was a shower at Laleham, otherwise a first class weekend.

Distance covered: 94 miles

SATURDAY 23RD JULY – WEEKEND TOUR
An evening with Wayfarer and co
HAMMERSMITH – HENLEY-ON-THAMES – DORCHESTER – NEWBRIDGE – BURFORD

We took the usual short road to Burford (Maidenhead, Henley, Dorchester, Abingdon and Newbridge) and arrived at the 'Swan' at 9.30 p.m. having had to contend with a strong headwind and 1½ hours' worth of drenching rain. We found "Wayfarer[1]" along with companions W. Borwick (nicknamed "Lame Dog") and E. Parry ("Wayfarer's unpaid private secretary) there and so had a pleasant evening, it being nearly midnight before we got to roost in the top attic.

Tea at the 'Fleur de Lis' and Bass at the 'Rose Revived' as usual and distance as usual *75 miles.*

SUNDAY 24TH JULY
A short cut to Sonning
BURFORD – STANTON HARCOURT – CUMNOR – ABINGDON – NUFFIELD – KINGSTON – WINDSOR – WRAYSBURY – HAMMERSMITH

A grey morning did not dampen our spirits and we enjoyed a pleasant breakfast in the good company we had at supper. We took affectionate leave of "Wayfarer" and company, who were going back to Birmingham by starting off in the opposite direction about 10.30 a.m. We got on the road at 11 o'clock, making first for Brize Norton and then turning left via Lew, Curbridge, Ducklington and Hardwick to Stanton Harcourt (a lovely village) across the ferry at Bablock to Eaton and Cumnor for bread and cheese at the 'Vine'.

Down to Abingdon and the usual road to Wallingford after which we adventured on a new route, a steep and rough road to Nuffield after which we badly wanted tea and had our wants satisfied in the beautiful gardens of the 'Bricklayer's Arms' at Kingston, a first rate tea place. About a mile further on we found a road to Sonning, which was undoubtedly a short cut and from thence by the usual Twyford, Waltham St. Lawrence, Windsor, Wraysbury, Staines, Laleham, Shepperton way. It was past 11 o'clock when we got home, a nail in E.B.P.'s front tyre and half an hour's shelter from a storm having delayed us. A very first class weekend. *Distance covered: 93 miles*

1 The renowned cycling journalist, WM Robinson, also known as "Wayfarer"

1927 HOLIDAY TOUR – MERLIN CYCLE 2413

SATURDAY 6TH AUGUST

No harm done

HAMMERSMITH – ESHER – STAINES – WINDSOR – WALTHAM ST. LAWRENCE – READING – NEWBURY – WEST SHEFFORD – WANTAGE – FARINGDON – BURFORD

Got away about 7.30 a.m. in a heavy storm which lasted about half an hour and contrary to our usual practice took the road to Kingston and Esher. Taking the short cut round Kingston I came to grief by braking too hard on the wet road to avoid a milk cart but, exempt for skin off prospecting parts, no harm resulted. From Esher we made across to Laleham and Staines to Windsor and then the usual Waltham St. Lawrence road going on to Reading and the Bath road via Theale to Newbury, having had our first refreshments at 'The Star' at Waltham St. Lawrence.

After Newbury, bread and cheese etc. became essential. We stopped at a likely pub – the 'Five Bells' – and though it sported a C.T.C. sign, after we had ordered beer they informed us it had no bread and cheese so we had to go on another three miles towards the Lambourn stream where our wants were satisfied at the 'Bell'.

We now took things easy, pausing to examine the Lambourn at West Shefford before taking the somewhat strenuous road over the Downs to

Wantage and through the Wiltshire Vale to Faringdon, where the 'White Hart' supplied us with an excellent tea. Here we met two different tandem pairs, whom we had run across on our last Sussex weekend. Having time to waste we made for our objective by a round about way via Lechlade and Filkins arriving at Burford about 7.30 p.m., just making *100 miles* of it.

SUNDAY 7TH AUGUST

A most amusing pair of artists

BURFORD – STOW-ON-THE-WOLD – LOWER SWELL – WINCHCOMBE – ANDOVERSFORD – PUESDOWN – NORTHLEACH – BURFORD

Sunday was to be treated as a day of rest as it was nearly 12 when we set out first for Stow-on-the-Wold, that glorious ten miles of Cotswold road. From Stow we ran down to Lower Swell for our midday refreshments at the 'Golden Ball'. We then took a very rough and tough road via Condicote and Temple Guiting, large portions of which were walked and ended up in a precipitous descent into the pleasant town of Winchcombe. Here we refreshed with lemonade and cakes at 'Whitley's' taking the proprietor's advice as to our return journey via Charlton Abbots, Brockhampton and Sevenhampton to Andoversford. It was certainly a beautiful and unsequestered road but hardly a speedway, the surface being mainly composed of small stones and it being necessary to open a gate every few hundred yards.

From Andoversford we got on the main road, which took us speedily to Burford over Puesdown through Northleach and we rolled in to tea about 6 o'clock. We spent most of the evening in conversation with other tourists who had turned up at the 'Swan' for the night and with two artists, John Higgins and William Willets, an extremely amusing pair with many quaint anecdotes, the day's riding having been *45 tough miles.*

MONDAY 8TH AUGUST

The famous trifle

BURFORD – PUESDOWN – ANDOVERSFORD – CHELTENHAM – COOMBE HILL – TEWKESBURY – LEDBURY – TARRINGTON – WHITNEY-ON-WYE

We had a long and fairly tough journey to do today so were not pleased to get up to a proper soaker. However, this did not delay our start and we were on the road soon after 10 o'clock swathed in our Pagets in the usual holiday optimistic spirit, which was justified as we were able to shed them just outside Northleach and take the long pull up Puesdown in comfort. From here we continued on the main road via Shipton Solers and Andoversford (first refreshment at 'Andoversford Hotel') to Cheltenham where the sun was already drying up the tramlines.

From Cheltenham we took the Tewkesbury road by way of Uckington and Coombe Hill, and were greeted with another shower, which soon passed, as we enjoyed our midday refreshment at the 'Old Swan', just outside that ancient town.

The road from Tewkesbury to Ledbury over Hollybush Hill and Eastnor is now a familiar one. We struck Ledbury in the sunshine for once and I was able to get the photograph of Church Street, which I had been trying to obtain for three years. Tea was now getting an urgent requirement but we remembered the 'Foley Arms' at Tarrington, which as on an occasion last year amply satisfied us so that thus fortified we were not long in getting over the 15 miles from Hereford via Bridge Sollers. From here, we went on to Staunton-on-Wye, Willersley and Winforton, to the famous 'Stowe Inn' at Whitney, having taken refreshments at the 'Kite's Nest' on the way. The 'Stowe Inn' gave us a huge supper including the famous trifle praised by Wayfarer, and so (after much pleasant conversation) to bed in much content, the 75 *miles* from Burford having been covered in very easy fashion.

TUESDAY 9TH AUGUST
Slow progress
WHITNEY-ON-WYE – HAY-ON-WYE – GLASBURY – PETERCHURCH – DORSTONE – WHITNEY

Morning broke in anything but promising fashion but we made up our minds to explore the Golden Valley which has a reputuation for dowsing its explorers. We had first to make for Hay over the toll bridge, the keeper of which has to remember everyone who passes over it and pays as they may return for free!

We had to go on the Brecon Road nearly as far as Glasbury before finding a road in the direction we wished to go pointing to Peterchurch. This proved to be a very pleasant way though not without some toilsome hill climbing. It soon began to drizzle which continued while we explored the pretty village of Dorstone where the 'Pandy Inn' supplied us with some very welcome refreshment amidst a curious company including a railway porter from Victoria Station on holiday. We were strongly advised by the landlord to take a steep and thorny path up a neighbouring mountain, but on looking at it and the rain having increased in power, we decided against it this time and took the road onto Peterchurch where the 'Boughton Inn' gave us our customary midday bread and cheese.

The road was particularly tough up through Vowchurch over Brampton Hill where the gentle rain became a perfect drencher, which drove us to shelter for about an hour and we decided to take what looked like a short cut towards our base. Two miles of it was enough as it appeared to disappear in a sheep track so we turned back and retraced our way to Whitney. Another bye day, the mileage only amounting to a paltry *42 miles.*

WEDNESDAY 10TH AUGUST

A mountain torrent

WHITNEY-ON-WYE – PRESTEIGNE – NORTON – KNIGHTON – NEWTOWN – CAERWYS – LLANBRYNMAIR – MACHYNLLETH

As usual a gentle rain was falling when we awoke but we had learned by now to take no heed of the weather. We made our early start taking the road through Willersley and the stiff climb from Erdisley to Kington where we had a watery sun for a short period continuing until we arrived at Presteigne where we refreshed at the 'Radnorshire Arms' before tackling the 1200 foot climb from Norton over Llanwen Hill to Knighton. Before we had reached the top a good drencher set in and we had the pleasure of coasting down the steep descent into Knighton in our trusty Pagets.

The 'George and Dragon' supplied us with our midday bread and cheese and alcoholic fluid before we went on our way in a light drizzle. This speedily became heavy rain culminating in a cloudburst before passing through Beguildy and Felindre and more than a cloudburst at the highest part of the pass where shelter was absent and the sheep looked astonished to see human beings without umbrellas!

The run down into Newtown in the face of the driving rain and the rutty road turned temporarily into a mountain torrent was one of the most hectic experiences we had had so far and we found a welcome railway bridge at the outskirts of Newtown where we wrung ourselves out and emptied the water out of our shoes. We proceeded in a steady and more comfortable rain to Caerwys where we found shelter and an excellent tea at the 'Buck Temperance Hotel'. The rain now ceased so we decided to push on via Pontdolgoch, Clatter, Carno, Talerddig, Llanbrynmair, Cemmaes and Penegoes to Machynlleth, stopping at the 'Wynnstay Arms' Llanbrynmair for refreshments.

At Machynlleth, we tried in vain to find a billet in a licensed house but 'Ferndale' where we put up for the night proved quite comfortable. A very wet and strenuous *72 miles.*

THURSDAY IITH AUGUST

Panorama walk

MACHYLLNETH – PENNAL – ABERDOVEY – TOWYN – LLANGELYNNIN – LLWYNGWRIL – DOLGELLEY

As usual it was raining brightly when we had breakfast with a walker who was making through the mountains. The rain made us decide to take a longer and less strenuous road, our objective like his being Dolgelley. We therefore made for the beautiful Dovey road, now very different from the condition it was in when last we traversed it. The rain had ceased by the time we had reached the unlovely village of Pennal and the estuary of the Dovey looked at its best and singularly reminiscent of the Exe.

At Aberdovey where we filled up with buns, a cloudburst overtook us but we were able to get shelter under a friendly railway arch for about twenty minutes until the storm abated and allowed us to go to Towyn, a seaside resort of no outstanding interest. From here the road is a fascinating one with a lovely view of the river and mountains from the bridge over the Dyffryn Dysynni (the Dysynni Valley), upon which we lingered for ten minutes or more and should have remained longer but the pangs of hunger made an inn very desirable.

At Llangelynnin the road comes out on to the coast and we were sorry to have to hurry over it. Our hunger and thirst were appeased at a beautiful little village, Llwyngwril, where the 'Garthangharad Hotel' supplied us with the best of bread and cheese and beer. We continued onto Barmouth, walking across the long railway bridge over the Afon Mawddach (the River Mawddach) to that very pleasant town which after an exploration trip we left by the Panorama Walk (well named) to Dolgelley stopping only to admire the charming little village of Bontddu with its picturesque waterfall and mill. At Dolgelley[2] a pleasant but ordinary little town – very Welsh – our first thought was for tea and a stopping place both of which we found at the 'Torrent Walk Hotel' which proved an admirable choice.

A lovely evening was spent on the glorious Torrent Walk and on our return journey we met two men of the C.T.C. who we had seen at Burford on the previous weekend and after parting with them ran into our walking friend of breakfast time. This had been one of our best days so far and though the *mileage was only 39*, each of those miles will bear repeating on our next year's tour.

FRIDAY 12TH AUGUST

Pure joy

DOLGELLEY – BALA – BETHEL – BETWS-Y-COED – LLANRWST – CONWY

We had ordered an early breakfast with the intention of making one of the other "lions" of Dolgelley, the precipice walk, part of our route, but a relentless downpour caused us to abandon that idea. We set off in our Pagets northward bound leaving Cader Idris[3] with his crown swathed in rain clouds, taking the Bala road via Bontnewydd and Drws-y-Nant.

The rain ceased before we reached Bala and we were not greatly impressed with the Lake, which has no surroundings and is a lame sheet of water. Nor did the town of Bala prove very attractive. However, we had a Bass and some biscuits at 'The Goat' before proceeding on the Corwen road. We found the most delightful little inn – 'The Boot' – at Bethel where we had an excellent tea in the bar or kitchen, whichever it was, where bread making and much appetising cooking was in progress.

From Bethel to the Holyhead road, which we struck about two miles beyond Corwen, was pure joy – a rundown of about four miles with a perfect surface. The main road as far as Cerrig-y-Drudion[4] is of a most ordinary description though very fast but the surroundings improve afterwards. Betws-y-Coed was as usual full of charabancs and other motors, orange peel and paper. Here we left the Holyhead road on the left and went onto Llanrwst where the 'King's Arms' gave us an indifferent tea.

---

2 Now more commonly known as Dolgellau
3 A mountain of 2930 feet lying on the southern end of Snowdonia
4 Also known as Cerrigydrudion

From Llanrwst we found the Llandudno traffic rather trying and at Glan Conwy we decided to cross the old suspension bridge into Conwy, which, with its picturesque Castle, looked very enticing. What we saw of it on entering the town decided us to go no further for today and we speedily found comfortable quarters at the 'Blue Bell Hotel', spending the remainder of the evening in the Castle – one of the best of the Welsh Castles – and after that closed at 8 o'clock along by the river. A very pleasant day of *62 miles cycling* in spite of the wet start.

SATURDAY 13TH AUGUST
An 18th century landlord
CONWY – LLANDULAS CASTLE – ST. ASAPH – LLANRHAEADR – RUTHIN – LLANDEGLA – GOBOWEN – NESSCLIFFE – MONTFORD BRIDGE

A brilliant morning made us linger in pleasant Conwy and it was about 11.30 a.m. when we passed out over the bridge vowing to return some day.

We took the road to Colwyn Bay, having no desire to sample Llandudno, and this section of road as far as Old Colwyn was peculiarly and unpleasantly rough, tram lined, and inhabited by all the roadhogs in the universe. We stopped to read the inscriptions over the gateway of Llanddulas Castle, which claims to have seen more bloodshed than anywhere else in Wales.

At Abergele we got rid of most of the traffic by going on the road to St. Asaph, a town of no great attractions though the 'Old Railway Inn' gave us excellent bread, cheese and onions. We passed through Denbigh, which was also a plain town. Some miles beyond, at Llanrhaeadr, we struck a delightful little pub the 'King's Arms', with an underground bar-kitchen full of romantic corners from which emanated Welsh talk from hidden lurkers and a landlord who looked as though he belonged to the 18th century. Here we had a most comfortable half hour over the usual midday rations before making our way through the picturesque town of Ruthin, one of the few Welsh towns that can be so described, and then up the Nant-y-Garth pass (mostly walked) through the Clwydian Mountains turning aside for a wonderful tea at the 'Crown' at Llandegla.

Then the ascent began over the Llantysilio Mountains and when we got to the highest point where the slate quarries are, the rain began in the best Welsh Mountain fashion and we were robbed of the lovely views coming down the Horse Shoe Pass by the solid rain, which also made this steep descent with its hairpin corners exceedingly tricky. Nevertheless we thought it desirable to stop halfway to let our hot back rims cool down a bit before descending into tripperised Llangollen where we did not stop but sped on through the rain through Chirk and Gobowen stopping only for a Bass at the 'New Inn' midway between those towns. Being out of Wales (it being Saturday night) we made our way Shrewsbury-wards via Whittington and West Felton trying in vain to get put up out of the rain at the 'Three Pigeons' at Nesscliffe. However the 'Wingfield Arms' at Montford Bridge (about four and a half miles out of Shrewsbury) was able to take us in and proved a most comfortable billet.

Distance covered: 72 strenuous miles

SUNDAY 14TH AUGUST

Lingering in the sun

MONTFORD BRIDGE – SHREWSBURY – MUCH WENLOCK – CORVE DALE – CLUN

We got up to a regular soaker for a change. Nevertheless it did not deter us from getting on the road soon after 10 o'clock after repairing a punctured front tyre, making first for a half drowned Shrewsbury where it finally stopped raining and quite a brilliant sun made its appearance.

We left the town over the English Bridge via Cound and Cressage and over the very steep Harley Hill to Much Wenlock, one of the most beautiful of the many beautiful Salopian[5] towns. Here we lingered for over an hour in the sun, having our midday sustenance at the 'Talbot', a very comfortable inn. We had no plans for proceeding and after much discussions seated on the kerbstone made up our minds to seek quarters at the 'Buffalo' at Clun for the night before turning once more into Wales. This meant getting down to the unlovely Craven Arms first via Bourton, Shipley, Munslow and Diddlebury through the lovely Corve Dale.

At about 3 o'clock the rain started again in its usual venomous manner and we soaked through it to Craven Arms where it abated sufficiently for us to remove our capes. We arrived at Clun moderately dry and were soon enjoying the excellent tea which the 'Buffalo' can be relied upon to supply. The evening was a somewhat damp and clammy one but we were able to explore the ancient castle ruins which are much more interesting at close quarters than they appear from the distance.

Distance covered: 43 miles

---

5 Salop is an old term for Shropshire.

A GOLDEN AGE OF CYCLING

MONDAY 15TH AUGUST
Newspapers for damp knees
CLUN – CLUNGUNFORD – LEINTWARDINE – LLANFIHANGEL-NANT-MELLAN

Once more rain greeted us for breakfast which we had in the company of two elderly 'motorfolk' – the unmotorish kind who were distinctly agreeable. I searched the town for brown paper and string to send home some used up underclothing, and finally succeeded in obtaining those articles from the landlady of the 'Buffalo', finally getting away about 11 o'clock in a rainy mist, which speedily became a steady downpour. I took the road back through Aston-on-Clun and turning to the right by the way of Clungunford to Leintwardine where as usual we made for the 'Swan' for some of the excellent bread and cheese which is always to be obtained at that inn.

As we left Leintwardine the sun came out to our great joy but it was, however, short lived, for within half an hour the rain came down harder than ever so we took the road via Lingen, Kinsham, Knill, Walton and New Radnor to Llanfihangel-nant-Mellan. Here, at the 'Red Lion', Mrs Williams immediately provided us with some newspapers for our damp knees and lit a huge fire which was not unwelcome, so we decided to go no further, spending the evening over the mass of reading matter which is always to be found at this, one of the most comfortable of 'cyclist' homes, while the rain continued with unabated fury. Our shortest and wettest stage so far, with *34 miles covered.*

TUESDAY 16TH AUGUST
A miracle!
LLANFIHANGEL-NANT-MELLAN – PENYBONT – RHAYADER – ELAN VALLEY – LLANFIHANGEL-NANT-MELLAN

We found the rain still coming down as though it had no intention of stopping. We thus spent some little time weather-proofing our machines, before making a start, having arranged to return to supper about 8 o'clock. When there is any rain about, the Elan Valley is the place to get it at its best so to the Elan Valley we made up our minds to go. We had battled against the rain through Penybont and taken some refreshment at the 'Gwystre Inn' when a miracle happened! As we approached the wet town of Rhayader the sun came forth and swept away the rain clouds, and after an excellent lunch at the 'Eagle' we made our way to the Valley and did the grand tour of the lakes in brilliant sunshine, a treat which very few who visit this spot ever experience.

After an excellent tea at 'Webbers', the run back over that road of stupendous views was a glorious one and so was the supper, which Mrs Williams had got ready for us when we arrived back to the 'Red Lion' after our pleasant *50-mile ramble*.

WEDNESDAY 17TH AUGUST

A fine morning at last!

LLANFIHANGEL-NANT-MELLAN – BUILTH WELLS – CILMERY – BEULAH – LLANGADOCK – CARMARTHEN

A fine morning at last!!

After an exceptionally heavy breakfast we got on the road about 10.30 a.m. taking the Builth road, loitering through that fashionable spa and calling in at the 'Prince Llewellyn' at Cilmery for our first refreshment. The 'Carpenter's Arms' at Beulah did us proud in the way of bread, cheese and beer, and put us in good fettle for the longish climb up from Llanwrtyd Wells to the top of the Sugar Loaf[6], the view from which this sunshiny day was magnificent and contrasted strongly with our last passage of this road some years back in a thunderstorm.

The four-mile coast down was a joyful one, the surface of the road now being like a track and we were in to Llandovery, where we were on that other occasion nearly drowned speedily. We made up our minds to try the 'Red Lion' at Llangadock for tea. It was a curious place with curious people but the tea was first rate. The landlord – an ex-professional pianist – entertained us with some wonderful music while his daughter sang to us in a powerful mezzo-soprano voice which may or may not be worth pounds when she grows up as she is at present only 13 years of age. After tea we were conducted round the garden and farmyard and altogether it was an interesting visit. We went on our way through Llandilo to the large straggling town of Carmarthen where the 'Bird in Hand' (a temperance

---

6 A 1955-foot mountain situated 2 miles from the town of Abergavenny

house) put us up indifferently. A stroll round the town before supper did not reveal any hidden beauties and our previous impression of Carmarthen as a 'one horse town' remained unaltered.

Distance riding: 63 miles

THURSDAY 18TH AUGUST

14 dangerous hills

CARMARTHEN — LLETHRACH — BANCYFELIN — ST. CLEARS — KILGETTY — PEMBROKE — MILFORD HAVEN — NEYLAND — HAVERFORDWEST — PELCOMB CROSS — SOLVA HARBOUR — ST. DAVIDS

The time had come for parting with E.B.P. as he was due at Burford on Saturday so I went on alone on the westward road through Llethrach, Bancyfelin and St. Clears finding the long pull up via Llanddowror to Red Roses somewhat easier with a following wind than on the last occasion.

The first refreshment was taken at the 'Commercial Inn' and at Kilgetty I decided to leave out Tenby and go straight onto Pembroke via Redberth, Sageston, Carew Cheriton and Milton, none of which villages had an inn that looked as though it kept good bread and cheese — which was then becoming an urgent matter. However, the 'Kings Arms' at Pembroke supplied this need and I was able to stable my horse[7] there while inspecting the interior of the castle. Following a few enquiries I at length found my way to Hobbs Point, from which the ferry took me across Milford Haven to Neyland on the opposite side. There being a dearth of finger posts[8] it was somewhat difficult to find a road to Haverfordwest.

The road via Johnston, Pope Hill and Merlin's Bridge was a steep and rough one, and probably not the best. Haverfordwest, where I had an indifferent tea at 'Varleys', struck me as being a town ripe for exploration, but I had no time for it on this trip and hope to visit it again. I had been warned that the road from Haverfordwest to St. Davids was a rough one, with, I think 14 dangerous hills, therefore I was agreeably surprised to find it eminently rideable (for the first ten miles at any rate) although it made me slightly uneasy as to my direction being right as there were no finger posts nor anyone of whom to enquire. However, I reached the 'Cross Inn',

---

7 A reference, perhaps, to parking one's bicycle.
8 Traditional signpost consisting of a post with a number of arms, known as fingers, pointing towards various named locations.

which I identified as Pelcomb Cross, showing that I was on the right road. I went inside to make sure and early though it was (before 6), I got a Bass and heard "Uncles and Aunts" from Daventry on the wireless.

It is a good road onwards until the precipitous drop down to Newgale Sands after I had turned aside a mile or two to investigate Roch Castle. Newgale Sands is a wonderful country though with continuous views of sea and rugged coast and Solva Harbour in the evening light presented a dream of beauty.

I reached St. Davids about 8 o'clock and succeeded in getting a billet at 'Martins', No. 5 Royal Terrace, a boarding house that gave first-rate accommodation. I had just time before supper to stroll round and become convinced that St. Davids with its Cathedral and many ruins is a gem of the order.

Distance covered: 61 miles

FRIDAY 19TH AUGUST

A happy miscommunication

ST. DAVIDS – FISHGUARD – NEWPORT – NEVERN – CARDIGAN – CENARTH – LAMPETER

A stormy night brought a bright and sunny morning and I was out early after breakfast, busy with my camera photographing the lions of St. Davids. It was past eleven before I got on the road to Fishguard via Croes-goch and Mathry, taking the right hand road beyond the latter village to Lower Fishguard.

First refreshments at the 'Pendre Inn' kept me going. Lower Fishguard is a wonderful place and I loitered there for about half an hour before walking up the steep hill towards Dinas where the 'Glan Hotel' did me well in regard to the midday mainstay. Further on is Newport, a thriving little watering place on the estuary of the Afon (River) Nevern, and Nevern, a charming little town after which there is a somewhat strenuous stretch to Cardigan.

Cardigan is a very pleasant town and quite picturesque from the bridge. Here I attended to my correspondence before seeking tea at the 'Glanavon Hotel' after which I pursued the beautiful Teifi Valley road via Llechryd and Cenarth (a lovely spot) to Newcastle Emlyn, which appeared to have no outstanding features. The Afon (River) Teifi is still followed through Henllan to Llandysul where I has some idea of putting up for the night but was not much attracted by the town and consequently decided to risk the failing light and unknown road (for I had no map) by continuing on to Lampeter.

The start was far from encouraging for it was a walk up a steep hill with the surface nothing but potholes and ruts. In fact the first five miles was a most strenuous character both on account of gradient and surface. About here I found another 'Cross Inn', which I entered with the intention of enquiring about the road but couldn't find anyone there who spoke English. However, a request for Bass was understood but 'biscuits' was beyond the landlady as she looked puzzled and went away returning in a few minutes with a happy smile and a huge platter of bread and butter and a lump of cheese!

Though I was tied for time, I was also very hungry as usual and speedily finished up this good fare. The road onwards improved wonderfully and though I passed through the largish village of Llanbydder, I did not attempt to seek quarters for the night there and it was quite dark when I reached Lampeter so that I had to light my lamp to find my way about. However, I spotted the welcome C.T.C. sign at 17 High Street and just dropped in to a hot fish supper which went down very well.

Distance covered: 65 miles

SATURDAY 20TH AUGUST

Before a genial sun
LAMPETER – LLANDOVERY – BRECON – HAY-ON-WYE – WHITNEY-ON-WYE

The usual Welsh morning – raining in torrents – but I had to get out of Wales for the weekend. I donned my trusty Paget directly after breakfast and took the Llandovery road, the first three miles of which runs up to some 1064 feet, which, in the face of drenching rain and clad in a hot and steamy cape, is no particular joke. The road beyond this point is a magnificent one and I regretted that the rain prevented the full enjoyment of it.

At Llandovery the rain was still in full cry but as there were signs of a break in the sky I made up my mind to stoke up with bread and cheese, before tackling the rising road to Brecon. I entered the 'Bear' and was informed that if I wanted bread and cheese there was a restaurant further down the road. I said what I thought of them and traversed onwards to the 'Kings Arms', which satisfied my wants admirably and supplied some excellent company so that I spent nearly an hour there.

It was still raining when I went on my way on the lovely Brecon road. However, about five miles on my way the rain disappeared before a genial sun and I was finally able to shed my Paget and enjoy to the full the beautiful panorama on either side on the gentle rise to Trecastle. I arrived in Brecon about 3.30 p.m. and had plenty of time for exploration of that pleasant town before an excellent tea at the 'Bell' (one of the cheapest and best).

The rain started once more as I set out from Brecon on the road to Hay. This is a fine stretch with the frowning Black Mountains very prominent on the right all the way. At Bronllys I called at the local universal providers with the object of acquiring a pair of shoe laces and had to be satisfied with the ladies' variety (about 1½ inches broad), which however served their purpose admirably.

I continued on through Three Cocks to Hay with the objective of purchasing some "Aertex" underwear but after searching that thriving town through could find no shop that stocked it and so in disgust I turned back to Glasbury and crossed the bridge. I then made my way to Whitney via Clyro – the rain having ceased temporarily giving place to a wonderful sunset. The 'Stowe Inn' engulfed me about 8.30 p.m. so that I was soon gorging on the ample fare provided by the doyen of inns, which strange to say I had all to myself. *Distance covered: 71 miles*

SUNDAY 21ST AUGUST

A thorough drencher!

WHITNEY-ON-WYE – HEREFORD – ROSS-ON-WYE – MUCH BIRCH – GOODRICH CASTLE – WHITNEY-ON-WYE

Bright sun greeted me on rising, an ominous sign. However, it was nearly 10 o'clock before the usual rain started. Being an optimist this did not interfere with my plans and I took the now familiar road to Hereford with the rain ceasing just before I entered that most pleasant city and being superseded by a brilliant sun which held out during the hour and an half I spent there.

I travelled over the bridge to Ross, stopping on the way for my bread and cheese and, of course, beer at the 'Axe & Cleaver' at Much Birch. While at Ross I made up my mind to go and have a look at Goodrich Castle and see how the work of restoration is proceeding. I found the Castle rather full of tourists of the 'Yankee' variety. The light being in the wrong direction I was not able to get the photograph I wished and as I was coming away one of the wettest thunderstorms I have ever encountered came up quite suddenly without any warning and lasted for about 1½ hours, a thorough drencher! Tea was becoming an urgent matter when this gave over and a particularly good one was obtained at the 'Axe & Cleaver', after which the weather remained fine for the trip back to Whitney where at the 'Stowe' several more cyclists had arrived to share my supper but as usual there was plenty for everybody.

Distance covered: 69 miles

MONDAY 22ND AUGUST

No great shakes

WHITNEY-ON-WYE – HAY-ON-WYE – BRECON – BWLCH – CRICKHOWELL – ABERGAVENNY - PONTYPOOL – PENARTH – BARRY

I had rather a strenuous trip in view today so was not over enjoyed to find a particularly venomous rain falling against which it was necessary to fortify the machinery with much oil.

I had intended to take the Black Mountains on my way but a look at them persuaded me to go around them instead. I took the short road to Hay over the toll bridge and onto Brecon, battling against a strong headwind in my Paget. The rain thinned down sufficiently to justify the removal of the cape and the wind being somewhat aslant made it easier work on the uphill road to Bwlch, where the 'Farmer's Arms' supplied the usual midday refreshment. However, the rain soon resumed operations for the long run down to Crickhowell while the appearance of the normally pleasant town of Abergavenny was too damp to tempt me to linger there, so I continued straight through taking a road to the right about a mile out of the town pointing to Pontypool.

This proved a good, easy road though on the upward trend and I was able to dodge the smoky town of Pontypool by getting a road above it and its, if anything, smokier neighbour Pontnewydd. A most pleasant inn outside Pontypool named the 'Horse & Jockey' lured me in to tea but the tea was "no great shakes'"": no eggs, no jam and only tinned apricots and bread and butter. Unsurprisingly, Newport was a dismal horror on such

---

9 Early 19th century expression meaning "nothing out of the ordinary"

a wet day and I hurried over the desert waste, which constitutes the new speedway from Newport to Cardiff via Castleton and St. Mellons with the rain having shut off for the night. There is always some difficulty in finding the Barry to Cardiff road. However, I got through via Penarth and Cadoxton, and arrived at 'Tallan' about 8 o'clock receiving the usual warm welcome and good entertainment from Mabel and Guy Paice after a *very strenuous 80 miles*.

TUESDAY 23RD AUGUST

A rough crossing

BARRY – WENVOE – CARDIFF – NEWPORT – CAERWENT – CHEPSTOW – BEACHLEY – AUST – IRON ACTON – YATTON KEYNELL – LACOCK

This was a much more promising morning and though a heavy shower was in progress when I took leave of my kind hostess (who had dried my sticky Paget and relieved its stickiness with a flour dredger overnight), this was the only rain I had all day. This time I took the road to Cardiff via Wenvoe and was amazed at the procession of charabancs on their way to Barry Island. I should imagine Cardiff has more charabancs to the acre than any other town.

I sped over the grisly horror road to Newport so as to make a more leisurely journey on to Chepstow via Llandevaud, Llanvaches and Caerwent, where I took my midday rest and nourishment at the 'Coach & Horses'. At Chepstow I tried in vain to get a map of Somerset and Dorset and also made enquiries as to how to get across the Severn, the recommended advice being to go by the ferry from Beachley which runs once an hour.

Beachley, which is about three miles south east of Chepstow on the shores of the Severn, is a charming spot but I had not long to observe its beauties as the ferry was due to cross in ten minutes. The placid water in Beachley Harbour left one unprepared for the rough time to come and the little motor ferry boat was soon tossing about like a bit of cork in a glass of Eno's Fruit Salt. In fact several of the passengers were glad to lighten their stomachs before the boat reached the other side and we were all well drenched with salt water.

It was somewhat difficult getting a heavily laden bicycle ashore at Aust but this was safely accomplished and I passed by the cluster of inviting tea shops in that village as it was somewhat early a decision which I subsequently regretted as the country I had to pass through was somewhat lonesome and neither the villages of Elberton, Olveston or Tockington gave me any hope and it was nearly 6 o'clock before I was able to get tea at a wayside cottage in Iron Acton.

I now decided to try and reach the much talked of village of Lacock, though by the map the road seemed rather a tricky one. However, from Yate through Chipping Sodbury, Old Sodbury, Acton Turville, Burton, Castle Combe and Yatton Keynell the road was a splendid one. At Yatton I lingered rather over long at the 'Bull' with a Bass so that by the time I finally reached Lacock it was dark. An enquiry at the 'Red Lion', being the only hotel there, was greeted with the reply that it was full up. Things began to look desperate until a man in the bar suggested I might try Miss Jenkins at the 'Corner House' on the bridge. This I duly did, only to be informed that Miss Jenkins was out. However, her cousin who was in charge of the house surmised (quite rightly) that I was hungry and I was soon seated in front of a very first rate supper of cold beef and salad, a fruit tart and a large pot of very excellent coffee to which I did full justice, so that when Miss Jenkins arrived home I declared that if she could not put me up I was sufficiently fortified to go on riding through the night. However, there was no need for this and I was soon snugly asleep in one of the quaintest bedrooms I have ever been in – very content after a *diversified 74 miles*.

WEDNESDAY 24TH AUGUST

Descending into the pit of Hell

LACOCK – MELKSHAM – WARMINSTER – MAIDEN BRADLEY – BRUTON – YEOVIL – CREWKERNE

The morning was ominously bright and clear when I took my early walk round the lovely village of Lacock, and I was not surprised at the usual rain starting immediately after breakfast so that I was foiled in my further explorations. My hostess held me in conversation and insisted that I must have some coffee and hot, newly made cakes, before I went. Consequently I was not ready to make a move before nearly 12.30 p.m., by which time the rain had died down to a drizzle. I had to move a bit if I wished to get to Lyme Regis, which was my intention. More time was lost in Melksham trying to get a map to help me on my way but I was able to get through Semington, Westbury and Upton Scudamore to Warminster before bread and cheese time at the 'Nag's Head'.

1927 HOLIDAY TOUR

From Warminster to Maiden Bradley the road is a beautiful one and then comes a long pull up with a sharp run down into Bruton. Before I got into Bruton a thunderstorm turned up from nowhere and running down into the town looked like descending into the pit of hell so black was the sky. I sought shelter out of the rain and for tea at the 'Blue Ball' – the only C.T.C. house – where a meagre tea cost me 2/– with an extra 3^d being charged for four very thin slices of bread and butter. The thunderstorm continued through Sparkford, Queen Camel and Mudford to Yeovil and though it had died down to a drizzle by the time I got to Crewkerne (via West Coker) I decided not to go on the unknown 16 miles to Lyme Regis in the gathering darkness. So I put up at the 'King's Arms', just dropping in to a hot fish supper which was very acceptable.

Distance covered: 59 miles

THURSDAY 25TH AUGUST

The New Forest proper
CREWKERNE – LYME REGIS – BRIDPORT – PUDDLETOWN – RINGWOOD – ROMSEY

A nice bright morning for once and a very excellent breakfast sent me way about 9.30 a.m. well content on the thorny road to Lyme Regis via Marshwood and Uplyme. Lyme Regis did not strike me as anything beyond the ordinary small seaside town very full of the ordinary seaside people, and the road up to Charmouth (Timber Hill) is a strenuous one and not improved on this occasion by being under repair. Charmouth sprouts petrol pumps at every point and I plugged up the long grind to Chideock and into Bridport before taking my midday refreshment at the 'Globe Inn'.

After my break I tackled that most strenuous stretch via Winterbourne Abbas to Dorchester but on this occasion I had the wind astern. Knowing no satisfactory tea place in Dorchester I went on to Puddletown with memories of a wayside cottage visited many years ago where the tea was as cheap and excellent as ever, and I spent rather more time than I ought to have done in conversation with other travellers, so that I found myself with over 50 miles to do after 6 o'clock if I wished to reach Winchester. I had happy memories of the splendid road via Bere Regis and Almer to Wimbourne and this stretch did not take long nor did the eight miles to Ringwood where at the 'George' a Bass put new life into me. Then began the road across the New Forest proper. Darkness was rapidly coming on so that by the time I reached Cadnam it was complete but I determined to push on to Romsey. That eight or more miles to Romsey seemed like a lifetime in the puzzling light or rather darkness of the Forest, and it was nearly 10 o'clock when I reached Romsey just as the local cinema was discharging its crowd. I tried several places before being fairly satisfactorily put up at a baker's shop after a rather *strenuous 90 miles* of up and down country.

FRIDAY 26TH AUGUST

One of "the" tea places

ROMSEY – WINCHESTER – SUTTON SCOTNEY – WHITCHURCH – LITCHFIELD – BURGHCLERE – NEWBURY – WOOLSTONE – FARINGDON – LECHLADE – FAIRFORD – BURFORD

I had to reach Burford this day whatever the weather so made an early start leaving Romsey at 9 o'clock with a bright sun for a change, making short work of the road to Winchester via Hursley and spending about an hour in Winchester before striking north on the long rise to Sutton Scotney with first refreshment at the 'Coach & Horses'. The sun had now gone for good and rain seemed imminent but it kept off, the road onward being through Whitchurch, Litchfield and Burghclere where the 'Carnarvon Arms' was irresistible – and a very nice bit of bread and cheese it supplied too!

The rest of the way to Newbury is as picturesque bit of road as you could wish for and, after a stroll through Newbury, I went on the road upon which we started this tour. Instead of turning off to Wantage I continued straight on through Lambourne to Ashbury and took rough and uncharted ways (I had no map) through Woolstone (into which you drop down a hill reputed to be 1 in 4) and other charming villages to Faringdon where I arrived as I intended to at 5.30 p.m., precisely making for the 'White Hart' – one of "the" tea places. After tea I wandered on through Lechlade and on the road to Fairford, the evening having turned out bright and sunny, before turning back on the familiar stretch from Lechlade to Burford via Filkins. I arrived at the 'Swan' about 8.30 p.m. ready for the supper that was awaiting me having covered an *easy 84 miles*.

1927 HOLIDAY TOUR

SATURDAY 27TH AUGUST

A long-awaited lunch at the Swan

LITTLE BARRINGTON – GREAT BARRINGTON – GREAT RISSINGTON – LITTLE RISSINGTON – TAYNTON – FULWOOD – SWINBROOK – WITNEY – EYNSHAM – BURFORD

This was to be a bye day as I was under contract to visit the Ing family at Oxford in the afternoon and so I arranged to come back for lunch at 1 o'clock, having never actually had that meal at the 'Swan' before. I wandered out prospecting round the neighbouring villages starting at Little Barrington, Great Barrington, Great and Little Rissington and Taynton getting back punctually at 1 o'clock for that lunch which proved well worth being punctual for, as a large company turned up for it too and it was rather a jovial meal.

I felt quite heavy for the trip to Oxford. However I took the bye-way, the rough road through Fulwood and Swinbrook coming out on the main road close to Minster Lovell from where with the wind behind all was plain sailing in Witney and Eynsham. I started back from Cowley about 7.30 p.m. and on my return to the 'Swan' found a goodly company assembled including E.B.P. ,who had run down for the weekend so that it was latish when we finally retired to roost.

Distance ridden: 56 miles

SUNDAY 28TH AUGUST

The Windsor Trumpet

FARINGDON – BUCKLAND – KINGSTON BAGPUIZE – WINDSOR – STAINES

The last day of a damp but very satisfactory holiday dawned bright and sunny and we set off for the last stage by taking the Brize Norton to Bampton road and landing by mistake in Faringdon. We however speedily found our road through the delightful Buckland where we refreshed on the usual midday fare before going on by the now familiar road via Kingston Bagpuize, Abingdon, Sutton Courtenay and Appleford to Wallingford taking the rough and steep road to Nuffield and Stoke Row where my back tyre came to complete grief, a sharp stone cutting two large gashes in it.

We turned in at the 'Bricklayer Arms' at Kingston for tea, repairing one while tea was being got ready, only to find the second hole after tea necessitating more repairs. We were not long getting down to Sonning and Twyford when we ran across A. J. Aisling (known at the 'Swan' as the "Windsor Trumpet" on account of his talking propensities) at Waltham St. Lawrence and riding with him into Windsor. We decided on taking the Staines route as darkness owing to tyre delays had descended, but the same tyre gave way again in the same place causing still further delay. By the time we had felt our way into Staines and along the main road to Bedfont (a very trying piece of road in the dark) it was nearly 11 o'clock and midnight struck a few minutes after we arrived home after an *eventful 90 miles*. The full tour totalled *1500 miles*.

1927 ANNUAL REVIEW

A record year in terms of mileage with the holiday tour amounting to 1500 miles and further summer tours in May, June and July adding 2954 miles to the overall total. Whilst there was a reduction in the number of Sunday rides (43 compared to 51 in 1926) the overall mileage and average was improved to 2755 miles and 64 miles respectively. The touring average was also improved from the 1926 figures with 65 miles being the average daily mileage for our August touring holiday.

The holiday tour was one of the wettest since we began recording our adventures. We can only be thankful for our trusty Pagets being so reliable, although I can only hope we do not need to rely on them as much next year. The 'Swan' and 'Stowe' proved yet again the mainstays of accommodation providing us with the usual high standard of fare and company.

The new machine 'Merlin' proved to be an excellent purchase and was the 'work horse' of 1927 covering some 5102 miles of the 6326 miles cycled this year.

CYCLOMETERS AS OF DECEMBER 31ST 1927:-

Chater-Lea – 7185 miles
James – 8474 miles
Merlin – 5102 miles

1927 HOLIDAY TOUR

CYCLING STATISTICS FOR 1927 BY MILES AND NUMBER OF RIDES PER MONTH

MONTH	NUMBER OF RIDES			MILES RIDDEN				AVERAGE MILES PER RIDE			
	SUNDAY	TOURING	OTHER RIDES	SUNDAYS	TOURING	OTHER RIDES	TOTAL	SUNDAYS	TOURING	OTHER RIDES	ALL RIDES
Jan	5	-	-	191	-	-	191	38.20	-	-	38.20
Feb	4	-	-	176	-	-	176	44.00	-	-	44.00
Mar	4	-	3	213	-	24	237	53.25	-	8.00	39.00
Apr	6	-	6	451	-	96	547	75.16	-	16.00	45.58
May	3	4	9	257	325	163	745	85.66	81.25	18.11	46.56
June	3	4	9	303	322	180	805	100.03	80.50	20.00	47.35
July	3	6	7	289	507	140	936	99.33	84.50	20.00	58.50
Aug	-	23	-	-	1500	-	1500	-	65.21	-	65.21
Sept	3	2	1	281	145	14	440	93.66	72.50	14.00	73.33
Oct	4	2	-	265	155	-	420	66.25	77.50	-	70.00
Nov	4	-	-	178	-	-	178	44.50	-	-	44.50
Dec	4	-	-	151	-	-	151	37.75	-	-	37.75
Totals	43	41	35	2755	2954	617	6326	64.00	72.04	17.62	53.16

Bwlch-y-Groes

1930 EASTER WEEKEND RIDE

SATURDAY 19TH APRIL – EASTER WEEKEND HOLIDAYS

A roaring evening

HAMMERSMITH – FAIRFORD – CRICKLADE –ASHTON KEYNES – MALMESBURY – CIRENCESTER – BURFORD

Anything more appalling than the breakfast time outlook it would be difficult to imagine – bold rain interspersed with snowflakes is hardly the sort of thing to expect in the latter half of April. However, with superb optimism we set out along the Lechlade road about 11.45 a.m. and turned off the Cirencester road just before Fairford, through the straggling village of Marston Meysey to Cricklade just before arriving at which town we had shed our capes during a temporary lull in the rain. We dismounted in Cricklade to buy some tobacco and a very intense block of rain drenched us before we could get into our capes again.

We hurried onto Ashton Keynes having vivid remembrances of excellent bread and cheese and Stroud ale at the 'Forester's Arms' there and we were not disappointed. While so indulging, the rain really did cease and decided us to go on to Malmesbury. As we reached that town the sun came out for a very brief visit lighting up the old Abbey enough to show the shocking state of disrepair it has been allowed to get into.

Black clouds looming up to windward warned us not to linger and we had scarcely got a mile on the way to Cirencester when we were once more ploughing through heavy rain which accompanied us as far as the 'Great Western Inn' about four miles from Cirencester, where we had designed to have tea. An armchair in front of a log fire was most welcome while tea was being prepared. The tea was a first rate one and when we had just finished we were joined by two mixed tandem pairs from Bristol bound, of course, to Burford.

We got no more heavy rain on the fast piece of road through stately Cirencester, Ampney St. Peter and Fairford to Lechlade but the last stage to Burford was again all a plug. However we arrived fairly dry and very hungry – quite ready for the eating match with a crowd of South Roads and Unity C.C. men, with the former we had a roaring evening, but the Unity men were a stuffy old crowd, keeping themselves very much to themselves. They will not be welcomed at the 'Swan' on any future occasion. Again we went to bed very satisfied with the day – that holiday feeling having triumphed over the wretched weather. *Distance covered: 63 miles*

EASTER SUNDAY 20TH APRIL

A famous police cat
BURFORD – STOW-ON-THE-WOLD – BROADWAY – MORETON-IN-MARSH – BURFORD

A slightly more cheery outlook so far as the weather went. True, there was not much sun, but it was not raining and the wind, though still blowing from the North, was not quite so strong. We decided on testing the wind's quality by digging into it over the immortal Stow road, and in spite of an exceptionally heavy breakfast of porridge and eggs and bacon, we succeeded in riding up the first rise out of Burford to the top of the ridge on our bottom gears, a thing we have never done before on normal gears. The next five miles, all up hill, was heavy work but we reached Stow-on-the-Wold, looking as bleak as usual, in the usual hour.

It being nearly bread and cheese time we rode straight onto the 'Coach and Horses', that retiring little inn which is so easy to miss. Here we found a very footsore walking party and two exceptionally quaint greybeards, whose dialect was very difficult to understand. The landlord, once a London Policeman, produced his famous cat which he alleges to be 28 years of age. She is a small person weighing about 2½ lbs and the only evidence of her advanced age is faulty eyesight. It is only when you look closely at her that you realise she is no spring chicken like so many of the elderly ladies of today.

After fuelling up we continued north until we reached the summit of Fish Hill, the view from which was spoilt by a murky atmosphere but the jagged ridge of the Malvern Hills was plainly visible. And so down into Broadway. But alas – poor Broadway! Much booming by the Press has brought it prosperity no doubt, but prosperity has turned its head and will very speedily prove its ruin. It is like a beautiful woman bedecked with cheap and tawdry ornaments, petrol pumps of all colours and Kodak advertisements being the chief offenders. The broad main street is full of cars and charabancs, the occupants of which industriously spew litter on the rather too neatly kept sidewalks. The decline of Broadway makes one thankful for the unchangeability of our own Burford, which still remains, in the estimation of all who know it, the gem of the Cotswolds.

I had been looking forward this Easter to seeing the Vale of Evesham in its glory. It was a truly marvellous sight looking over miles and miles of plum blossom but close investigation of the trees shows that the bitter north east wind has done its foul work – the petals are all tinged with brown and the stalks are turning yellow. There will be few plums from Evesham and Pershore this year. At Evesham we turned to get the wind in our backs, taking the Chipping Campden road which takes us many miles through plum trees via Bretforton, Weston-sub-Edge and Aston-sub-Edge, and finally over the Edge Hills before dropping us into the picturesque Chipping Campden, alas, suffering from earthworks, probably water pipes, through the whole length of the town.

One more climb out of Campden and we made all haste along the perfect surfaced road which leads through Bourton-on the-Hill to Moreton-in-Marsh. Surely that little tea house (Webb's) at the first corner as you enter the town, is the only one of its kind in England. A long table runs down the centre and Mrs Webb directs operations from an armchair at one end. The table is loaded with everything good to eat that you can think of. You are requested to sit down and help yourself. "Dad" (aged 84) is ordered by the presiding genius to bring you a large pot of tea, and you set to work and eat until you are tired. When you feel sufficiently recovered to totter away "Ma" collects 1/3[d] from you and hopes you have had enough to eat!

After this experience our progress on the five miles which separates

Moreton from Stow-on-the-Wold, was slow and stately, but the last ten miles, with the wind behind over the that lovely Cotswold road dropping finally into snug old Burford, was worth much hard labour to achieve.

Distance covered: 57 miles.

EASTER MONDAY 2IST APRIL

A dumbstruck school master

BURFORD – ABINGDON – STEVENTON – WANTAGE – BAYDON – ALDBOURNE – STRATTON ST. MARGARET – LECHLADE – BURFORD

Distinct improvement in the outlook – wind round to the West and of small force. E.B.P. had to return home so I set off with him about 11.30 a.m. as far as Abingdon, taking the familiar Brize Norton, Bampton, Buckland, Kingston Bagpuize and Tubney road. Stopped for bread and cheese at the 'Black Horse' just outside Abingdon before continuing through the town over the bridge to Sutton Courtenay. Here I parted from E.B.P. turning right through the village to Steventon, a pretty enough village but not looking at its best with the local loblolly boys[1] standing about in their best Bank Holiday garbs on the village green.

My objective was further exploration of the delectable Berkshire and Wiltshire Downs and for this purpose I cut around through East and West Hendred to Wantage and skirted the ridgeway road, looking for a favourable opportunity of plunging into the wilderness. This came close to the village of Sparsholt from which a track ran at right angles to the main road snaking away in zigzags until it disappeared miles away over the crest of the Downs. This was exactly what I wanted, so I put on my little gear and prepared for some hard work. I was very soon taking walking exercise, for not only were the upgrades steep, but the whole length of the track was rutty and became boggier and boggier the higher it went. Thus alternately riding and walking I reached the top in just over four miles, and here I met the first human beings I had seen since leaving the main road – a party of four cyclists wrestling with a punctured tyre in the mud. They were making for Wantage so as their spirits seemed rather depressed I cheered them up by telling them what they had to go through before they got there.

---

1 An assistant to the ship's surgeon on a Royal Navy ship; the expression is often used to refer to a sailor in uniform. 'Loblolly' was a thick porridge served (by Loblolly boys) to sick sailors to help expedite their recovery.

1930 EASTER WEEKEND RIDE

For about two miles I bounced and bumped, finally coming on a clump of trees which seemed strangely familiar. As I surmised I was only a few miles from Lambourn to which town all was plain sailing. Resisting the temptation to look for tea I prepared for some more hard work taking another snaky lonesome track which, I was informed, led to Aldbourne. It was all uphill for the first four miles to Baydon, a village which at some time or other seems to have owed a lot to the late Baroness Burdett-Coutts, and then there is a glorious smooth run down to the remote village of Aldbourne, a large compact village with some fine old thatch and much opportunity for photography given favourable circumstances. However, the sun, which had shone steadily from midday, failed me, and Aldbourne must be photographed at some future time. Tea at the 'Crown' left nothing to be desired and prepared me for the way back to Burford.

The road to Swindon seemed the right direction and every road meant more uphill work but after such a tea as I had had there was no such thing as hard work. Mostly small gear took me to Liddington and having no desire to visit Swindon I found a short cut which took me on to the Ermine Street to Stratton St. Margaret. Leaving the Downs behind, top gear came into use and the miles through Highworth and Inglesham over the Halfpenny Bridge into Lechlade soon passed. Lechlade Church said 7.45 p.m., and with the wind behind me, the remaining 9 miles to Burford took exactly 25 minutes. I found Wood already arrived at the 'Swan' together with 11 other cyclists, one of whom a Birmingham school master aged about 24 gave us much amusement by waxing eloquent on the proper methods of cycle touring as though we were all ignorant of that art. It was only when I let out that I had been at the game for the past 30 years that he became dumb for the rest of the evening. Wood and I and a seasoned old North Roader named Holcombe went out for half an hour's stroll about 11 p.m., the rest having gone to bed and Wood and I were the last to turn in about 12.30 a.m.

A thoroughly satisfactory day of *74 happy miles.*

TUESDAY 22ND APRIL

Meandering homewards with an insatiable companion

BURFORD – KELMSCOTT – WANTAGE – WEST SHEFFORD –THEALE – WALTHAM ST. LAWRENCE – WINDSOR – HAMMERSMITH

A perfect day at last – sunshine, genial air and what wind there was coming from the west. Wood and I who were joining forces for the homeward run decided to make a day of it and ambled gently off about 10.30 a.m., not exactly in the direction of London, for it was Wood's desire to visit certain delectable villages before getting on that track and I had no objection to spinning out the journey.

And so we circled round to Kelmscott, the home of William Morris, being however unable to find his tombstone in the churchyard; finally coming out on the main road by St. John's Bridge, and making for Faringdon. There I took command, the road through the White Horse Vale to Wantage and beyond there across the Downs being new to Wood. Wood was beginning to get hungry (weighing 14 stone he requires a lot of keeping up) so we hustled over the nine miles down the Vale of the White Horse to Wantage finding the rise to East Challow a very tough bit. We did not anticipate any difficulty in finding something to eat in Wantage but after trying two different large sized commercial hotels we had to go to the 'Bear' after all. We certainly did very well there but I had misgivings as to the result in my case, being unused to anything more substantial than bread and cheese at midday when cycling.

I had been down into Wantage from Shefford many times but never in the reverse direction and on top of that heavy feed, we were both glad to walk the last few hundred yards to the top from which it is easy work to the headland where stands the monument to Major Philip Musgrave Neeld Wroughton. Here we dismounted to drink in the champagne air and survey the wondrous expanse of the Berkshire Downs, we being the only human inhabitants to be seen in that vast arena. We soon ran down to West Shefford and spent a considerable time on the bridge over the Lambourn at Welford Park. Here Wood began to feel hungry once more and we made up our minds to tea at the 'Red Lion' at Theale some twenty miles further on.

Once through Speen and out on the Bath Road at Newbury we made things hum and that thirteen miles from Newbury to Theale was made mincemeat of, Wood getting very hot in the process. I had never had tea at the 'Red Lion' before but they seem to have an excellent idea of feeding cyclists. We started on two eggs each with buttered toast, waded through an immense plate of bread and butter with jam, followed by half a dozen rich pastries of different kinds. Even then Wood felt a vacancy and we supplemented this with half a dozen bananas taking two away with us in case we got hungry again before reaching home.

The evening was a glorious one and we had only 42 miles to go so took things easy through Reading and Twyford turning aside to have a look at charming Waltham St. Lawrence. By the time we got to Windsor it was lighting up time and the innumerable turns in the Datchet, Stanwell, Bedfont, Feltham road slowed us down somewhat so that it was nearly 11 o'clock when we got to Hammersmith and 2.15 a.m. before Wood (after some more grub) left us for his home at South Tottenham.

An easy and enjoyable run of 95 *miles* to finish up the Easter holidays.

1930 HOLIDAY TOUR – MERLIN 3

SATURDAY 9TH AUGUST

The cure for all ills

HAMMERSMITH – WALTHAM ST. LAWRENCE – WINDSOR – THEALE – HUNGERFORD – ALDBOURNE – STRATTON ST. MARGARET – BURFORD

General conditions were not too auspicious for starting a long tour. E.B.P. had been during the week much troubled by his varicose veins while during the same period my internal arrangements had been completely deranged.

We therefore both took the road in a somewhat doubtful frame of mind about 8.30 a.m., our destination for the first day being Burford. As we had all day to do it in we started out through Richmond Park, Ditton and Molesey to Staines and then the usual Waltham St. Lawrence road from Windsor to Reading. My interior was beginning to settle down now and E.B.P. was gaining confidence in his leg. At Theale we took our midday refreshment of bread and cheese and ale as usual at the 'Red Lion' after which we made short work of the miles on the Bath Road to Newbury, which as usual on a Saturday was very crowded, as we continued along the Bath Road for the further nine miles to Hungerford. Here we took the right hand road through Chilton Foliat to Aldbourne where the 'Crown' supplied us with its usual excellent tea. This was E.B.P.'s first visit to the sequestered town of Aldbourne and he was impressed accordingly.

I had something more to show him in the beautiful Swindon Road skirting the Wiltshire Downs with its series of stiffish climbs up to Liddington and then the sudden drop down into the valley, the disappearance of the Downs, and scenery more reminiscent of Warwickshire than Wiltshire. At Stratton St. Margaret, a Bass came very welcome before taking the last stage via Highworth and Lechlade and then the ever-joyful nine miles from the latter town and the drop down the steep High Street to the hospitable 'Swan' without the slightly depressing feeling of having to return on the morrow. The *101 miles* we had covered had quite banished my internal pains while E.B.P.'s swollen ankle was diminished in size.

Supper was, as usual, everything that could be desired and we got to roost early (just before midnight) for another fairly strenuous stage tomorrow.

SUNDAY 10TH AUGUST

A poor substitute for our midday mainstay

BURFORD – NORTHLEACH – PIFF'S ELM – TEWKESBURY – LEDBURY – HEREFORD – WHITNEY-ON-WYE

A fine morning and the usual heavy breakfast of porridge, eggs and bacon and toast finished off with a thick layer of bread and butter and jam sent us off in good fettle about 10.30 a.m. There is always something attractive about the Gloucester road especially on a fine morning such as this, up the long slopes and corresponding coasts through grey old Northleach with the final plug to the summit of Puesdown where top gears came into use so that the pace at times approached 'evens' (20 mph). On we went through Shipton Solars and Andoversford until the tram lines at Charlton Kings warned us of the near approach of Cheltenham, and it is necessary to go warily through the main streets of the town as its inhabitants seem to have a habit of always walking in the middle of the road.

We have often had to hurry somewhat on the plain but good road which leads to Tewkesbury but on this occasion we had bags of time and arrived at 'The Old White Swan' at Piff's Elm before 1 o'clock. Here we had a setback for they had no bread and cheese so we had to content ourselves with biscuits, a poor substitute for our midday mainstay. We were in Tewkesbury by 2 o'clock which gave us plenty of time for the remainder of our journey. However, the road from Tewkesbury to Ledbury amid the orchards of Worcestershire is made for fast travelling and we were soon on the steep part of Hollybush Hill where we surveyed the prospect for some time before dropping down through Eastnor to Ledbury, which as usual on a Sunday afternoon was very much asleep.

We accordingly rode straight through intent on the early tea, which our somewhat scanty lunch made desirable. We had often admired 'The Old Trumpet Inn' and no less a person than "Wayfarer" had had tea there so we thought we should not go wrong in trying our luck. The result was most gratifying and in the future we shall not pass 'The Old Trumpet Inn' especially if it is near tea time. A storm came on while we were having tea but this spent itself before we were ready to restart.

The remainder of the road to Hereford via Stoke Edith, Farrington and Lugwardine is an easy one and we were early in Hereford City which presented its usual Sabbath atmosphere of sleepy calm. The old familiar 15 miles by Kite's Nest Bridge, Sollens, Willersley Cross and Eardisley to the 'Stowe Inn' with one stop for shelter from a short-lived storm, was soon accomplished and after a wash we sat down to an excellent hot supper or late dinner in the company of two other cyclists from the Midlands.

After the heavy feed, a stroll in the dark made us eager for retirement. The 'Stowe Inn' being full up we slept at a farm nearby, a most opulent looking farm with a baronial hall ornamented with numerous cups won at the various cattle shows. This billet proved most comfortable and there we rested content enough after an easy run of *73 miles*.

MONDAY IITH AUGUST

Ever changing scenes of rural beauty

WHITNEY-ON-WYE – CLYRO – TALGARTH – CRICKHOWELL – BRECON – FLAGBURY – CLYRO – WHITNEY-ON-WYE

A brilliant morning made us hopeful of a dry trip over the Black Mountains Pass, which was our design after an excellent breakfast. In this the most delectable corner of the United Kingdom there is no more beautiful road than that upon which we were bent today. We have traversed it many times before and I trust we do so many times again.[2]

Going straight ahead instead of turning left over the toll bridge the road

2 Sadly for Charles James Pope, this would not come to pass as his brother, Edward Brownfield Pope (E.B.P.) died on 30th November, 1930.

trends gently upwards past the renowned 14th century 'Rhydspence Inn', by no means one of the least picturesque inns around. The panorama on the left presents ever changing scenes of rural beauty with the silver Wye as the central feature until the village of Clyro is passed and the river is crossed at Flagbury Bridge from which there are wonderful views from either side.

Three miles further past the 'The Three Cocks' on the road to Brecon is a sharp turn to the left with finger post pointing to Talgarth. The road rises the greater part of the way to the plain town of Talgarth with a few down grades, then there is a continuous rise for the next four miles to the summit of the pass. And here, most fortuitously situated is the 'Castle Inn' where is to be obtained the pleasant flavoured and thirst quenching Alton Court Ale and very excellent bread and cheese. It is difficult to see how anyone having come up the pass from either side by their own labour can resist the appeal of the open door of the 'Castle Inn'. We certainly did not.

After filling up the magnificent prospect over the mountain was too good to hurry away from. We strolled gently for a considerable distance and when we did mount it was with brakes on, to spin out the seven mile coast via Cwmdu and Tretower to Crickhowell. Tea was the next thought and with Brecon only some 14 miles away 'The Bell' in that pleasant town occurred to us as being the place for that meal. The 14 miles from Crickhowell to Brecon is by no means a speedway but for a main road with its expansive views of the Brecknock Brecons it is one of the most beautiful in Wales.

We found our low gears very useful on the long pull up to Bwlch which is a fatiguing climb on normal gears. As we entered Brecon a heavy shower loomed up (I seem to have entered Brecon many times in the rain!) so we made straight for the 'Bell' where the tea was as usual here one of the best. The rain spent itself while we were having tea.

We took the Brecon-Hay Road back as far as Flagbury preferring here to cross the Wye and go by way of Clyro where we visited the 'Baskerville Arms' for a drink of Bass and biscuits arriving "home" at the 'Stowe' about 8 o'clock to find hot roast duck and peas waiting for us. This was followed by one of those perfect apple tarts for the 'Stowe' is so famous so that we envied not even King George the Fifth.

A glorious run of *60 miles* in some of the finest country in Great Britain.

TUESDAY 12TH AUGUST

Welcomed as old friends

WHITNEY-ON-WYE – KINGTON – PRESTEIGNE – CLUN – BISHOP'S CASTLE – MONTGOMERY

There is always a feeling of regret on leaving the 'Stowe Inn' for fresh fields and we left our Redditch friend and his pal who were putting in a full week there. However we had prepared our ground ahead and as our day's run would not be a long one we set out with light hearts in spite of decidedly inclement weather.

We had to take the road through Willesley Cross and Eardisley to Kington and this means plenty of collar work with very little compensating runs down. From Kington to Presteigne via Titley is moderately easy road and we called in at the 'Barley Mow' of Presteigne for our midday sustenance. Here we were greeted as old friends and the bread and cheese washed down by Wellington Ale was more than ordinarily good.

We went on through Kinsham and Lingen across to Brampton Bryan taking the left hand road about 1½ miles on the Knighton Road by way of Bedstone and Bucknell, Aston on Clun and Clungunford. The 8 miles from Aston Clun to Clun was all a push in the face of a strong headwind and we were quite ready for tea at the 'Buffalo' when we got to Clun. Here also we were now welcomed as old friends and the tea we had was of the best.

We rode quite a long way up the hill out of Clun on the road to Bishop's Castle and then became involved in a very heavy storm which sent us to shelter for nearly half an hour. We had no sooner got on our way again when E.B.P.'s back tyre collapsed and it was only just repaired when another shower overtook us and we entered Bishop's Castle under somewhat moist conditions.

After we had climbed out again the weather cleared somewhat and the sun appeared. It was however only a temporary visit and we soon found it necessary to put on our capes for the first time since we started our tour. We were able to remove the said garment before entering Montgomery where we were glad to find our usual rooms at the 'Old Bell' were ready for us and that Mrs Maddox still preserved her fascinating rotundity. By the time we had had a wash and brush up there was one of those wonderful little legs of Welsh mutton with suitable vegetables all ready for us, and we were certainly ready for it! This, and the pudding which followed occupied us a full hour so that it was nearly dark before we took our stroll round the town before turning in for the night being lulled to sleep by the 'music' of the owls which seem to make Montgomery their home, and they are not bad judges either.

The day's riding only amounted to *52 miles.*

WEDNESDAY 13TH AUGUST

The "Old Squire"

MONTGOMERY – WESTBURY – ATCHAM BRIDGE – SHREWSBURY

It was a nice, bright morning that greeted us and after the heavy Montgomery breakfast we were in no hurry to get on the road. There is no particular beauty in the town but its situation is unique and the one picturesque street is Arthur Street wherein lies the 'Old Bell' under the hill upon which is all that remains of the once great stronghold of the Herberts, now reduced to a few fragments of the walls amidst which sheep graze.

The thanks of the burgesses[3] is due to the lady who owns the garden beneath the castle which presents a wonderful bank of flowers along the roadside. It was particularly beautiful this cool and flowery summer. We had made up our minds to have a quiet day by running into Shrewsbury and it was well past 11 a.m. before we started. The Shrewsbury road from Montgomery is a joyful 22 miles, always unequalled as to surface and just sufficient undulations to make it interesting. We passed through Chirbury and Marton to Westbury where the 'Lion', having been many times visited in the past was visited once more for it was near enough to bread and cheese time to make it advisable. We have met many strange characters in this old inn and this time the "Old Squire" himself was there, a bucolic old fellow who looked more like a moderately contented and well-to-do farmer. He was holding court and treating all and sundry in the far parlour and it was only the respectful "Sir" prefaced to everything said to him by the assembly which betrayed his quality. He had been arranging the village sports day and chuckled consumedly at the idea of the old women's race (1st prize 1lb of tea and 1lb of sugar) the course of which he had selected running uphill.

After he had gone we were informed by the landlady he was the Hon.

---

3 Decorations organised by freemen (burgesses) of the borough

John Ashworth, a large landowner and proprietor of two Shoots, shooting being his main hobby. I dare say he was a thorough old scamp in his way and rarely went to bed sober but after all such men who live on their own estates and mix freely with their tenants have some value to the country.

We got into Shrewsbury via Worthen and Yockleton about 1.30 p.m., and after some necessary shopping, crossed the Severn by the English Bridge and along that perfect road via Atcham to Wellington, where we spent about half an hour before making our way back to tea with Mrs Dodd at Atcham Bridge which we reached just as it began to rain. Mrs Dodd was as usual full of small talk and the kitchen fire was also as usual roaring up the chimney.

When we left Mrs Dodd's it was raining steadily and it became so heavy just outside Shrewsbury that, having plenty of time, we sheltered for half an hour in preference to riding on in our capes. It, however, passed off into a mere drizzle by the time we had got a few miles on the Montgomery Road so that we reached the 'Old Bell' for supper in a dry condition and remained fine enough for a stroll round the town before going to bed.

Distance ridden: 65 miles

THURSDAY 14TH AUGUST

Glorious mountains in the evening sun
SHREWSBURY – WELSHPOOL – LLANFAIR CAEREINION – DINAS MAWDDWY

We were moving on into wild Wales today and the weather conditions appeared none too propitious, a stormy sky dropping heavy showers at intervals, and though we had only a short if somewhat rugged stage to do, we were prepared for a rough time.

It is plain sailing as far as Welshpool via Garthmyl crossing the ubiquitous Severn, the road running for some distance by the side of the Shropshire Union Canal. Then comes a long and trying push up Golfa Hill to Llanfair Caereinion. It rises sharply out of Welshpool for about half a mile and you think you are at the top but this is not so. There is at least three miles steady grind uphill and in the face of a stiff headwind with occasional rain on this occasion it was no mean undertaking even on 47" gears.

Llanfair was *en fete* for the Flower Show which looked likely to be spoilt by the foul weather. It was rather early for lunch but we thought it best to be on the safe side so we adjourned to the 'Goat' for some of that curious cheese with bread and of course beer for which this town seems famous, before turning nearly due west. This road is mainly uphill and though the surface is excellent, the wind which was now half a gale, made it most strenuous. We were content to crawl on low gears against the wind and rain, which occasionally gave place to a glimpse of sunshine, which when Cann Office, Llangadfan and Garthbeibio were passed and we emerged into the mountain road which led to Mallwyd, made the surrounding beautiful indeed and was some consolation for the gruelling head wind.

We reached Dinas Mawddwy just after 5 o'clock quite ready for tea at that comfortable stopping place Celyn Brithion where we had booked up. Old Mr Jones was seizing the opportunity of the fine weather to do a little hedge clipping and informed us that it had been raining for the past three weeks in Dinas and he had no doubt it would start again very soon "yas". However we had a fine evening for a stroll along the Dolgelley road as far as the third milestone, the mountains looking glorious in the evening sun. Had we struck some fine weather for the trip up Bwlch-y-Groes which we had planned for tomorrow?
Distance covered: 35 (tough) miles

FRIDAY 15TH AUGUST
"Impassable for Motors"
DINAS MAWDDWY – LAKE VYRNWY – LLANWDDYN – GARTHBEIBIO – DINAS MAWDDWY

It was a brilliant morning that we got up to with a most autumnal nip in the air. We felt that the unbelievable had really come to pass in spite of the croakings of the aged Jones: "It is much too bright for early morning, it is sure to rain before midday, yas". We started off in brilliant sunshine on the rocky road to Bala, the first five miles through Aber Cywarch and Llanymawddwy on our comforting little gears in a series of sharp ups and downs until the corner is reached where the ascent begins in earnest.

After this there is no more riding though E.B.P. mounted for a few yards so that I could photograph him in the act of riding up Bwlch-y-Groes. Compared with our last year's ascent of this fearsome pass when we had a bitter wind and rain in our faces, this was easy work. About a mile from the summit we overtook a party of four cyclists from Huddersfield and immediately on joining forces with them the rain commenced, a drizzle at first but very soon a steady downpour which made us all seek protection in capes. We parted with the Huddersfielders at the top taking the track on the right with the welcome sign *"Impassable for Motors"* at its commencement. We tried to ride some of it but never spent more than a few minutes at a time in the saddle having every few hundred yards to cross streams with rocky beds running across the road while a roaring cascade, which must have looked very beautiful in fine weather, accompanied us on the right hand side.

We were prepared for squalls about four miles on the way when two large sheepdogs came bounding down the mountain side. However, on our talking to them they proved to be "friendly natives" and accompanied us for nearly two miles on the way before going off on other business. The track eventually brought us out on the shore of Lake Vyrnwy – the largest sheet of water in Wales, used as a reservoir to supply water to Liverpool.

We struck this vast lake at a most desolate point and there was no indication which way we were to go to find civilisation (in this case meaning a pub) and E.B.P. had forgotten to bring a map. However we turned right along a good road which skirted the lake. After about six miles there is a bridge across the narrow end and there was supposed to be a hotel somewhere thereabouts. We failed to find it but we found the next best thing, a small general shop which appeared to sell everything in a small village called Llanwddyn.

Here we filled up with lemonade and large quantities of buns, cakes and custard tarts. Being mapless and finding a road to Cann Office we adjudged it better to make for that mythical place. This involved much heavy uphill work in the rain which still fell in some abundance and it was 4.30 p.m. before we came out on the main road leading from Llanfair to Dinas Mawddwy. We were getting extremely hungry and were therefore very pleased to obtain an excellent tea at a tea house at Garthbeibio kept by a Mr James. After this the rain ceased and we were able to see the beautiful mountain road from here to Dinas under the best conditions in the evening sun.

Before supper we explored Dinas Mawddwy village and spent half an hour over a Bass at the 'Buckley Arms' watching the natives playing rings.
Distance covered: 38 miles

SATURDAY 16TH AUGUST
Saved from a smokeless Sunday
CELYN BRITHION – DINAS MAWDDWY – DOLGELLEY (DOLGELLAU) – BONTDDU – BEDDGELERT – LLYN CWELLYN – RHYD DDU

We left Dinas Mawddwy, not without some regret soon after 10 o'clock taking the road to Dolgelley over the Drws Pass. This is not so strenuous as Bwlch-y-Groes but it is tough work nevertheless and unsurpassed for beauty and today we were favoured by bright sunshine, though old Mr Jones had sent us off with his usual gloomy prophecy that it would rain before long "yas".

There is a glorious run from the top of the Pass down to the plain town of Dolgelley which it being Saturday was very crowded with shoppers. We took the Barmouth road over the bridge across the Mawddach at Penmaenpool from whence the road runs alongside the Mawddach Estuary. There are few lovelier roads in Wales than this, though it is often infested with the worst kind of motorist who seems to delight in driving along the narrow twisty road so fast as to risk his own worthless life (which does not matter) and endanger the lives of other people. The time being between 1 and 2 o'clock there was a scarcity of traffic on this occasion.

At Bontddu we called in at the 'Halfway House' for our customary midday sustenance before proceeding into Barmouth and up through the town on the picturesque coast road which runs north via Llanaber, Tal-y-Bont and Llanendwyn to Harlech. We have visited Harlech before but have never been much impressed with it and the castle is spoilt by the poor buildings in its vicinity.

At Harlech the road leaves the coast road and for some miles is level until the unsavoury village of Penrhyndendraeth is reached. Here there is a stiff hill to be negotiated, part of which it is advisable to walk. There then follows a very beautiful stretch which finally brings you to the romantic Pont Aberglaslyn[4] – one of the most beautiful spots in Wales – but sadly over crowded these days with stinking cars and unsightly motorists.

The short Pass of Aber Glaslyn to Beddgelert is decidedly steep. At Beddgelert we made for "Wayfarer's" favourite stopping place 'Plas Colwyn' for tea. The tea was a truly excellent one but 'Plas Colwyn' did

---

4 A well-known 17th century bridge over the River Glaslyn

not strike us as an ideal place of which to stop – rather too much of the seaside boarding house type. From Beddgelert we took the Carnarvon road which goes uphill for several miles and in due course we arrived at the village of Rhyd Ddu. Here we had been recommended to 'Bron Eifion' (kept of course by a Miss Jones) as an excellent stopping place. We found 'Bron Eifion' at the end of the village.

Miss Jones was out but old Mr Jones, her father, was at home and though as he explained he had very little English we were made thoroughly at home until the return of Miss Jones, and the old gentleman was particularly anxious to know if we would like an 'ufel' (fire, I assumed) it being a somewhat cool evening. However after finding Miss Jones for quarters for the night we went for a stroll down the village primarily to get some cigarettes but we could find nothing in the nature of a shop where such things were sold. As tomorrow was Sunday (a Welsh Sunday!) we were at last driven to drink at the 'Cwellyn Arms' where after consuming a Bass, we enquired for cigarettes only to be told they had none but could send out for some. In about ten minutes a small boy came in with packets of various brands so that we were saved from a smokeless Sunday, but where they came from we knew not.

We strolled along the Carnarvon road as far as Llyn Cwellyn – a really beautiful sheet of water surrounded by rugged mountains – and all the more beautiful in a florid sunset. By the time we got back to 'Bron Eifion' we were very glad to find a good *"ufel"* had been lit and were also very glad of the excellent supper which was waiting for us.

This had been another day of *small mileage – only 47*.

SUNDAY 17TH AUGUST

Four shillings and sixpence!

RHYD DDU – LLANBERIS – BETWS-Y-COED – GLASFRYN – CHIRK – MONTFORD BRIDGE

It was a bleak prospect that greeted us on rising. A fine Welsh rain enshrouded everything in a dense mist. Snowdon, in front of our windows, was invisible until sometime after we had finished breakfast and then only bits of it appeared from time to time through the mist.

We got on the road about 10.30 a.m. taking the Carnarvon road past Llyn Cwellyn through the villages of Betws Garmon and Waunfawr where

Summary 1932.

Month	Number of Runs			Mileage				Averages			
	All day out and home	Touring Weekends	Other Runs	All day out and home	Touring and Weekends	Other Runs	Total	All day out and home	Touring and Weekends	Other Runs	All Runs
January	4	2	15	332	124	564	1020	93·00	62·00	37·60	48·57
February	3	6	9	275	488	397	1160	91·66	81·03	44·11	64·44
March	3	11	11	286	735	432	1423	85·33	66·81	39·27	56·94
April	6	5	15	569	405	592	1566	93·33	81·00	39·46	60·23
May	4	12	10	367	940	377	1684	91·75	78·33	37·70	64·78
June	4	7	15	394	596	653	1643	95·50	85·14	36·86	59·34
July	3	4	19	495	561	730	1686	165·00	90·25	43·68	64·84
August	2	9	18	165	678	502	1345	84·00	95·33	33·46	51·86
September	2	—	25	175	—	653	828	87·50	—	28·39	33·12
October	3	2	22	246	129	673	1048	82·00	64·50	30·59	38·87
November	3	2	22	268	180	1046	1464	89·33	75·00	49·50	56·30
December	3	2	23	215	114	841	1170	71·66	57·00	35·56	41·42
Total and General Average	40	62	201	3760	4720	7460	15940	94·00	76·12	37·12	52·66

Like most cyclists, Charles was a stickler for recording his cycling mileage.
Charles rode nearly 16,000 miles in 1932, according to his diaries.

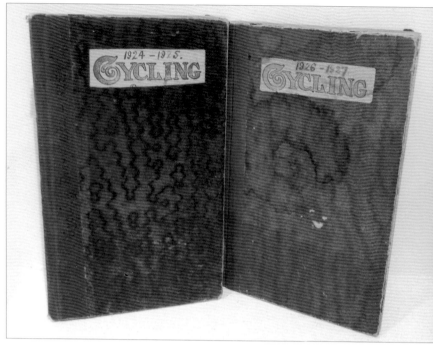

Charles' original handwritten diaries for the years 1924-1927

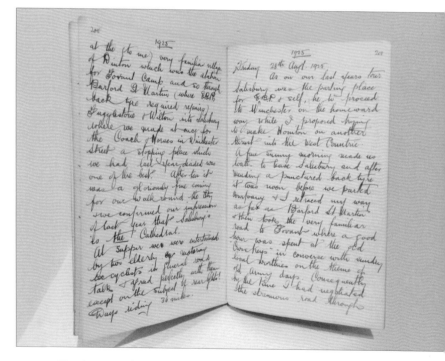

Handwritten diary entries recording Charles' adventures during his
summer tour of 1925.

The cursory chat among cyclists before starting the day's riding, Charles and friends outside his last night's abode.

Charles posing in his formal cycling garb complete with tie and C.T.C. emblem badge.

A warm welcome was always guaranteed at a Cyclists' Touring Club hostelry.

Running repairs – with no Kevlar inner tubes punctures and minor adjustments to tyres were common place on rough tracks. Thankfully, Charles was a dab hand at roadside maintenances.

Left: 'Cyclealites' — A contemporary advert for bells and lamps by the Lucas Company of Birmingham featured in the C.T.C. Gazette.

Below: Brooks saddle advertisement from the Cyclist's Touring Club Gazette. Brooks are still making quality leather handmade saddles today from their Birmingham factory.

The allure of the open road, new discoveries await around every corner.

A scene which could be drawn from Charles' diaries: the British weather
sometimes proved a tough foe

The yearly, essential companion for every touring cyclist – the C.T.C. Handbook.

The Cyclists' Touring Club membership card from 1929.

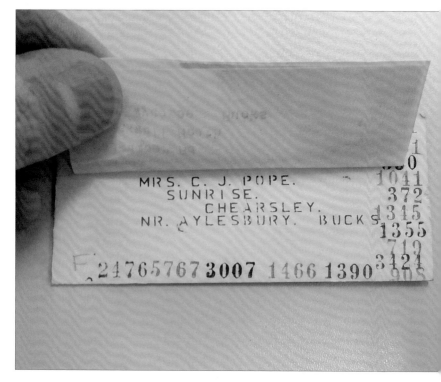

Charles' much stamped C.T.C. members index card. Charles was a Life Member of the C.T.C.

instead of continuing towards Carnarvon we turned sharply to the right. This was a rather strenuous but pleasant road which brought us out on the Carnarvon–Llanberis road about three miles west of Llanberis, which as a town is not particularly inspiring. The sky was leaden so that we did not see the two lakes, Llyn Padarn and Llyn Peris at their best.

After the village of Nant Peris the hard work begins for 3½ miles – it is a steady grind even on a 47" gear and at one time I very nearly gave up and took to my feet. At the top of the Pass of Llanberis there is a large hotel, the 'Gorphwysfa Hotel'. It was nearly 1 o'clock, it was Sunday and we were hungry. The door was open as we entered in search of bread and cheese and whatever we could get to drink. We waited about half an hour and were then ushered into a glittering room. A loaf of bread and a cheese dish with some indifferent cheese was placed before us with two very small glasses of lemonade. We refreshed ourselves on this festive fare and then enquired what there was to pay. Four shillings and sixpence! We paid and came away more or less dazed.

The run down from Pen-y-Pass to Capel Curig was a most exhilarating one though my back brake began to cluck ominously before we got down to Betws-y-Coed, that very crowded and Southend-like town. We had no plans and the question arose "Where to"? Memories of the joyous Holyhead road had the day, and we decided on making a dash for England. After the uphill 3½ miles out of Betws, top gears came into operation through Pentre Voelas to Glasfryn where tea at 'Bryn Tirion' was not to be missed. And it was a tea, quite up to the standard of the one we had here last year.

When we restarted after this enormous 'stoke up', the rain which had been threatening all the afternoon came on in earnest and compelled us to seek the protection of our capes. It is not the final time we have done this road in pouring rain and it is a tradition from many years ago that it is always wet when we have occasion to pass through the unlovely town of Corwen and nearly always through the Vale of Llangollen. However, soon after leaving Llangollen the rain began to grow less violent so that just outside Chirk we were able to take off our coverings to our great content.

There was the usual crowd making out of Welsh Chirk for the 'Bridge Inn' just inside the English border, but we had a fair wind behind and were on top gear and even the fact that we had been total abstainers all day did not tempt us to stop. From Gobowen to Shrewsbury is always a cake walk and we sped on through Whittington, West Felton and Nesscliffe to Montford Bridge where we hoped to come to rest at the 'Wingfield Arms', which had sheltered us more than once before. However, this time it was full up but only a few more miles towards Shrewsbury we found the 'Four Crosses' displaying the P.R.H.A.[5] sign. The exterior did not look promising but the "question" received an affirmation and feeding – especially the supper – was up to the best traditions of P.R.H.A. houses. And so to bed after a most *exhilarating run of 86 miles.*

MONDAY 18TH AUGUST

The ideal place for peace and quietness

MONTFORD BRIDGE – SHREWSBURY – CHURCH STRETTON – LEINTWARDINE – WIGMORE – AYMESTREY – KINGSLAND – EARDISLAND – PEMBRIDGE – BROXWOOD – KINGSLAND

After a very excellent breakfast a few miles found us once more in Shrewsbury, the first of the towns which we once more entered over the Welsh Bridge. After a wander round its always delightful streets we quitted it by the English Bridge taking the Hereford road up to Bayston Hill through Dorrington and Leebotwood to Church Stretton stopping two miles short of Craven Arms at the 'Traveller's Rest' for the usual midday sustenance.

Many times in the last few years have we travelled this road (and it would be difficult to name a more glorious stretch) but never can I remember having passed the 'Traveller's Rest' and we spent at least an hour in sporting chat with the landlord, a man of mighty valour, late of the R.A.F. and holder of many parachute records.

At Craven Arms we took the right hand road up to Clungunford and then the rough and strong track leading to Leintwardine. Only the first mile is now rough and stony, the remainder has been "improved", which made us quake for what might be happening in our old favourite village of Leintwardine. Alas, our fears were fully justified – the beautiful old bridge over the Teme has been demolished and a wide stone and iron one is being built. Thus is the curse of the internal combustion engine gradually ruining the countryside everywhere.

Passing over the bridge we took a road about a mile and a half signposted to Wigmore. It is mainly uphill though not fiercely so; nevertheless we found our little gears very useful. Wigmore is a sweet village with much

5 People's Refreshment House Association

quaint and antique architecture but it is much marred by corrugated iron garages and hideous petrol pumps. The road onwards runs steeply downhill for a space and then the villages of Yatton and Aymestrey, the latter a dream of beauty, but it requires a watercolour artist to do it justice; my camera was unequal to the task.

A few miles from Mortimer's Cross, with two stops for shelter from brief but heavy storms, brought us to our stopping place the hospitable 'Angel' in the fascinating village of Kingsland. I visited Kingsland for the first time last year and my first impression was one of supreme contentment at having found the ideal place for peace and quietness. Subsequent visits strengthen this impression. It is difficult to account for the attraction of this village. Many would vote it a deadly hole. Though full of quaint old houses it has not the beauty of many of the surrounding villages, consisting as it does if one long straggling street, yet to sit in the front garden of the 'Angel' looking across the orchard opposite towards the ancient church is to me the acme of content.

We had a wash and tea, ordered supper for 9 o'clock and set out for an evening in the enchanting villages of Eardisland and Pembridge as the showers has passed and the evening was fine and sunny. From Pembridge we explored on a mile or so to the village of Broxwood, a peaceful spot as all the villages in this delightful corner of Herefordshire are but with no outstanding features.

It was then back to supper at the 'Angel' a cold supper of beef and salad followed by stewed plums and cream and gorgonzola in prime condition, such a supper that leaves a feeling that there is nothing more to be desired, waited on by a small child of about 12 years of age named Dora in a most efficient manner. This had been one of the most pleasant days of our tour, in this lovely district which, with its rural charm, is such a complete contrast to the stern grandeur of North Wales from whence we had so recently covered.

Distance covered: 56 miles

TUESDAY 19TH AUGUST

A marvellous show of rainbows

KINGSLAND – EARDISLAND – KINGTON – NEW RADNOR – LLANFIHANGEL-NANT-MELAN – RHAYADER – LLANGWIG – LLANFIHANGEL-NANT-MELAN

We reluctantly left the 'Angel' about 10.30 a.m. after having taken the opportunity of lightening our toil by posting home our cast off underclothing. I found some difficulty in finding the entrance to Kingsland Post Office but was finally directed to go down the garden and in at the back door.

The outlook was somewhat watery but the sun favoured me when passing through Eardisland and I was able to photograph the Staick House from a new angle. We went on through Pembridge to Kington where it being market day there were considerable crowds. We were bound first for the 'Red Lion' at Llanfihangel-Nant-Melan but as we left the New Radnor the usual Radnor Forest rain began in the usual way. It did not look as though it would last long so we took shelter in the hedge but after half an hour decided to put on our capes and push on. We found the 'Red Lion' full up but Mrs Williams was able to arrange for a bed at a nearby cottage down the road and in about 20 minutes we had the "use" of a large joint of beef at which we cut many a time and oft. There were the usual stewed plums to follow.

About 3 o'clock we stopped eating and drinking and, as the rain had given over, made up our minds to run over to Rhayader. There was a powerful wind against us up the long slope to the summit of the pass which also acted as a brake downhill. However we had no more rain on this pleasant road via Penybont to Rhayader which was as usual full of sheep and cattle. We had only time to go a mile or two along the road to Llangwig before returning to tea which we intended obtaining at 'Webber's'. Alas, we found 'Webber's' was no more – it had been renamed the 'Kimberley Temperance Hotel'. The tea was quite a good one but nothing like the bountiful spread which Miss Webber and her assistants used to provide. While we were having tea the rain came on once more but it had practically ceased when we started for home with the wind behind.

The ride back to Llanfihangel was remarkable for a marvellous show of rainbows of the most vivid kind. To see two rainbows at once is not unusual but when we saw four simultaneously we wondered whether it was only tea we had drunk at Rhayader! When we arrived back to the 'Red Lion' we were not sorry to sit in front of the stove before having another cut at that cold beef for supper. It was somewhat of an adventure going in search of our sleeping quarters and it was certainly one of the most curious places I have ever slept in, access being gained up a curious ladder like staircase. However the bed was good and we slept soundly enough after another quiet day of 59 *rather damp and windy miles*.

WEDNESDAY 20TH AUGUST

The unexpected Wolverhampton music makers

LLANFIHANGEL-NANT-MELAN – SHOBDON – LUDLOW – MUNSLOW – MUCH WENLOCK – BRIDGNORTH

After a breakfast of that remarkable 'Red Lion' bacon and eggs, we made our way once more down to New Radnor and on to Kington. From there it was our wish to get to Shobdon and we got rather involved in various byroads through Staunton-on-Arrow where there are many uncharted crossroads. Local enquires produced results more confusing than helpful but we arrived there eventually and in time to obtain nourishment at the 'Bateman Arms' a largish pub with a most wonderful fire place in the bar with a piscine[6] on either side surmounted by curious angels. We were informed that this had been the idea of an architect who had been doing restoration work to the church about 200 years ago and the faces of the angels were supposed to be portraits of the landlord of that time and his wife.

From here we made for Ludlow via Croft and Orleton and up through the woods from Richard's Castle and the run down to Ludford Bridge. We made through Ludlow and out of it down Corve Street turning sharply to the right at Bromfield over the railway. This took us past Stanton Lacy lying back off the road and looking as though it would repay exploration, then on to Diddlebury and Culmington. The time had arrived for tea and also the opportunity at 'The Crown' ('The Hundred House'[7]) at Munslow. This had been a very fast 11 miles from Ludlow and we were ready for the excellent tea 'The Crown' gave us.

The road still remained very fast. We were bound for Much Wenlock but it was too close if we followed the direct road from Shipton so we took

---

6 A shallow basin usually placed near the altar of a church.
7 A 'hundred' was a former division of a shire used for administrative and military purposes; a 'hundred house' was used as a court and taxation counting house.

the Bridgnorth road through Monkhopton and Morville turning sharply off to the left just past the latter village, a somewhat lumpy five miles. We intended to have stopped the night in Much Wenlock but it was early closing day and the town looked so depressing that we decided making tracks for Bridgnorth where we anticipated no difficulty in finding a "sliop" [8] as the Handbook contains many appointments there. In this we were mistaken and after visiting at least five C.T.C. houses and being told they were full up, we went down to the Low Town to see what the 'Vine Hotel' to which we had been recommended looked like. We put the question and received a satisfactory answer.

After a wash we proposed a stroll and enquired if there was likely to be anything to eat about 9 o'clock (it was then about 8.30 p.m.). We were informed there was hot duck and peas going if we liked to have it now. Naturally we needed no pressing and we had a joyous feed in company with three young men from Wolverhampton for whom the duck had been cooked. After supper, music was proposed. One of the men produced a violin and apologised as it only had two sound strings; another one sat down at the piano, a much better instrument than one usually sees in country pubs. We rather expected the usual kind of modern jazz noise and it was thus that the show started but the dexterity of both performers led us to expect something better and we began to make suggestions. Liszt's 'Liebestraum' led to Chopin's nocturnes and waltzes all played in the manner of virtuoso. We had a remarkably pleasant evening, with the Classics being interspersed with songs of more or less merit.

There was an elderly man in the room who had told us he had come from Shrewsbury for peace and quietness from the excitement of the Flower Shows. He did not look pleased when the show began but sat up and took notice when the violinist went out and brought back an ordinary carpenter's saw from which with the aid of a penholder he produced notes of a marvellous sweetness. Towards the end of the evening the elderly man began joining in the songs in a fine bass voice and it turned out that he was choirmaster at one of the Shrewsbury churches.

The Wolverhampton music makers departed to their grimy habitat at 11.30 p.m. and we went to bed thoroughly pleased with our quarters and entertainments.

Distance covered: 46 miles

---

8 Unknown term.

THURSDAY 21ST AUGUST

Grub fit for a king

BRIDGNORTH – STANTON LACY – LEOMINSTER – DILWYN – WHITNEY-ON-WYE

An excellent breakfast confirmed the good impression we had formed last night of the 'Vine Hotel' and the extremely moderate charges made it desirable to add this house to the C.T.C. list to which the proprietress, Mrs Travers, was quite agreeable.

It had been raining all night and there was still a drizzle when we left about 10.30 a.m. taking the road back to Ludlow when bread and cheese became desirable. This we obtained at the 'Royal Oak' close to Stanton Lacy and it was good and plentiful. I had designed to replenish my stock of pocket handkerchiefs in Ludlow, but when we arrived there we found that it was early closing day and so I hoped for better luck in Leominster. We were bound by the main road via Brimfield and Ashton, a good but uninteresting road. However, Leominster was also 'early closed' through we did succeed in finding a tobacconist open and were able to replenish in that direction.

On the grounds that you cannot have too much of a good thing we decided to make for the 'Stowe Inn'. We accordingly turned into the wind once more on the fine stretch of road which runs within sight of Weobley without going through that picturesque town and through the village of Dilwyn. Here we were badly in want of tea. It is a sleepy sort of village and the one inn (the 'Crown') was enjoying deep slumber. I assaulted the front door fruitlessly and then tried to gain access at the back without result. We were just going to move sadly away when a head appeared at an upper window. Our enquiry as to tea was satisfactorily answered. The tea was a gorgeous one and sent us on battling against the gale joyously through Kinnersley and the right turn at Willesley Cross to the haven which is the *Mecca* of all good cyclists with good appetite, the 'Stowe Inn'. Miss Williams and Mr Taylor gave us the usual warm welcome, assuring us there would be something to eat at 8.30 p.m.

We had a little time to spare so decided to see what the gale behind us felt like and so once more into the breeze over Whitney Bridge to the not too prepossessing town of Hay. Ten minutes in Hay and then a dash back to supper on top gears. In spite of some minutes' conversation with the tollgate keeper on Whitney Bridge, that five miles only took us 14 minutes.

The something to eat proved to be a hot roast chicken followed by one of those famous apple tarts and cream. King George himself could not have better grub than that provided by the 'Stowe'. And so to bed after *an arduous run of 62 miles.*

FRIDAY 22ND AUGUST

Conquering Whitchurch Hill

WHITNEY-ON-WYE – HEREFORD – MONMOUTH – REDBROOK – CHEPSTOW

There was no more speculation as to where was to be our next stop, for our joint holiday was coming to a close and Chepstow had to be made tonight. We took the muchly familiar road back to Hereford via Willesley and Bridge Sollers and as usual loafed for an hour in that pleasant city so that soon after leaving it bread and cheese was required. This we received at a pleasant little inn – the 'Angel' – a few miles on the road, the bread and cheese being supplemented by tomatoes and celery – a welcome addition. When we had finished this and got on our way through Much Birch on the road to Ross it began to rain, and though it left off as we reached Wilton Bridge, we dismounted as usual to enjoy the distant view of Ross.

As we restarted for the town a terrific downpour drove us to shelter by the river for about twenty minutes. When this had ceased we went on up into the town turning round by the Market to Walford and then over the Kerne Bridge for Whitchurch and Monmouth. We rode all the way up Whitchurch Hill for the first time in our lives, of course on our bottom gears. We did not linger in Monmouth but passed straight onto Redbrook where we thought the 'Bell' might provide a decent tea. In this we were not disappointed.

The ride up the glorious Wyndcliff was marred by storms. At Brockweir we stood up under a thick tree for quite half an hour and the rain continued through Tintern and up to St. Arvans and only ceased down a bit as we ran down into Chepstow where we made at once to the 'Bridge Inn'.

A short stroll before supper prepared us for the excellent feed of steak and chips which Mrs Wilding had ready for us.

Distance covered: 57 miles

SATURDAY 23RD AUGUST

Carried on swift wings

CHEPSTOW – ROSS-ON-WYE – PUESDOWN – BURFORD

With regrets that we could not stay longer at the 'Bridge Inn' we quitted Chepstow about 10.30 a.m. climbing once more up to St. Arvans for the run down the Wyndcliff. We were unlucky for the famous view was shrouded in a thick rain mist and Tintern was glistening with moisture.

There was nothing to linger for so we rode straight on through Monmouth on the road to Ross stopping only for bread and cheese and of course beer at the 'Weston Cross Inn' just outside Ross. From Ross to Gloucester we had the wind behind us down through Huntley, and the same fair wind carried us on its wings swiftly over the eight miles from Gloucester to Cheltenham. Even up the steep slope to Andoversford and Puesdown, we were able to keep on our 84" gears.

The 'Puesdown Inn' supplied us with its usual excellent tea and we soon ran into Burford where the 'Swan' was expecting us.

Distance covered: 73 miles

SUNDAY 24TH AUGUST

Lovely Lacock

BURFORD – LECHLADE – CRICKLADE – MALMESBURY – LACOCK

It was a fine morning and Burford was looking at its best, so much so that E.B.P. could not be induced to leave it until past midday.

Our way out was the familiar Lechlade road via Filkins and on to Fairford taking a road to the left pointing to Marston Meysey. As it was such a late start we were quite ready for bread and cheese at the 'Three Horseshoes' outside Lechlade before making our way through the villages of Kempsford and Whelford to Cricklade, which town was in Sabbath slumber.

A slight following wind made it easy work through Minety to the ancient town of Malmesbury where a shower made lingering unprofitable so we continued on our way via Hullavington to Chippenham. We were getting hungry but my suggestion of tea in Chippenham was turned down by E.B.P. as we were within easy reach of our base, turning off two miles along the Bath road out of the town by the side of the railway through the small village of Notton to Lacock. Here we were expected by Miss Jenkins at the 'Corner House' and tea followed as a matter of course.

Miss Jenkins and E.B.P. found so much to talk to about after tea (it was their first meeting) that it was already dusk before we got out for a stroll. Nevertheless E.B.P. was struck with the marvels of this wonderful village which, though so close to the city of Bath and the big manufacturing towns of Chippenham and Melksham, appears to be ignored by them all and so is allowed to live its own life and to retain the beauty of its ancient architecture unsullied by the bill poster and the petrol pump. Someday no doubt it will suffer the fate of its beautiful neighbour Castle Combe but at present it is "a gem of purest ray serene"[9]. An excellent supper awaited us on our return and we were able to inspect the wonderful oak panelling in the dining room of the 'Corner House' which some vandal at some remote period had covered with white paint!

Our bedroom was the ancient spook room with a tombstone mantel-piece which I have slept in on other visits, but we slept sound enough nevertheless.

Distance covered: 46 miles

MONDAY 25TH AUGUST

Down to Devon

LACOCK – TROWBRIDGE – FARLEIGH CASTLE – FAULKLAND – WELLS – LYNCH – BAMPTON

This was the morning of our parting – I had still a week's holiday to run but E.B.P. had to return to work.

It had been my intention to make across to Peterborough and then on to York but the west exerted its force and I had to obey by turning in the opposite direction. After seeing E.B.P. off on the homeward route I lingered yet another hour in lovely Lacock upon which the sun was now shining.

I had no large scale maps for the west and had to go mostly by guesswork making first for Melksham and then via Semington to Trowbridge. Here I had some difficulty in finding the way out, finally taking the road to

---

9 From the first line of Thomas Gray's "An Elegy Written in a Country Churchyard", published in 1751

Radstock. After passing Wingfield, Farleigh Castle struck my eye and I felt bound to turn aside to explore it. It has been taken over by the National Trust and the sixpence I paid to inspect the interior of the ancient chapel was money well spent. This delayed me nearly an hour and by the time I reached the small village of Faulkland, bread and cheese at the 'New Inn' was welcome.

The road onward to Radstock via Writhlington is a somewhat arduous one. At Wells I was accosted by an elderly gentleman in plus fours who informed me he was Alderman Wheeler C.T.C. Consul for Somerset, aged 72. I loitered around with him for some time and by the time I got beyond Glastonbury, tea was an urgent need. I stopped at a wayside cottage at Lynch (Mrs Bird) which did me well. The easy road over the lowlands to Taunton was taken at speed and I decided to thrust into Devon before nightfall. There are some nice hills to tackle on the Barnstaple road through Milverton and Wiveliscombe to Bampton where I put up at the 'Temperance Hotel'.

Distance covered: 80 miles

TUESDAY 26TH AUGUST

No ferry today

BAMPTON – SWIMBRIDGE – BARNSTAPLE – INSTOW – BIDEFORD – APPLEDORE – MONKLEIGH – HOLSWORTHY – STRATTON – HOLSWORTHY

Got an early start and found the road much easier through South Molton and Swimbridge (where I stopped for refreshment at the 'Coach and Horses') to Barnstaple where an early midday refresh at 'The New Inn' on the road to Bideford left me plenty of time for Bideford and Appledore in the afternoon.

At Instow I was disappointed in finding thick fog in the estuary and the tide so low as to make it impossible to ferry across to Appledore so I had to continue on and cross the bridge to Bideford first and then through Northam to Appledore. Though Appledore was covered in a sea fog blanket it was bright enough in Bideford so I returned there and continued my journey on the road to Holsworthy via Monkleigh, Frithlestock and Stibb Cross. The 'Bell' at Monkleigh gave me an early tea and I arrived in Holsworthy about 6.30 p.m. receiving the usual warm welcome from

Pere, Mere et filles[10]. As the evening was young I ran over the familiar road to Stratton just into Cornwall and, after a Bass at the 'Kings Arms', returned to supper.

Distance covered: 79 miles

WEDNESDAY 27TH AUGUST

Sorely disappointing Tintagel

HOLSWORTHY – WAINHOUSE CORNER – BOSCASTLE – TINTAGEL – BOSCASTLE – BUDE – STRATTON

I took a dive into Cornwall taking the coast road out of Stratton via Marhamchurch, St. Gennys and Wainhouse Corner to Boscastle and onto Tintagel.

At 'Wainhouse Corner Hotel' I just escaped being served with Simonds Ale[11]. Tintagel I found most disappointing and the crowds of charabanc parties and 'picknickers' making for the Castle kept me away from it. After a meagre lunch at a C.T.C. refreshment house I made my way back to Boscastle and after a short interlude strolled mostly up Penally Hill. The tea I had at Mrs Butler's 'Perrotts Post' was nothing great and I took the rough road to Widemouth Bay – a pleasant spot – and so into Bude. A Bass at the 'King's Arms' Stratton sent me back to the 'South Western Hotel' for an early supper and bed.

Distance covered: 59 miles

THURSDAY 28TH AUGUST

A kindred spirit

STRATTON – HATHERLEIGH – SAMPFORD COURTENAY – BOW – EXETER – SEATON

With great regret I took my departure from the 'South Western Hotel' about 10.30 a.m. taking the road by way of Highampton (now a spoilt village) to Hatherleigh, also spoilt by having the old bridge removed and replaced by an

---

10 This relates to the Jollow family who managed the South Western Hotel at Holsworthy. 'Pere' is Alfred Jollow, 'Mere' is Mary Jollow and the 'filles' would be Evelyn and Gladys Jollows. There were five daughters but in the 1930s only Evelyn and Gladys would be at the Hotel. There is no French connection to the Jollow family. The parents were both born in Devon and were farmers prior to the move into hostelry.

11 Simonds were a well-known brewer based in Reading and specialised in pale ales.

ugly new stone and iron one. The landlord of the 'Bridge Inn' informed me it was a great improvement but I kept silence on the point.

I was relieved to find Exbourne and Sampford Courtenay (where the 'New Inn' gave me midday grub) were still unspoilt. North Tawton still presents its "suivey"[12] aspect and in Bow I found a long strip of the tread of my back tyre unstuck. At a small general shop I got some black tape and bound it up and it was not until I got to Exeter some hours later I found I had left my repair box and all my tools on the greensward at Bow.

The tea I had at Cowles between Crediton and Exeter was 'no great shakes'. At Exeter I went all over the town to try and get a new repair box but with only partial success. I was undecided where to make for the night so turned coastwards a few miles out of Exeter on the Honiton road. On Salcombe Hill I ran into a young man named Parnell in the same undecided condition of mind. We had some idea of trying for Charmouth but when dusk was approaching Seaton being near we decided to try our luck there. Our hopes were low when we got down to the town and found its crowded state. However, we ran against some other C.T.C. members and with the aid of the landlord of the place where they were staying succeeded in getting a bed for the night, feeding at 'Vile's Restaurant'. We met our friends after supper for a stroll round and retired early.

Distance covered: 65 miles

FRIDAY 29TH AUGUST

Mighty climbs

SEATON – LYME REGIS – CHARMOUTH – MORCOMBELAKE – CHIDEOCK – DORCHESTER – WIMBORNE – RINGWOOD – FORDINGBRIDGE

Our first job this morning was to get out of Seaton – a mighty climb. We hoped to by-pass Lyme Regis but found we could not so we dropped down into it and had another enormous climb out of it to Charmouth. I had done the furthest climbs up to Bridport and Chideock so was prepared for them but we were glad of some beer at the 'The Ship Inn' Morcombelake before we had our midday food at the 'Traveller's Rest' Chideock.

The road onward to Dorchester is much simpler and some bananas eaten on the way took us to Puddletown where the little cottage on the right gave

---

12 This could be Charles' attempt at a Devonish accent for survey (general view).

us the usual bountiful tea. Here Parnell met an old school friend and other cycling acquaintances turned up. Consequently we had to foot it[13] if we had any hope of reaching Salisbury today. The fine back road through Bere Regis and Sturminster Marshall to Wimborne was taken at well over evens (20 mph) and some ten minutes was spent in Wimborne getting tyre levers in which we were both deficient.

It then became a grim struggle against time on to Ringwood but we got there before 8 o'clock and, after a drink at the 'Royal Oak', ran into our Seaton friends. Parnell wanted a battery for his lamp but he let 8 o'clock go and the shops were shut. This made Salisbury a hopeless proposition and we just got into Fordingbridge by lighting-up time and before the commencement of a heavy thunderstorm which continued for some hours.

The cold meat for supper at the 'Greyhound' was found to be somewhat "passe" after I had eaten some of it, for which I duly suffered during the night and next morning.

Distance covered: 69 miles

SATURDAY 30TH AUGUST

A scorching day

FORDINGBRIDGE – SALISBURY – AMESBURY – UPAVON – PEWSEY – HUNGERFORD – LECHLADE – BURFORD

We did not take long over the miles from Fordingbridge to Salisbury and, after a run round the city, took the beautiful road to Amesbury alongside the Avon through Woodford and Wilsford in preference to the shorter main road.

After a drink at the 'Royal Oak' Amesbury, we made off across the plain via Netheravon to Upavon where at the 'Ship' the bread and cheese and a "Usher"[14] was so good and the company so amusing that we loitered far longer than we should have done. It was a scorching day and we took it very gently through Manningford Bruce to Pewsey loitering still further over bananas with our feet in the cooling stream that runs through that town.

After about an hour of this we woke up to a desire for tea making a hurried dash to the 'Red Lion' at Hungerford. After this we made up to Aldbourne, climbed the slopes to Liddington and slid down Swindon-wards

---

13 Speed up
14 Ushers were a brewery based at Trowbridge producing pale ales.

taking the customary bye way to avoid the "Railway Town"[15]. At Lechlade, Parnell wanted a reviver so we visited the 'Three Horseshoes' arriving at the 'Swan' Burford to find E.B.P. already there and a large assembly of other cyclists.

Distance covered: 72 miles

SUNDAY 31ST AUGUST

Trailing behind

BURFORD – BUCKLAND – ABINGDON – KINGSTON – OAKLEY GREEN – HAMMERSMITH

As Parnell was coming the same way as E.B.P. and myself, I warned E.B.P. not to try and take it out of him up hills as he was too tough even for him. E.B.P.'s reply was that his leg was much too weak for him to want to do anything of the sort.

We took the Brize Norton to Bampton road and at the stiffish rise to Buckland I was left at least a quarter of a mile behind! We had refreshment at the 'Black Horse' Abingdon then made our way via Sutton Courtenay to Wallingford up to Stoke Row for tea at the 'Bricklayers Arms' Kingston. A drink at the 'Braywood Inn' Oakley Green carried us back to Hammersmith where Parnell, after a light supper, departed for his home at Hornsey.

Distance covered: 81 miles and a tour of nearly 1500 miles.

---

15 Swindon's nickname, owing to the presence of the railway works, completed in 1843 by the Great Western Railway.

The Grand Avenue, Savernake Forest

Near New Radnor, on the road to Aberystwyth

1931 SOUTH WALES TOUR – MERLIN I

THURSDAY 23RD APRIL

A series of drenching showers

HAMMERSMITH – HORTON – DORCHESTER-ON-THAMES – NEWBRIDGE – ABINGDON – STANDLAKE – BRIZE NORTON – BURFORD

Started off about 11.30 a.m. in a series of drenching showers which necessitated taking shelter on occasions and decided me to take the shortest route. I had poached eggs for lunch at the 'Five Bells' Horton after which the rain ceased down for a bit and enabled me to get to the 'Fleur de Lis' at Dorchester for tea fairly dry. After this it was fairly easy work by the usual route through Abingdon with a call at the 'Rose Revived' Newbridge for a glass of Bass.

At Standlake I decided to dodge the main Gloucester Road stretch by going via Bampton and Brize Norton, the "bye-road" through Cote and Aston being in a first rate condition. Arrived at the 'Swan' about 7.30 p.m. finding Mr and Mrs Barnes, who I had met before, being the only other visitors.

Distance covered: 77 miles

FRIDAY 24TH APRIL

A trip to see the plum trees

BURFORD – STOW-ON-THE-WOLD – EVESHAM – STANWAY – BOURTON-ON-THE-WATER – BURFORD

Had set aside this day for a trip down the Vale of Evesham to see the plum trees in full bloom. The outlook was very unpromising when I took the Stow Road after breakfast and after reaching Stow I soon had my trusty cape on. The 'Fish Inn' provided me with my midday sustenance and the rain had all but ceased sufficiently to enable me to negotiate Fish Hill and Broadway uncaped.

I found the plums not more than halfway out but even so they would have been a fine sight with better weather conditions. At Evesham the sun shone for about five minutes but it was the only sun I was to see all day. The rain came on as though it meant it and I made up my mind to take the shortest route to Stanway for tea via Sedgeberrow and Toddington. The rain and the wind combined made it a hard plug even on a 49" gear.

At Stanway Mrs Stratford gave me the usual magnificent tea, which put such a lot of beans into me that I rode up Stanway Hill in the teeth of the gale. At Ford, the rain having ceased decided me on dodging Stow by making for Temple Guiting through Bourton-on-the-Water and Little Rissington. At the latter village I must have taken the wrong turning for I eventually found myself at the top of Maugersbury Hill about three miles from Stow. However it did not take me long to polish off the seven miles to Burford and supper.

Distance covered: 60 miles

SATURDAY 25TH APRIL

A prayer to St. Christopher

BURFORD – CHIPPING NORTON – GREAT TEW – BICESTER – CHARLBURY – BURFORD

I had to meet Wood today at Bicester and needless to say I did not intend to take the direct route to that town though the weather still showed no promise of better things. My route was by the way of Fulbrook and Shipton-under-Wychwood to Chipping Norton where I made up my mind to visit Great Tew. Bread and cheese and beer at the 'Falkland Arms' gave me the idea of a weekend in a fortnight's time with Wood at this ideal village and Mr Ives of the 'Falkland Arms', though he could not put us up himself, thought it might be done.

From Great Tew I made my way in the rain to Ledwell and Duns Tew, North Aston. Somerton and Bucknell into Bicester. It was far too early for Wood to arrive so I listened to the Cup Final by wireless for some time and then set off on the Aylesbury road to meet him. I had covered some seven miles of the uninteresting Akeman Street before he came into sight and we made for the 'King's Head' of Bicester for an indifferent tea.

It was raining steadily when we resumed our journey and we made one or two false starts before striking the road Wood wanted to take to Burford via Charlbury. At any rate it was a rough and stony way with several hard uphill grinds in the face of the rain and wind before Charlbury was reached. Here we fortified ourselves with refreshments at the 'White Hart' before tackling the strenuous country between Charlbury and Burford.

I had found it tough on a normal summer's day but in the tempest of wind and rain in the dark this night the negotiation of the ever upward slope with the red lights of Leafield always to the fore might be classed as a most valorous deed. When I started vowing wax candles to St. Christopher if we reached Burford without mishap, Wood thought I was getting delirious. It was about 10.20 p.m. when our haven finally came into sight and we soon had newspapers tucked around our knees and enjoyed our well-earned supper in borrowed slippers.

Distance covered: 72 miles

SUNDAY 26TH APRIL

Ups and downs
BURFORD – CHELTENHAM – GLOUCESTER – NEWNHAM – CHEPSTOW

Today I was to resume my way towards South Wales but it was about 11.30 a.m. before I started after parting with Wood. The wind, and as usual, the rain were against me.

By the time I had struggled through Northleach over Puesdown through Andoversford to the purlins[1] of Cheltenham I was fairly waterlogged and at the 'New Inn' the usual refreshment came very welcome. Though the rain

---

1 A horizontal beam along the length of a roof

had nearly stopped it was all a push from Cheltenham to Gloucester and I decided on the shorter though more strenuous Severn route, taking the left hand road about two miles beyond Gloucester. A great part of this road, being under reconstruction, is very rough.

Once through Westbury the trouble begins on the steep ups and downs out of Westbury into Newnham (where I had a satisfactory tea at 'Roseville') and from Blakeney into Lydney so that I had had quite enough by the time the 'Bridge Inn' at Chepstow came into sight.

Distance covered: 58 miles

MONDAY 27TH APRIL

A few days with the Paices
CHEPSTOW – NEWPORT – CARDIFF – BARRY

It was a pleasant surprise to find the sun shining in the morning and as I only had a short stage to do I left it until nearly 12 o'clock before getting away. The wind was still very strong and dead against me so it was hard work to Newport via Caerwent, Llanvaches and Penhow. After refreshment at the 'Royal Oak' about three miles outside Newport I had plenty of time to go to Cardiff. In fact I spent about an hour admiring the show parts of that fine city before going on to Barry, via the toll bridge and Cadoxton, to stay with Mabel and Guy Paice for a few days.

Distance covered: 40 miles

TUESDAY 28TH APRIL

A damp day
BARRY – ST. BRIDES MAJOR – BRIDGEND – LLANTWIT – BARRY

I went on by bye-roads through Aberthaw, St. Athan, Llantwit Major, St. Donats and Marcross to St. Brides Major up through Ewenny and some miles on the road to Porthcawl, but the rain being steady, I returned via Laleston to Bridgend to St. Brides and then via Wick to Llantwit – a damp and unpleasant day with much wind.

Distance covered: 47 miles

WEDNESDAY 29TH APRIL

A welcome stroke of luck

BARRY – CARDIFF – LLANDAFF – LLANILLTERN – COWBRIDGE – BARRY

Took the Cardiff road via Wenvoe to Canton and Llandaff to inspect the Cathedral with which I was not greatly struck. Here I found my back tyre had encountered something sharp which somewhat made further progress a problem. The situation was made more difficult by the fact that except for a little odd bit of silver I had left my money behind in Barry. However, after a few miles of careful progress I found a shop in the outskirts of Cardiff which had one 26"x1¼ inch cover of unknown make at 2/6d. I joyfully took this, made a quick change and returned to Llandaff for lunch at the 'Maltster's Arms'.

After lunch I took the road to Llantrisant via Capel Llanilltern. Llanilltern on the top of its mountain looks attractive from the distance but when, after much toil, the town is reached it is a most sordid place though the view from the church is magnificent. From Llantrisant I made my way through various mining villages namely Talbot Row, Pontyclun and Ystradowen to Cowbridge, a town consisting of one long street mostly of public houses. From here I took the main Cardiff road, then found a pleasant bye-road just beyond Bonvilston, which took me back to Barry and tea.

Distance covered: 41 miles

THURSDAY 30TH APRIL

Tar troubles

BARRY – NEWTON-NOTTAGE – PORTHCAWL – BRIDGEND – BARRY

I set out once more for Porthcawl, the weather having set fair. I got involved in a road tar trap on the road from Llantwit to St. Brides which drove me on to the main road where it took at least an hour to scrape some of the tar from the machine and tyres. There is a by-pass cutting out Bridgend. This I took but it was not only tarry as well but also very rough and I was glad to get on the Porthcawl bye-road beyond Laleston via Tythegston and Newton-Nottage, where I lunched.

Porthcawl like Barry has a jungle of merry-go-rounds and such like things but the west side is magnificent country consisting of a wide stretch of open common with fine sea views, while the sandy shore rivals Ramsgate itself. To keep clear of the tar fiend I kept to the main road through Laleston, Bridgend, Cowbridge and Bonvilston on the way back taking the bye-road to Barry as yesterday.

Distance covered: *50 miles*

FRIDAY 1ST MAY

The smokiest town in South Wales

BARRY – PYLE – MORRISTON – PONTARDULAIS – LLANDDAROG – CARMARTHEN

Today I brought my visit to Barry to a close, my destination being Carmarthen en route to St. Davids. I was not anticipating a particularly picturesque trip as it meant going through a great part of industrial Wales. However it was fairly countrified as far as Pyle where the 'Old Wine House' gave one satisfactory bread, cheese and beer, then the smoke and chimneys soon come into sight; Port Talbot, Aberavon, Briton Ferry and Neath all present chimney stacks of unrivalled size and quantity all doing their best to darken the atmosphere.

I did not much want to go into Swansea so took the road across from Neath to Morriston – surely the smokiest town even in South Wales and there is a hill just outside it where it can be surveyed in all its grim magnificence. Gorseinon, Pontlliw and Pontardulais are the last of the large industrial towns and at the last mentioned I was surprised to come on a most useful little tea shop kept by a Miss Williams, just when I wanted it.

The road onwards to Carmarthen through Cross Hands and Llanddarog though extremely strenuous is pleasant enough, and in spite of some delay taking lessons in Welsh pronunciation from a young Welsh 'soubrette²' in the 'White Hart' at Llanddarog, I arrived at Carmarthen in good time and got a satisfactory 'put up' at the 'Nelson Hotel'.

Distance ridden: *65 miles*

---

2 A soprano singer

SATURDAY 2ND MAY
A transcendent show of spring wildflowers
CARMARTHEN – WHITLAND – HAVERFORDWEST – NEWGATE – ST. DAVIDS

I got on the road just before 10 o'clock but just past Bancyfelin I had to make a halt to consider my front wheel bearing which was obviously in a 'dicky' state, judging by the explosion which emanated from it from time to time. However when it had been packed with Chemic Chain Grease it was much more silent.

At St. Clears I had got about two miles on the Red Rose road before discovering my error and I had to get across to the Haverfordwest road. The crossroad I took exhibited the most remarkable show of spring wildflowers I have ever seen: primroses –(yellow and pink ones), violets, bee orchids, ox slips, cuckoo flower, wind flower and many brilliant blooms whose names I do not know. Everywhere in these West Welsh counties, wildflowers were prodigious but this lane transcended anything I had seen elsewhere.

After passing through the large village of Whitland there is a steep hill which brought me out of the saddle, and after a considerable walk, the sight of an inn at a place marked on the map and also on a sign as "Commercial", was welcome. The inn was signed as 'Parkyandy Inn' and as no cheese was forthcoming, a large plate of Welsh bread and butter satisfied me. Here I was entertained with tales of the ring by an ex-champion lightweight, a one-time professional to a London Amateur Boxing Club.

The remainder of the road to Haverfordwest via Robeston Wathen is fairly simple. It was market day here and the steep streets were thronged with some fine examples of Welsh rural types. I walked up the steep bit onto the St. Davids road and a few miles further on, while I had stopped to put on my cape as protection against the characteristic drizzle of these parts, a man driving a jig asked me to speak to his horse as it refused to pass me until it knew I was safe. A few words of encouragement had the desired effect.

At Newgate the 'Sands Café' provided an excellent tea but it did not put enough power into me to enable me to ride out of the west side of the bay. The trying bit of road from Newgate and some time spent in Solva made it nearly 8 o'clock when I arrived in St. Davids to find the sun shining and everything beautiful in that enchanting city, where Mr Martin, as in the past, gave me bed and board.

Distance covered: 49 miles

SUNDAY 3RD MAY

A gloriously sunny Sunday

ST. DAVIDS – WHITESAND BAY – SOLVA – ST. DAVIDS

I was determined to make this a day of rest in the brilliant sun, which lasted from sunrise to sunset. I spent the morning mostly in Whitesand Bay, a charming spot, and after an excellent dinner I made for Solva where I left my bicycle at the 'Cambrian Arms' and wandered over the coast on foot. I returned to the 'Cambrian Arms' to tea and then back to St. Davids down to Porthstinian and round many bye-roads.

Distance covered: a paltry 18 miles

MONDAY 4TH MAY

No butter!

ST. DAVIDS – LOWER FISHGUARD – NEVERN – CENARTH – LLANYBYER

I left St. Davids still in the sunshine about 10 o'clock by the Fishguard road with the wind behind finding many sheep and cattle on the road through Croes-goch, Mathry, Jordanston. Lower Fishguard in the sun held me for some time and I made my way through Dinas and Newport to Nevern before stopping for lunch at the 'Trewern Arms', the bar-kitchen being one of the quaintest I have been in.

I had no need to hurry up the steep rise out of Nevern and I was in Cardigan before 3 o'clock. The road along the Teifi Valley through Llechryd to Cenarth was wonderful in spring garb and the hour and a half in Cenarth included tea at the 'Three Horseshoes', quite excellent but without butter!

By putting a little ginger in it I got through Newcastle Emlyn and Henllan to Llandysul by 7 o'clock and paused on the bridge for a few minutes to gather energy for the climb up the Lampeter road, a good three miles stiff rise. At Llanybyther[3] the 'Black Lion' received me in its usual hospitable fashion and a roaring fire combined with a good supper put me on good terms with myself for the last few miles downhill had been bitterly cold.

Distance covered: 61 miles

---

3 Now more commonly known as Llanybydder

TUESDAY 5TH MAY

Fortune favours a familiar customer

LLANYBYTHER – LAMPETER – LLANDOVEY – BRECON – CLYRO – WHITNEY-ON-WYE

With thoughts of the "Stowe Inn", Lampeter to Llandovey was my first objective. Lampeter had a cattle market on and livestock were everywhere. The climb up Lampeter Cwmann from sea-level to 1024 feet is rather more than one wants after breakfast and there seems no adequate compensation for it in the way of a run down; in fact near Pumsaint there is still steeper rise.

At Llandovey (all up for road repairs) the 'Kings Arms' supplied the usual midday necessaries before I tackled the nine-mile rise to Trecastle. A sharp shower overtook me in Trecastle and rendered a cape desirable for the run down through Senny Bridge to Brecon. Brecon had a fair on the main streets and was full of all kinds of shows, so only the narrow side turnings were available for traffic. Most of the adult population seemed to have had enough and some even too much! Prospects of tea at the 'Bell' seemed remote but the landlady, recognising me as an old customer, decided she must do it somehow. Two Cardiff men on a tandem shared in my good fortune.

With the wind astern the Hay road through Bronllys was lazy and I turned over Glasbury Bridge for the longer but pleasanter road through Clyro overlooking the Wye. About a mile after Clyro I picked up a Nottingham cyclist, and as he had never been to the 'Stowe' before I had no difficulty in persuading him to accompany me, and we had a pleasant evening discussing the 'Stowe Inn' fare and other things.

Distance covered: 68 miles

WEDNESDAY 6TH MAY

One of the most picturesque houses in Herefordshire

WHITNEY-ON-WYE – WEOBLEY – NEW RADNOR – LLANFIHANGEL-NANT-MELAN – WHITNEY-ON-WYE

I meant to have left the 'Stowe' for another base today but just as I was starting I changed my mind and decided to stay another night returning first for lunch. The black and white town of Weobley was my morning objective and I reached there via Winforton and Willersley Cross before 11 o'clock. Exploration and photography occupied all the morning including The Ley, surely one of the most picturesque houses in Herefordshire.

The lunch of roast fowl and rhubarb tart made an afternoon start before 2.45 p.m. unwise so I was all the more gratified to be able to ride up the slopes on the way to Kington without flattering. My next move was through Walton and New Radnor up to the 'Red Lion' at Llanfihangel-nant-Melan for tea. Conversation with the Williams family kept me until past six but I had little difficulty in getting back to the 'Stowe' by 8.30 p.m. for supper in company with a young tandem pair, Mr and Mrs Dean of Bournemouth.
Distance covered: 61 miles

THURSDAY 7TH MAY

An accompanying tandem

WHITNEY-ON-WYE – HEREFORD – ROSS-ON-WYE – GLOUCESTER – PUESDOWN – BURFORD

Today I had to get to Burford on the homeward track meaning to take the Ledbury-Tewkesbury route. However the Deans wanted to see Ross and I was easily persuaded to accompany them. Hereford via Bridge Sollers and Kites Nest was reached very quickly but strong head winds and long hills made the stage to Ross somewhat more difficult especially for the tandemists.

However we got to Ross in just the right time for lunch and did very well at the 'Swalia', Mr Pugh being very pleased to see me after some year's absence. We had the wind behind us from Ross to Gloucester with a clear five miles coast down from Huntley and after inspecting the Cathedral the tandemists, though new to cycling, decided they might as well come on with one to Burford. A cheap and excellent tea at the 'The Pheasant' outside Cheltenham put plenty of power into them for the climb over Puesdown and we arrived at 'The Swan' in good condition about 8 o'clock and more than ready for supper. I rather annoyed the local policeman by taking a walk with the electric lamp after 11 p.m.
Distance covered: 76 miles

FRIDAY 8TH MAY

Dubious tales of otters and foxes

BURFORD – MORETON-IN-MARSH – WARWICK – MORETON-IN-MARSH – BURFORD

Business in Burford kept me from making a start until 12 o'clock and I set off on the Stow road going from there to Moreton-in-Marsh to have lunch at 'Webbs' and listen to a recital of Old Frankie's adventures[4]. My destination was Warwick but so long did I loiter over lunch that it was 4.30 p.m. before I got there. However, by then the rain clouds, which had been threatening all afternoon, had passed over and the sun shone once more.

It being rather late I decided to return by the same route as I had come (via Wellesbourne, Ettington, Halford, Stretton-on-Fosse, Moreton and Stow). Two miles beyond Wellesbourne I had marked a village with a tea sign up, which did me quite satisfactorily but at a cost of 1/4d! I was somewhat delayed at Ettington in conversation with an ancient man who told me some rather tall stories about otters and foxes but got back to the 'Swan' in good time for supper.

Distance covered: 73 miles

SATURDAY 9TH MAY

A grudge against the grey squirrel

BURFORD – CHIPPING NORTON – SWERFORD – BANBURY – BLOXHAM – BUCKINGHAM – GREAT TEW

Having arranged the weekend at Great Tew with Wood with rendezvous at Buckingham for tea I set off through Shipton-under-Wychwood to Chipping Norton. Here my cyclometer which had got some tar in it on the 30th April run jammed and had to be removed.

The 'Mason Arms' at Swerford seemed a desirable place for lunch and there I met a farmer who had a grudge against the grey squirrel, not only because it had exterminated the native brown squirrel but he declared it was killing off the stoats and weasels and that two of them had actually killed his cat! This is rather too much to stomach!

As there was time to spare and the weather was fine I decided to go on

---

4 'Old Frankie' was perhaps the elderly owner of Webbs' Tearooms.

to Banbury via South Newington and Bloxham instead of to Buckingham direct. The long slopes on the road to Buckingham via Farthinghoe, Brackley and Westbury were somewhat trying with a strong headwind but I reached Buckingham well ahead of time. When Wood turned up we had tea at the 'Grand Junction Hotel' and then after one or two false starts found the road we wanted via Croughton, Aynho and Deddington turning right at Swerford and eventually finding ourselves at Great Tew.

After a drink at the 'Falkland Arms' we proceeded to our quarters where a pleasant surprise awaited us for we were greeted there by Mr and Mrs Emery. Our resting place kept by Mrs Matthews, the saddler's wife, proved a great success and we retired to roost after an excellent supper, very content.

Distance covered: 66 miles

SUNDAY 10TH MAY

Loiterers in the act of loitering

GREAT TEW – BICESTER – LONG CRENDON – PRINCES RISBOROUGH – AMERSHAM – EASTCOTE –SOUTHALL – HAMMERSMITH

After breakfast, I spent some time with the Emerys in exploration and then took the road to Bicester I had travelled on the 25th. We had a very indifferent lunch at a restaurant and then proceeded about 2½ miles along the Aylesbury road before turning right for Blackthorn, Oakley, Long Crendon and Thame spending some time in Long Crendon photographing the Court house.

The seven miles to Princes Risborough was unexpectedly tough and it being past 5 o'clock we decided on tea at the 'Buckingham Arms' before tackling the 'mountain' between Risborough and Missenden. Once over this obstacle and on the main road we soon bowled along through Amersham and Chorley Wood to Rickmansworth. Wood on his 35" gear insisted on riding up Moore Park Hill while I walked and at the top found a party of his Northern Section loiterers in the act of 'loitering'.

At Eastcote we had light refreshment at the once famous cyclists' house the 'Ship' now also a boozing den for all and sundry. As usual I got mixed up at Greenford and eventually came on to the Uxbridge road at Southall leaving us a nice trafficky seven miles home which we reached about 9.30 p.m.

Distance covered: 76 miles

1931 EARLY SUMMER 'TOURLET' – MERLIN I

THURSDAY 18TH JUNE

Most romantic woodland

HAMMERSMITH – WINDSOR – WALTHAM ST. LAWRENCE – HUNGERFORD – RAMSBURY – MARLBOROUGH – HUNGERFORD

In spite of a sore toe I decided on a four day easy 'tourlet'.

I took the usual Windsor, Waltham, Twyford route to Reading stopping for bread, cheese and beer at the 'Bell' Waltham St. Lawrence. The Bath road from Reading was fairly empty on a Thursday afternoon and at Hungerford I turned right. At Chilton Foliat a heavy shower delayed me in a dry and pleasant spot by the River Kennet for about half an hour before I resumed my way to Ramsbury where the 'Bleeding Horse' gave me a first class tea, though it could not put me up for the night.

From Ramsbury I returned to Chilton and passing over the bridge turned right at the bottom. This took me through some most romantic woodland skirting Littlecote Park and after much climbing over rough roads eventually brought me out at Froxfield on the Bath road. The evening being fine and the road good I went on to Marlboro' but having no handbook with me I decided to return to the safety of the 'Red Lion' at Hungerford for the night, which I found satisfactory quarters.

Distance covered: 84 miles

FRIDAY 19TH JUNE

A thundery evening

HUNGERFORD – EAST GRAFTON – PEWSEY – DEVIZES – TROWBRIDGE – LACOCK

After breakfasting off haddock and poached eggs I left Hungerford about 9.30 a.m. and after a mile or so of the main road I turned left to Little Bedwyn and Great Bedwyn and by bye-roads to East Grafton, a charming scattered village consisting entirely of thatched dwellings.

Eschewing Burbage and the main road I took further lanes through Easton Royal and Milton Lilbourne, which brought me out into Pewsey. Here a heavy storm drove me to shelter for about half an hour. Instead of the direct road to Devizes in Woodborough I preferred what looked on the map something more strenuous by way of Alton Priors. Stanton St. Bernards attracted me off the road but it proved a disappointing village, too much new red brick having cropped up among the original stucco and thatch.

Soon after regaining the road the storm which had been threatening all the morning overtook me but had spent its force in about half an hour which I spent in a cowshed, and I was able to proceed into Devizes where the 'Unicorn' gave me a lunch of beef which went down rather well. The rain had nearly ceased when I continued on the road to Trowbridge via Seend and Semington.

About five miles from Trowbridge my back tyre expired with a sigh and I had to retire down a side lane for repairs. Trowbridge presented its usual busy aspect and I retraced my way for two miles and then turned left through Hilperton and Staverton to Melksham arriving at Lacock's 'Corner House' for tea just before 5 o'clock. A thundery evening made photography difficult as about 8 o'clock I toiled to the top of Bowden Hill marvelling at the extent of the view in the clear atmosphere after the thunderstorms.

Distance covered: 54 miles

1931 EARLY SUMMER 'TOURLET'

SATURDAY 20TH JUNE
Calamity at Tetbury
LACOCK – COMPTON BASSETT – MALMESBURY – TETBURY – CIRENCESTER – FAIRFORD – BURFORD

There is no more difficult place to leave on a sunshiny morning than Lacock and by the time I had conversed with practically everyone in the village and taken some more photographs it was nearly 12 o'clock. Once more did I toil up Bowden Hill taking the short cut to Calne from whence about two miles along the main London road a left turns leads to Compton Bassett, a charming village with architecture of the Castle Combe type. Here I loitered at the 'White Horse Inn' until nearly 2.30 p.m. before making my way by various tortuous lanes via Hilmarton, Beacon Hill and Foxham to Christian Malford.

Time forbade me from going onto Castle Combe, which had been my intention, so I made for Sutton Benger and took the direct road through Seagry to Malmesbury. The tea I had at the "Abbey Café" was neither cheap nor bountiful but sufficient and having bags of time the familiar direct road to Cirencester did not appear. I accordingly went round via Tetbury, a plain sort of town but with a rather picturesque market place. The town was in a state of excitement, with the local picture palace having been burnt out during the afternoon and the ruins still smoking away.

From Tetbury to Cirencester is a very fast stretch and the views of Cirencester in the evening sun coming into the town off this road, though most impressive, refused to adapt itself to photography. Cirencester to Lechlade through Ampney Crucis, Poulton and Fairford is always a fast stretch and in spite of half an hour at the 'Three Horseshoes' I reached the 'Swan' at Burford soon after 8.30 p.m., Mr and Mrs Sissons arriving about ten minutes after.

Distance covered: 64 miles

SUNDAY 21ST JUNE

Gorging on strawberries

BURFORD – BUCKLAND – KINGSTON BAGPUIZE – ABINGDON – GORING HEATH – WALTHAM ST. LAWRENCE – WINDSOR – FELTHAM – HAMMERSMITH

The longest day gave promise of a real summer's day at last. Wood who was expected to breakfast failed to appear but Mr Emery had made a night or rather early morning, run of it from Watford and turned up about 8 o'clock.

The Sissons and I loitered until nearly 12 o'clock before getting on the road, and the road via Bampton, Buckland, Kingston Bagpuize and Tubney to Abingdon was new to them. We gorged on strawberries at Kingston Bagpuize and it was 1.30 p.m. before we reached the 'Blue Boar' Abingdon for lunch (steak pie, peas, spinach and potatoes and banana trifle). It was 3 o'clock when we left there on the Dorchester road, turning over Sutton Courtenay Bridge through Appleford to Wallingford.

We kept up a steady pace and arrived at the 'King Charles' Head' Goring Heath at 4.45 p.m. for tea. The same steady pace took us down to Caversham across the Great West road through Twyford and Waltham St. Lawrence, Windsor, Horton, Stanwell, Bedfont, Feltham and Twickenham in excellent time. I arrived home at 9.30 p.m., the Sissons who were lamp less, proceeding on their way to their home at Regent's Park.

Distance covered: 85 miles

1931 THE CONTINENTAL TOUR – FRANCE, GERMANY AND AUSTRIA

FRIDAY 17TH JULY AND SATURDAY 18TH JULY

A wet and dismal evening decided me to take the train to St. Pancras Station instead of going by road as had been my intention. I had got my specially prepared machine (Merlin 3) into the Guard's Van before discovering I had left my wrist watch behind. My mount had to be yanked out again while I returned to fetch the missing article. Nevertheless I was at St. Pancras 1¼ hours before the train started and a good half hour before Wood arrived.

The registration of the bicycles to Strasburg was a tedious process and by the time we got to the special boat train every seat was occupied. In the meantime we had picked up a young man with a bicycle (hereinafter referred to as Gerwinkle) who "had been there before" and proposed to know all about it. We finally got seats in the Guard's Van on various bales of goods, for the trip to Tilbury. At Tilbury passports had to be produced, the customs were passed (a pure formality in our cases) and we pushed on to the 'S.S. Picard' which already seemed fairly crowded. Gerwinkle, who knew all about it, led the way and as he much preferred climbing up the rigging to using stairways we temporarily lost him, my age and Wood's weight being rather against us in this exercise.

Jack and I finally came to rest on a seat in the forepart of the boat where we spent a damp and somewhat chilly night getting what comfort we could out of our capes. Once clear of the Thames the ship began to get somewhat lively. This had quite the reverse effect on many of the passengers and sounds of regurgitation were heard all around so that one instinctively made oneself as small as possible to avoid getting splashed. Sleep was rendered impossible by a noisy crowd nearby, one of whom in an advanced stage of combined intoxication and seasickness made himself a complete nuisance to everybody by staggering around falling over everybody's legs, falling down stairways and being carelessly sick in every direction. How he escaped going overboard is a mystery and had he done so everybody would have (if their stomachs permitted it) heaved a sigh of relief.

A watery dawn at last appeared. Gerwinkle was discovered wrapped in a blanket in a deck chair – a dry island surrounded by a sea of sickness. As desolate Dunkirk came nearer the sea flattened and the sick saw a new hope of life. We were badly placed for disembarkation and were somewhat late in getting through the French Customs. The obtaining of a *"permis de circulation"* for each of our bicycles was a tedious process so that we very nearly lost the train. However, we just achieved our object with the aid of two French porters, one of whom made Jack squirm by riding his beloved Sunbeam over the metals to save time, before hurling it into the luggage van.

We just had time to see my Merlin also pitched in "all ends up" before scrambling aboard just as the train was on the move. We were thankful to find breakfast about to be served and did full justice to our first Continental meal after which we settled down for the somewhat tedious journey across rain soaked France. When we had at last been permitted to remove our cycles from the Customs we had noticed Gerwinkle's machine standing against the wall neglected and concluded he was coming on by a later train. We were therefore surprised when he turned up in our compartment during the course of the morning. He was quite confident that his bicycle had followed him on to the train and that the formality of a *"permis de circulation"* was unnecessary and, in spite of what we told him, he seemed quite satisfied that it was in the luggage van.

The tedium of the journey was broken at 12.30 p.m. by a very excellent lunch of many courses and we at last reached Strasburg at about 3.30 p.m. Our bicycles minus much enamel were duly unloaded but an inspection of the luggage van by Gerwinkle revealed no trace of his mount and he at last came to the conclusion that his confidence was misplaced. He was going to Colmar so we never heard the end of his trouble but it is quite certain from what we had seen at Dunkirk that he found himself cycle-less when he got there.

Before embarking at Tilbury we had stripped our machines of everything removable therefore it was somewhat amusing to find that mine had acquired a pump en route. However I already had one in my bag so I left the acquisition at Strasburg Station. The rather trying journey had burdened me with a jumpy headache which was not improved by the four miles of pave through the grey streets of Strasburg to the Pont du Rhin where we crossed the Rhine into Germany. The French Customs people seemed somewhat excited before we were allowed to proceed but on the other side our reception was most urbane by an official who spoke perfect English.

The German town of Kehl opposite Strasburg presents a complete contrast to that city. Here all is bright and clean and though we had some trouble just outside the town owing to 'road-up'[5], it was a pleasant level country we ambled through with several clean looking villages on the way in each of which we noticed one or more "*gast hausen*" (inns).

At Offenburg, a largish town I got some cigarettes of curious flavour and in due course we arrived at our first stopping place, Gengenbach where we had been recommended to the *gast haus* 'Salinen'. Here we entered but all my knowledge of German evaporated and I did not know what to ask for. Interpreters were looked for in vain and at last I gasped out "*Wir sind Freundts von Herr Clarke*". This did the trick and we were soon in possession of "*Ein zimmer mit zwei betten*" and after a wash were sitting down to a "*Schnitzel von schweinefleisch mit kartofflen*" which was of course preceeded by a soup of unknown ingredients but of excellent taste. After this a German who knew some English came in, and from him we learnt some words and my first phrases for future use.

I was glad to get to bed soon after 10 p.m. my first experience of a German bed under which and not upon which you lie. This however did not keep me awake.

Distance covered by bicycle from Strasburg to Gengenbach: 22 miles.

SUNDAY 19TH JULY

Gengenbach was all astir on this Sunday morning long before we were – church bells were sending out their message to the faithful and while we

---

5 A road in disrepair.

were getting up we saw many weird and wonderful costumes – the peasant garb being quite picturesque and always finished off by an umbrella.

The usual Continental breakfast, of coffee and rolls was supplemented by an egg each and after this blow-out we inspected the town before preparing to flit. It is a particularly attractive one and especially so on a Sunday morning with all the peasants in their best clothes. At one corner on the top of a high chimney was a stork's nest which, though inconvenient to the owner of the chimney, is a very picturesque item. On our return to the *gasthaus* we were both photographed and of course returned the compliment by photographing Frau Maier and the three frauleins, the eldest of whom, Elsa, is well worth photographing. After this operation it started to rain with such goodwill that we delayed our start until 11.30 a.m., the rain then showing no signs of ceasing.

The road we took was an easy one as far as Hausach though we could see plenty of trouble ahead. At Hausach we were feeling in need of sustenance and found a *gasthaus* (zum Hirsch), which had a sideway, promising cover for our machines. In the *gasthaus* we were rather at a loss what to ask for with our limited knowledge of German. However I could only think of what can sometimes be obtained in English inns and by demanding "*speck und eier*" obtained an extraordinary looking compound of fat bacon and six eggs all in one forum. It had to be cut up in squares but we were in no mood to cavil at anything eatable and it went down with gusto. I found the beer an excellent lubricant, while Jack had to make do with "*mineral wasser*" – fizzy stuff with a funny taste.

The rain had ceased when we had finished this curious meal and as we were preparing to depart, a young German came up and greeted us profusely in moderately good English. He appeared quite mortified that we could not come back into the house and let him practise his English on us. We finally parted with much ceremony and good wishes not heeding his warning that the road to Triberg (our next move) was very steep. It did very soon begin to go up through Gutach and Hornberg but nothing to call bottom gears into action until the top of the town of Triberg, a largish, bright, clear place.

There was a path at the end of the town by the side of a waterfall which would have been taken had the weather been a little more promising but we preferred to stick to the road and the way it began to rise made bottom gears a fixture for some miles. At Schönwald we attained an altitude of 3000 feet. This town is a kind of health resort and winter sports ground and as such it is possible to imagine a very pleasant stay could be made there.

From Furtwangen, about five miles further on, there was a descent of a few miles after which we climbed once more finally reaching the 'Pension Zum Nene Eck' which was our stopping place for the night. Our request for "*ein zimmer mit zwei betten*" was favourably received and the suggestion of soup and 'wiener schnitzel' followed by tart commended itself to us favourably. The proprietor, who had a hairless head very suggestive of the egg of the extinct Aepiornis[6], wished us "*guten appetits*" I replied to show that he was understood "*wir haben grosses appetits*". This upset Jack who thought I was accusing him of having a gross appetite so that proceedings were delayed while I explained that "gross" is the German word for "large" and it would have been curious if we had not large appetites after the strenuous 40 miles we had covered with nothing to eat since lunch.

Distance covered: 54 miles

MONDAY 20TH JULY

The country around New Eck presented none too cheerful appearance in the morning though in fine weather the surrounding scenery must have been gorgeous. We had the usual breakfast of coffee and rolls with stuff they called "*hovey*" which was really some kind of vegetable spirit.

We took the road through Neustadt, the centre of the Schwarzwald (Black Forest) clock industry. Here we had an excellent lunch at the 'Gasthaus zum Engel' where we left our cycles while we explored the town. A long-threatened storm burst upon us just as we were preparing to resume our journey and we had to continue for some time in capes.

We wished to make for the Titisee and from hence onto Bonndorf. We found the Titisee, a somewhat tame lake, but took a walk along a path by the shore for some distance leaving our machines by the wayside. While we were contemplating a little photography two hikers came along, one of whom claimed acquaintance with Jack asking him if his name was not Wood and did not come from N15. On enquiry it appeared they had never met in England or elsewhere. We were somewhat mystified for a time but of course the stranger had seen the bicycles by the wayside weighed up the Sunbeam with Wood divided by two and got the correct answer.[7]

---

6 An genus of enormous flightless birds that once lived in Madagascar and produced the largest bird eggs ever discovered

7 The suggestion is the address on the bicycle was either Jack's or the retailer of the Sunbeam, probably in Wood Green which would have been in postcode N15.

From Titisee we took a rising road by the side of the lake in capes as the rain had started once more. At a fork in the road we were at a loss wanting to get to Bonndorf a place we could not find on the map. While we were under a tree considering the matter a German cyclist came up his cycling garb including (inter alia) a flowing frock coat. He got out a map and I intended asking him if Bonndorf was marked on it. I got as far as "*Haben sie Bonndorf*" when he not only indicated it on the map but drew our attention to a signpost pointing to that town which we had overlooked – a double fault on our part as we were also studying the wrong map.

The road took us through Rothaus, chiefly famous for its beer and by a hamlet bearing the suggestive name of Zeebruge near which at the 'Gasthaus zum Altglasshutten' we had some coffee accompanied by a kind of pudding (*Kuchen* (cake) was what we asked for), which was extremely palatable!

Hereabouts on a steep rise we were taken on by a couple of yokels but they were over geared and soon died away. This road skirted the Schluchsee, a large but uninteresting lake and we were constantly shaken by the reverberations of blasting operations in the vicinity. It was still raining when we reached Bonndorf, a large plain town and we went on to Dorfbull, a small muddy village which we reached after a precipitous descent.

At the 'Gasthaus zum Grunenberg' we were well received and the rain having ceased we ordered "*schinken mit eier*" *(ham with eggs)* at 9 o'clock and took a stroll through the woods along the Rutach but the weather did not justify our going as far as the waterfall at the bottom. The "*schinken mit eier*" was a strange compound but went down very well.

Distance covered: 42 miles

TUESDAY 21ST JULY

Dorfbull seemed full of hardworking cattle drawing heavy loads up steep and slippery slopes this morning. The crowning infamy of all was that the poor old cows, after they had done their duty in supplying the morning milk, were harnessed to heavy waggons with a lump of wire netting tied over their muzzles to prevent them taking any refreshment by the roadside to lighten their toil.

We left the "Gasthaus zum Grunenberg" with the usual good wishes and "*Auf Wiedersehens*" and there seemed nothing for it but to retrace our way at any rate to Bonndorf. The slope we had come down last night proved too much to ascend even with our bottom gears and we took the first compulsory walk of the tour for about half a mile.

As we were leaving Bonndorf we discovered a German operating on us with a cinematograph apparatus and we stopped at the top where he insisted on taking us together and stuck a bargain to supply us each with three prints on payment of two marks. We of course had to trust him to send on the prints but we had already learnt that the German is an honest soul and we had no misgivings on this score.

We proceeded nearly into Rothaus taking a road signposted to Grafenhausen. This proved rather a tough problem and at one time we were doubtful if we could get on. However it led us over a brickbat surface round a large electrical workshop placarded with all manner of notices of things that were *"verboten"* (prohibited). We had visions of being seized and treated as spies.

However a fierce and tough upward grade brought us back into civilization again and the 'Gasthaus zum Hirschen' at Staufen supplied us with much needed sustenance. Much roughriding brought us via Häusern to Sankt Blasien, a large and pleasant town. Here we spent about an hour. The church is the lion of the place with a dome rivalling St. Paul's. The interior is most richly decorated and is full of shrines to various saints with relics complete.

I succeeded in getting some so called American cigarettes but they tasted much the same as the native article. A very rising road past a large Sanatorium eventually led us to a high altitude from which there was a terrific descent with many hair pins into Todtmoos. Jack with his superior weight got there a good mile ahead of me and I found him cooling his brakes outside the 'Gasthaus Maiern' where we proposed spending the night. As usual the *"zimmer mit zwei betten"* was forthcoming and after a high tea we ordered *"abendessen"* *(dinner)* for 9 o'clock and set out to explore the town, a pleasant enough little place with a highly decorated church surrounded by fine rolling countryside.

The supper proved all that could be desired and we were glad to turn in after a short but strenuous *stage of some 38 miles.*

WEDNESDAY 22ND JULY

A pleasant sunny morning induced us to delay our departure from Todtmoos until about 11 a.m. Further delay was caused on the road to Wehr a few miles out of the town waiting for the sun to shine for photographic purposes. We had left our cycles by the roadside and ventured into a flowery meadow which seemed to be inhabited by every creeping, biting, flying and jumping insect including immense grasshoppers, evil looking but quite harmful creatures about an inch and a half in length. While we were there a German of the agricultural class on the road got very excited about something. We could not understand what he was driving at but probably we were trespassing and he thought we were doing so with evil intent perhaps with designs on the *"bloomen"* the plucking of which around Todtmoos is *"streng verboten"* (strictly prohibited).

The sun refused to be kind and we resumed our way along a particularly delectable road by the side of a river which led us to Wehr – a rather ordinary sort of town – and the road to Säckingen is also of the most ordinary description. From Säckingen we proposed taking a short train journey to Griessen preparatory to passing into Switzerland. It was about 12.30 p.m. when we got there and on enquiry we found there was no train until 3.23 p.m.. Luckily the town had many picturesque streets so the time passed fairly profitably.

At the 'Gasthuas zum Adler' where we met an English speaking German we did well with an excellent *"Schnitzel"* followed by *"obst"* (fruit) in the way of stewed cherries and then a large plate of fresh red currants each. The latter with plenty of sugar went down wonderfully.

Jack was anxious to cross the bridge over the Rhine into Switzerland but I feared complications with cycles and dissuaded him. When the train came in we duly put our cycles on board. By error we had taken 3rd class tickets instead of 2nd class. The seats were hard for the short but somewhat tedious journey but we did see all manner of people at each of the forty (more or less) stops before we reached our destination. It was nearly 6 o'clock when we arrived at Griessen and we might easily have ridden there and back on our cycles by the same time. We had coffee at the 'Gasthuas zum Krone' before taking to the road again.

At the German Customs House before passing into Switzerland we were mistaken for Dutch, the official apparently not recognising a British passport. However when we explained we were English, all was well. At the Swiss Custom House at Neuhausen our cycles were subjected to a strict scrutiny especially as to the maker's number but as usual we passed without any examination of baggage. A nice paved road with rampant tramlines runs down from Neuhausen to Schaffhausen – a fine bit of road to find out if there's anything loose on our cycles.

Schaffhausen is such a fine swank town that we were rather at a loss where to put up. We chose the 'Hotel Lowen' (Lion) and ordering supper for 9 o'clock went out to see the sights. We found Schaffhausen a very beautiful town and were especially attracted by the parts down by the bridge over the Rhine. There are innumerable picturesque streets, good shops and any amount of flowerbed-decked fountains.

When we returned to our hotel we were taken in charge by a sandy faced damsel who seemed to regard us both as a huge joke. However we fed well enough and our sleeping accommodation was all that could be desired. Before returning for supper we made enquiries at the railway station as to trains for St. Margrethen on the morrow. I did my worst in mingled French and German only to find the booking clerk spoke good English and we decided to leave by the 1.50 p.m. train tomorrow afternoon. *Our day's riding only amounted to 35 miles.*

THURSDAY 23RD JULY

We had the morning to amuse ourselves in Schaffhausen and as we were moving off the maps in our possession a further one was a necessity. After trying two shops we obtained one which while being nothing great, would suffice. On the further side of the Rhine Bridge we met two English cyclists with whom we spent about half an hour. When we parted from them we decided to settle up at our Hotel and go up to Neuhausen to see the Rhine falls.

The settling up process cleared us out of Swiss currency except for a few francs and we proposed to remedy this on our return from Neuhausen. We found the falls a magnificent spectacle and well worth the toil of getting there. There were a polyglot lot of spectators and I found Jack trying to conduct a conversation in bad German with a particularly hunnish looking old specimen until the latter and Jack discovered that they were both in fact English!

Having had some experience of registering cycles on Continental railways we thought it prudent to be at the station a generous time before the train started. Consequently we pelted down that vile four miles of road back to Schaffhausen with the consequence that my lamp became seriously deranged, so much so that that it took a permanent place in my bag.

Our first consideration was to change some sterling into Swiss francs and we were rather disturbed to find the banks closed from noon until

A GOLDEN AGE OF CYCLING

2 p.m. A Swiss damsel who spoke some English said her master would certainly change it for us and after enquiring of him informed us he would give us 70 centime for each English shilling (14 francs to the £). This was rather more than we could stand, the correct rate being something about 24, so the offer was declined and we subsequently obtained our exchange at the proper rate at an AA Hotel.

We were leaving Switzerland for good and after paying our fares we were so cleared out that we had nothing but a few centimes to tip the porter who looked after our cycles. I offered him two good German marks but he refused them and took the 10 centimes. The journey was of the usual slow continental kind with innumerable stops, the line running through not very interesting country alongside the Bodensee (Lake Constance).

After changing at Rorschach we duly arrived at St. Margrethen about 3.45p.m., having had no sustenance since a light breakfast at 8.30 a.m. except two bananas and some chocolate. Furthermore we had no Swiss money so to find a bank was the first importance. Closing time nearly arrived before we did so and I presented a French 5 franc note and got in exchange a few Swiss centimes. I had of course forgotten the poverty of the French franc and explained the error to the cashier who saw the joke and I got some more for a 50 franc note.

We satisfied our wants for the time being at a small gasthaus before going over the border into Austria. Here our formidable triptyques[8] came into operation and we got our first entry into Austria marked on sheet two at the Custom House, where we were treated with the same courtesy we had received in Germany. The cyclists we had seen this morning had mentioned a good stopping place at Bludenz, but when we reached Feldkirch, prudence made us decide to stay the night there. After looking around we decided on the 'Gasthaus zum Weisses Rossl' where we were received with the utmost urbanity. In the meantime our cycles were surrounded by a huge mob of critics and we had some difficulty in extricating them to put them away for the night. From a stroll round before supper we formed a very good opinion of our first Austrian town.

The *Wiener schnitzel* which we had with the usual trimmings for supper was quite excellent.

Distance covered: 22 miles

---

8 A customs permit serving as a passport for a motor vehicle

FRIDAY 24TH JULY

After an early breakfast notwithstanding some time spent in exploring and photographing the picturesque parts of the town, we got away at 10 o'clock as we knew we had a strenuous time in front of us. The road has a general upward tendency to Bludenz and after that town bottom gears became a permanent institution. This was the start of the Arlberg Pass and we had struck a nice hot day for it.

Jack was soon reduced to shirt and shorts but my coat being burdened with too many important documents had to remain on my back. About 2.30 p.m. at a small *gasthaus* where we called for light refreshment, Jack who had been perspiring freely, made a great discovery. Up to now his liquid refreshment other than coffee had been confined to mineral "*wasser*" (hereinbefore described). His great discovery at this unimportant hostelry was a sickly red compound called "*himmwasser*" or "*himbeer*". He felt much better after consuming many litres of this and henceforth his war cry at every gasthaus we visited was "*Haben sie Himbeer?*".

Fortified by this we continued our hard labour until Stuben, where the road goes up with a bang in a series of hairpins. We did a little walking here for the first time today and about halfway up to the first hairpin we found a car in distress, the owner of which was conveying water to it for the radiator in his hat. I noted the car bore an English number plate and made a remark to him as we passed to his apparent astonishment at being addressed in his own language.

After getting round the corner we got on our machines once again for a short distance but the gradient was too much even for our bottom gears and we walked to the top, a distance of about one mile. We encountered on the way two hikers, apparently Italians with whom we carried on a difficult conversation in several languages for a space before parting with best wishes.

There was a very fine view from the top and also it was apparent that a storm was approaching, which rendered it advisable not to linger too long. The descent for the first few miles is a very steep one with many hairpin bends, the surface of the road being very loose at each bend. The storm was obviously approaching and as we passed through St. Anton the rain commenced accompanied by thunder. We put on our capes and, coming to a village with a large gasthaus, decided to put up there for the night. The village was Pettneu and at the *'Gasthaus zum Hirschen'* we spent a somewhat amusing evening watching among other things the lads and lassies of the village dancing to the strains of a somewhat cracked gramophone. However we had an excellent *schnitzel* for supper and Jack was able to swill large quantities of his new discovery.

Distance covered: 44 miles

SATURDAY 25TH JULY

After a frugal breakfast we prepared to make an early start for the continuation of our journey down the Arlberg Pass looking forward to an easy day of mainly downhill work. There was much new snow on the tops of the mountains, the result of last night's storm and looking back the scene was a fairy-like one. As we anticipated it was mainly downhill as far as Landeck with the Rosanna river below on the right, a picturesque mountain road with indifferent surface such as all Austrian main roads have. We reached Landeck about 11.30 a.m., too early for a call at the 'Goldener Adler' of which the proprietor Herr G. Berchten is the Chief Consul of the C.T.C. for Austria. We however found a bank there and replenished the exchequer with Austrian currency of which we were running short.

The road onward is anything but downhill and as it commenced to rain at Imst, a fair sized town, we looked around for a suitable feeding station, selecting the 'Gasthaus zum Lamm' where we fared excellently at small expense. By the time our hunger was appeased the rain had ceased sufficiently for us to go on without capes. The road was still very rough and at one point disappeared into a heap of stones without any warning notice that we saw. We had seen very little in the way of motor traffic and this no doubt accounted for it.

We clambered over the rubble and picked up the road again on the other side and after crossing the river at Haiming it became not only comparatively flat but with quite a good surface. This made us rub our eyes and wonder if we really were still in Austria. Thenceforward the river now on our left broadened out considerably. We were able to move along this road faster than we had done for days and I almost pined for my 84" gear. We took our substitute for tea (coffee, rolls and marmalade made of red currants) at the 'Gasthaus zum Tranbe' in Pfaffenhofen and reached Innsbruck through Zirl about 6.30 p.m.

Our next business was to find the 'Goldener Adler' and when we found it we were rather appalled at its swankiness. However, our enquiry was answered satisfactorily and we were conducted to our "*zimmer*" by the porter. Before he left us he kept on reiterating what sounded like "Wey". At last we handed him the dictionary and he pointed to "*Juli*"– the German for month of July. We at once said "*ya*" and this seemed to make him happy but we never knew what he was trying to tell us.

Our evening stroll round Innsbruck revealed it as a very fine city indeed but it was cut short by the approach of a thunderstorm, which started very soon after we had reached the shelter of our hotel. We therefore at once went up to the dining room and obtained seats in an already somewhat crowded room, the centre of which was occupied by a small platform upon which was seated a gentleman of the entertainer species in full Tyrolese costume, who accompanied himself in his songs on the zither. His efforts were greatly applauded but it was our misfortune not to be able to understand his words. A verse of one of the songs was obviously an impromptu effort at Jack's expense, probably directed at the famous many coloured stockings and we should very much have liked to know what it was about.

The menu was yards long and quite incomprehensible to us so fortunately an elderly dame who appeared to be in charge of the culinary department and spoke good English came to our rescue and we did very well. Fancy dress seems customary in Innsbruck and there were some most extraordinary costumes in that room. When we had finished feeding, an old flower seller who might have been transported from Piccadilly Circus in the 1890s made her appearance. Her face would have made her fortune on the films and her capacity for beer was enormous. I think Andreas Hofer, the entertainer was considerably relived when she took her departure so that he could get on with his job.

Jack and I began to let our imagination play on the company. In an alcove on our left was a beautiful but unscrupulous Russian Countess with two simple looking men, obviously dangerous vampires exploiting her charms for stealing the plans of the very latest type of submarine from one of her dupes. Royalties in disguise abounded and poisonous blondes were in profusion. Neither of us would have been surprised to see the late William Le Queux[9] walk in arm in arm with E. Phillips Oppenheim[10]. Yes, that evening at the Goldener Adler was well worth the money and we both hope to repeat it someday.

Distance covered: 61 miles

9 William Le Queux (1864–1927) was a spy novelist, journalist, diplomat and traveller
10 E. Phillips Oppenheim (1866–1946) was a renowned writer of thrillers

SUNDAY 26TH JULY

We were out early seeing the Sunday morning sights of Innsbruck and endeavouring to stalk some of the more interesting specimens with cameras, and we almost felt disposed to spend the whole day in this fascinating town. However, our time was unfortunately limited so about 11 o'clock we decided to pack up and move on.

We had first to make our way back to Zirl and on the way thither a rather curious thing happened. On the left hand side of the road there was a sheer drop of a considerable distance and a German cyclist coming towards us and evidently riding carelessly, suddenly disappeared over the top. He could not have gone far for in a very few minutes he reappeared dragging his bicycle after him, remounted and went on his way as though nothing had happened.

In Zirl we turned right and then left and were very soon on our feet, the road going up like the side of a house. We continued walking, pushing and perspiring for about two miles when we came on a car with scotches under its wheels having a rest to cool down. It certainly appeared in need of a rest for its brakes were smoking furiously. An elderly lady within fired off a volley of German at us as we came up. We tried in vain to make something of it and at last took refuge behind "*Nicht verstehen English*". This drew shrieks of laughter from a brown faced young woman who was at the wheel and we were soon on the best of terms with what turned out to be an American party who had been wintering in Italy. I particularly appreciated their Gold Flake cigarettes as I had had nothing but the native article for some days. We stopped to talk to them for nearly half an hour until their brakes had cooled sufficiently for them to proceed.

We have often wondered since whether they got to the bottom safely for we found out that what they had done so far was nothing compared to what they had to do; in fact shortly after leaving them we were able to resume our saddles, on bottom gears of course.

The road goes up all the way to Seefeld where we had light refreshments at a wayside gasthaus and, shortly after getting through Scharnitz in the Scharnitz Pass, we took a temporary exit from Austria and passed through the German Customs at Mittenwald. Mittenwald is a most picturesque town, but we were unfortunate in striking it on a Sunday for it was full of motors and hikers, being somewhat of a showplace and within easy reach of the Oberammergau tourist district. Here our bicycles became a centre of attraction to a polyglot crowd.

We were out of the Austrian Tyrol into the Bavarian Alps and it was evident that the Bavarians are as dressy as their neighbours. At Kaltenbrunn we had coffee, rolls and marmalade (red currants again) followed in Jack's case by several litres of "*Himbeer*". I also tried this compound but found it rather nasty. When we mentioned we were going on to Partenkirchen, the good Frau of 'Gasthaus zum Kaltenbrunn' got very excited. It was evident she wished to warn us of some terrible danger that awaited us in that town and that we had much better stay where we were. With true British spirit we refused to be intimidated and proceeded on our way.

When we got to Partenkirchen we found this small but picturesque town en fete with crowded streets and everybody in their most fantastic garb. One of the first objects that met our eyes was a cow wandering down the main street with a wreath of flowers twined round its horns. We found that the cause of all this excitement was that the town had been indulging in a passion play which is the national sport of this part of Bavaria. We picked out the 'Gasthaus zum Melber' as being the most respectful hostel but it was full up. However they speedily found us 'B&B' quarters in a neighbouring house which proved one of the cheapest 'put ups' we had struck. We were told we must not fail to go up the "*Wank Bahn*" so we went and had a look at it before supper. This is a cable railway which slings you up to the top of a mountain like a cwt[11] of coal. It looked too terrifying but Jack was keen on it so with my heart in my boots I consented to accompany him on the morrow.

A young man at our billet who spoke some English informed us that we would feed both well and cheaply at the 'Gasthaus zum Melber'. So hither we repaired ordering a supper of many courses. It was an excellent repast but we were rather dismayed when the hors d'oeuvres consisting of six sardines sitting on a lump of butter, turned up last of all. Jack jibbed at his but I, concluding that it must be the custom of the country, gobbled down mine with gusto having a second "*gross bier*" to wash them down.

Distance covered: 34 miles

---

11 Abbreviation of hundredweight (112 lb)

MONDAY 27TH JULY

We had an early breakfast in our billet and after transacting some necessary bank business and shopping, repaired to the "*Wank Bahn*" Station and duly took our tickets for the first run. There were quite a lot of passengers and the car when it started was about as crowded as a Tube lift at a busy time of the day. It was not unlike a Tube lift – a sort of octagonal chamber but with windows that you could lean out of if you liked. I believe the trip only lasted ten minutes but it seemed like hours to me. In fact it was quite as unpleasant as I anticipated, especially as it passed over the standards and bounced so that your breakfast seemed to hit the top of your head. Perhaps the worst part of it is the last stage when the car goes up almost vertically creaking and groaning and swaying so that you fear either that it will stop and leave you forever hanging between earth and sky or that the suspending cable will break and let you down on the town some 6000 feet below.

When I got out at the top everything was swimming with me for a good ten minutes. The views over innumerable mountain peaks were prodigious and for 10 Pfennig one could gaze through a large telescope for a few minutes. We both had a go but my senses were too stirred up for me to see much. Reason tells me that all the nasty sensations I felt coming up were reasonless and I shall certainly try it again if the chance comes along.

An hour 'upstairs' was enough for us and strange to say the journey down was not half so unpleasant. Nevertheless I was very glad to find myself at the bottom. We settled up at our billet and got on the road about 11.45 a.m. making first for the neighbouring town of Garmisch. We had to enter Austria once more and passed over the frontier at Griessen. Unfortunately we had neglected to fill up at a gasthaus before doing so for we found no feeding station on the other side.

We made a false start at first and had to retrace our way, taking a very 4th class looking road. This got worse and worse until we were soon floundering on brickbats and loose stones. Jack's weight kept him steady but I came off twice, the second occasion necessitating the application of iodine to a broken shin. We at length came out on the shores of the Plansee, the lake we were seeking, and anything more entrancing to the eye can scarcely be imagined than this mountainous expanse of water of a deep emerald green sparkling in the sunshine. We regretted afterwards that we did not photograph the scene as it first appeared to us but the pangs of hunger were too great to allow us to think of much else.

We made for the palatial 'Hotel Forelle' and after a wash made our way to the restaurant. It was about 3.30 p.m. and hardly a suitable hour for lunch. However we explained matters to what I presume was the reception clerk, a most urbane young man who spoke some English and his suggestion of some trout from the lake was received with applause. That fish was delicious and was followed by a pudding of unknown brand. I consumed three litres of beer while Jack consumed a few quarts of his favourite "*himbeer*", the request for which occasioned some amusement.

Unfortunately when we had finished this feast it began to rain and continued until nightfall. Even so we strolled around sufficiently to fill us with enthusiasm for our surroundings. We had another big feed about 7.30 p.m. and spent the rest of the evening writing postcards to various folk.

Distance covered: 20 miles

TUESDAY 28TH JULY

It was alas still raining in the morning when we got up. It was small comfort to be told by the genial King George-like old gentleman who presided over the entrance hall and spoke a few words of English that 'it will be fine tomorrow'.

However we made up our minds to spend the day there and after breakfast went out in the rain in our capes for about 2½ miles along the bank of the lake taking a few photographs from sheltered spots. It was now that I found the inconvenience of plus fours as against shorts and soon hit upon the expedient plan of rolling up my plus fours as far as they would go and rolling my stockings down to my ankles.

We returned about 1 o'clock for some more grub (I think it was either a *schnitzel* of some sort or *schweinebraten* (roast pork)), and the rain having become a negligible quantity, encouraged us to have a trip up the lake in the Hotel launch 'Forella'. The fare was only two schillings so it was not an undue risk. The lake is swarming with trout and the chief amusement of the juvenile visitors after lunch is feeding the fish with pieces of bread or anything else that comes handy. In fact they will even swarm round a piece of paper or a cigarette end.

We started off on our boat trip about 3 o'clock and with two stops it took about an hour to get to the end of the Heiterwanger See (a smaller lake connected with the Plansee by a narrow canal which apparently required careful navigation). The views on the way were varied and beautiful, but we unfortunately did not see it at its best, the sky being overcast and the wind bitter.

We had about an hour ashore at the far end of the Heiterwanger See, part of which was spent in watching a small boy catching fish by inserting his hand with a small piece of bread in the palm of it and closing his fingers when there was sufficient fish nibbling at the bread. He seldom struck without capturing at least two or three.

The return journey was also very cold and we were glad to take refuge in the cabin for part of it. We had made up our minds to move on the morrow so determined to have a last tryst with the lake trout, ordering it in its most expensive form. It was I believe steamed, a large lump out of the middle of a fish as big as a small salmon and I shall remember the delicious flavour for evermore. The greater part of the evening was spent in writing more postcards and a stroll after dark revealed many brilliant glow worms in the undergrowth. *No cycling today*

WEDNESDAY 29TH JULY

As we had perforce to leave this enchanting place today the weather was of course brilliantly fine. However, after breakfast we settled up and prepared to depart feeling that the 100 schillings to which our bill amounted had been well spent having regard to the high living we had indulged in.

It was not only 'goodbye' to the Plansee but 'goodbye' to Austria we had to say today. Our send-off was quite touching and the hope that we might one day return was reciprocated by both of us. We took a rough road at the back of the hotel, which after passing through some miles of beautiful scenery brought us to the Austrian Custom House at Ammerwald where we obtained our final exit on the 3rd sheet of our passports, though not without some misgiving on the part of the Customs bloke who was unable to decipher the stamp of the Custom House where we had made our first entry.

From Ammerwald there is several miles of 'Zollstrasse' (neutral road) before Germany is officially entered at Linderhof but about midway there is a somewhat battered medallion erected on a post inscribed "*Königreich Bayern*" which presumably marks the actual boundary. A few miles beyond Linderhof we turned left for Oberammergau coming across many parties of hikers and tourists of all descriptions.

As soon as you enter a town a feeling of over civilisation or super sophistication strikes you. It is a large clean town and of course beautifully situated among the mountains, but there seems nothing to render it so attractive as to warrant the number of tourists of all nations which seemed to be gathered there. We entered a few shops where, after we had strained our throats by speaking our best German, we were addressed in very good English. This sort of thing takes the gilt off Continental travel and we soon took our departure via Unterammergau. For the rest of the day our way lay through just plain Bavaria, which except for the oxen transport, the peasants' garb and the wide eaved farmhouses might have been an English agricultural county.

The 'Gasthaus zum Weiss Pferd' (White Horse Inn) at Gschwend we lunched off real ham and eggs just like English ones which quite gave us nostalgia. At the large town of Schongau we took a steep and rough downhill road on the left which took us through much more plain country to Oberdorf where we refreshed with coffee and rolls before continuing on over similar country with plenty of hard pushing up hill until we reached a small one horse town called Obergünzberg. Here we decided to pack up for the night first making a tour of the town to find out which was the most imposing gasthaus.

We chose the 'Goldener Hirsch' and, though its imposing exterior concealed a somewhat plain and unvarnished interior which slightly peeved Jack, we did quite well there, one of the refinements being a bedroom with two basins with (real) hot and cold water laid on. There was no fault to be found with the grub either, the *schnitzel* being excellent. We were taken in charge by a most hilarious damsel who absolutely refused to take us seriously, being especially tickled when Jack demanded "*himbeer*" which failed to appear this time so that he had to fall back on mineral "*wasser*".

An inspection of the town revealed it as quite a pleasant little place well bedecked with flowers, some of the gardens being as good as anything we had seen in Germany so far. This had been our longest day's run – *61 miles*.

THURSDAY 30TH JULY

Apparently, it was a special Saint's day in Obergünzberg. The church was just opposite our bedroom and at an early hour its one bell (somewhat cracked) was busy. While we were dressing, an immense covey of nuns filed in followed by acolytes and apprentices.

We had breakfast at 8 o'clock sharp and called for the "*rechnung*" (bill). When this appeared it was so ridiculously small that we came to the conclusion that it must be for one only so Jack doubled it. This seemed to be the correct procedure for it was greeted by our damsel with immense hilarity. Jack then added the usual 10% for service but she struck this out with much gleeful chuckling so we let it go at that having anyhow come off very cheaply though Jack avers she charged us for one beer which I did not consume.

We took a somewhat strenuous road, which eventually brought us by way of Ottobeuren to Memmingen, a large and somewhat busy town. We had been advised to take the train as far as Ulm but decided to ride it. From Memmingen it was only a matter of 33km and there were no mountains in the way. It was also marked on the maps as a first class road but it was first class for only a few kilometres at a time. The remainder as to the surface was vile. It would improve for a mile or two and then a small town would come in sight and we would be bouncing through pot holes six inches deep.

Jack felt like packing into a train at one of the wayside stations but we finally decided to see it through. On one stretch we were taken on by a local speed merchant (l.s.m). After a mile or two Jack gave him a spot of 90" gear, leaving both the l.s.m. and myself. However the l.s.m. immediately crumpled up and Jack's spasm not lasting long I soon picked him up again.

We had lunch at the 'Gasthaus zum Rose' at a town the name of which I did not get. The approach to Ulm is marked by at least four miles of bone shattering pave. Ulm is a large and towny city with tramlines of the very best set in cobble stones. We proposed visiting the interior of the cathedral but finding a charge of one mark made for admission we sheared off. The road out of the city to Blaubeuren (this was not the direct road to Urach for which we were making) gave us another good four miles of pave and tramlines. However, Blaubeuren was a pleasant little town and we took "*coffee und kuchen*" at a very nice 'Gasthaus zum Lowen' where we were told we must not leave the town without seeing the Great Well of Germany which was close by. This was duly visited but we were not over much impressed by it.

We had now got out of plain ordinary Bavaria into Swabia, the country being much more akin to the Black Forest and therefore once more of the picturesque order. The road rises almost continuously from Blaubeuren and we had to do a good deal of it on our baby gears. The surface of the road was however quite good, which made up a lot for its strenuous nature.

It was nearly 8 o'clock when we arrived at Urach. The last few miles running downhill much steeper than was pleasant. Down at the bottom Jack found that one of his gear levers, the one that operated 'baby' had gone west[12]. This was something in the nature of a disaster as it was extremely improbable that we were going to get out of Germany without a few more hills.

We were received with open arms at the 'Pension Schoeneck', the *schnitzel* which we had for supper being exceptionally fine. There we met a middle-aged German who said he spoke a little English. We were anxious for news as our German was not equal to reading the papers and the last English newspaper we had seen was the 'Continental Daily Mail' in Innsbruck. He was quite ready to oblige and translated from the German paper into faultless English though he stated it was thirty years since he had visited England!

He gave us much interesting information about Urach and also about the customs of the Student's Guilds, Urach being a university town. He also told us that he spoke and read other European languages and if time had permitted we should like to have made further acquaintances with such an interesting character.

This had been a long and tough day's riding, the *85 miles* covered being as good as 120 miles on English roads.

FRIDAY 3IST JULY

After breakfast the first consideration was to try and get some wire to make a temporary repair of Jack's wounded gear level. A suitable piece of wire was obtained after some little difficulty in getting understood.

The town of Urach was well worth exploration and photography and it was about 11 o'clock before we took our departure in the direction of Reutlingen through Metzingen. There was nothing of particular interest

---

12 Died, or ceased functioning

in Reutlingen, the usual type of a fair sized clean German town with paved roads and a network of tramlines. It being near 1 o'clock the whole population seemed to be mounted on bicycles making their way to dinner.

We scouted around and eventually made our way to the next town, Tubingen. Here, feeling peckish we entered the 'Gasthaus zum Bahnhof' a very busy feeding station where we had a first rate blow out at the usual moderate charge. After this we took it easy to the next town – Rottenburg – this being the last of the big towns for the time being, of which we were glad as we were not out to see towns.

From Rottenburg the road ran mostly uphill. The mishaps to Jack's bottom gear (it would only work in fits and starts) rather undermined his morale, for on one particularly stiff bit a hefty workman mounted on the usual type of German machine required "downing". I did not like to take advantage of Jack's infirmity slipping into 'baby gear' so nearly killed myself by struggling to the top on middle gear (47"). There I had to wait for a pedestrian procession! Jack came first. He had got off thinking I was taking advantage of my healthy baby gear.

The descent into Horb was rather terrifying not only as to gradient but also surface. We had been advised to look out for the 'Gasthaus zum Baren' as a suitable place for 'tea' (I never really tasted tea after leaving Dunkirk) but probably owing to having to keep an eye on the road we missed it. However a few miles further on at Seewald our wants were satisfied at the 'Gasthaus zum Seewald' after which we made for Freudenstadt, a large modern town. There we looked around for the best hotel as had now become our custom and chose the 'Hotel Krone', quite a luxurious hostelry where the *schnitzel* was excellent. We loitered sometime in the evening in the principal square where the town band was performing passably.

The manager of the hotel who spoke good English promised us a treat for the morrow before we went to bed: "Ah gentlemen, you shall have eggs and bacon for breakfast tomorrow". And so we went to bed full of hope.
Distance covered: 55 miles

SATURDAY 1ST AUGUST

The promised eggs and bacon breakfast duly turned up. It proved to be of the usual German variety – all mashed up together and served in blocks.

The exchequer required replenishing and it took us quite a long time to find a bank where sterling could be changed into marks. We left by a road signposted to Freiburg, which after a short but tough climb up, gave us a glorious coast down off about 13 miles through the best Schwarzwald scenery, and eventually we came through Wolfach to very near our original starting point.

It was about 12.30 when we came into Hausach, our first lunch spot after leaving Gengenbach at the start of our tour. We had no intention of stopping at the 'Gasthaus zum Hirsch' but we were seen by the good Frau at that establishment and had no recourse but to enter. Here we were greeted most heartily and the best of *schnitzels*, soup *kartoffel* (potato soup) and *obst* was put before us. We fed in the company of three police captains, most humorous dogs, one of whom had a most chronic face. We discussed (or tried to) various topics and I was particularly warned against eating fruit and washing it down with beer.

We parted from the 'Gasthaus zum Hirsch' with no little ceremony and a large quantity of "*Auf Wiedersehen*" in various keys, and took the road to Haslach from whence the road commences to go up with a bang with many hairpins, each stretch being steeper than the last.

Jack's baby gear was very fractious and kept jumping up one so that I rode a mile at a time and then waited for him to come up. Naturally by the time he arrived I had recovered my wind and once more left him behind. At the top it gave me great joy to see a gasthaus into which I tumbled and bespoke "*Ein gross bier*" without the least hesitation. I soon poured this down and was sitting on the steps and was halfway through another when Jack appeared.

After several miles down to Freiburg, this road flattens out and becomes somewhat of the ordinary type, passing through many small towns of the agricultural type. We reached Freiburg in the late afternoon finding it a large city and very busy this Saturday evening – in fact it was too towny to suit us. We scouted around for somewhere to stay the night but seeing nowhere which appealed, made up our minds to move elsewhere.

We retraced our way for a few miles and then bore left eventually arriving at a largish town which seemed a suitable stopping place. This was Emmendingen where the 'Gasthaus zum Lowen' appeared to be the goods. As usual we had no difficulty in getting put up, our bedroom being provided with two basins with hot and cold water laid on. The town was quite a pleasant one with large public gardens where there is a magnificent show of tropical plants growing in the open. The *gasthaus* was attached to a butcher's shop and we had very excellent steaks for supper which went down well after a somewhat strenuous *68 miles.*

SUNDAY 2ND AUGUST

We took our departure from Emmendingen about 9.30 a.m. by the main road towards Offenburg. This was so badly infested by motor traffic that we were glad to turn off it after a few miles on a road of the 'rough and tough' description, which after much hard work brought us to Steinach. On the way we stopped at a small *gasthaus* after some very heavy climbing. Beer of course I got but poor old Jack could not even get any mineral *"wasser"* so had to go dry.

From this point it was mostly downhill through picturesque country and villages, and we were much intrigued by the Sunday costumes of the peasantry, especially of elderly dames in gilt headdresses. Personally I was very glad when we were once more through Haslach and approaching Gengenbach where we had a good welcome at the 'Gasthaus Salinen'. It was nearly 3.30p.m. before we were sitting down to a square meal of which I was urgently in need of having had nothing but the usual breakfast of coffee and rolls since 8.30 a.m. the preceding evening.

During the afternoon we were able to devote more time to the exploration of the charming little town of Gengenbach than we had been able to do on our first visit and also took a stroll along the banks of the river, which was in full use of bathing. Later on, while we were sitting in the Salinen, three elegantly dressed damsels (all three quite presentable) entered and sat down at a table near us. Jack was curious to know what they had come for. I said "beer" and beer it was, each of them calling for *"ein gross bier"* (one litre, about a pint and three quarters). We left them at it and went for a stroll among the vineyards and when we came back about an hour later the same three damsels were still there and still drinking beer. By then the Salinen was full, with complete families (mother, father and children of all ages) all drinking beer.

Jack thought he must sample the German wine before we left the country. We each had a glass of the most expensive brand and as I expected one sip of it was enough for him! It was hardly likely that anyone who could drink the sickly raspberry compound known as *"himbeer"* could have any appreciation for good dry Rhine wine, which is a taste I must confess, I have not acquired. However, I had to finish both glasses, of course.

Distance covered: 35 miles

MONDAY 3RD AUGUST

Much talk with Frau Maier and her daughters and further photography made it about 11.20 a.m. before we started on the last stage of our journey home. Just as were about to get under way, Jack's arms, which we were all hanging in rags with sun blisters, caught the attention of the good Frau. She straightaway sent her youngest to a neighbouring chemist for the where withal to render first aid (somewhat late) and he was well anointed with dripping and swathed in lint when we took our departure.

We started from the back of the house amid a perfect torrent of '*Auf Wiedersehens*' and as we came round to the front the amiable Maier family were all there to see the last of us and hand waves were exchanged until we were unsighted by a bend in the road.

From Offenburg to Kehl we had to make a considerable detour to avoid a section of road under repair which had caused us some trouble on the way out, and after getting rid of our German money at Kehl Station we passed out of Germany across the Pont du Rhin about 2.30 p.m., as usual feeling very hungry. There seemed nowhere to get anything to eat in Strasburg and it looked as though we must hope for the best on the train, which was due to leave for Dunkirk at 3.52 p.m.

In the meantime we got some light refreshments on the station platform, the registering of our cycles through to St. Pancras not being the weary process it had been on the outward journey. We were rather dismayed when the train arrived to find no restaurant car on it, though.

As this was a Bank Holiday in England, the train was not overcrowded and we got comfortably seated for the somewhat tedious journey. At Longuyon, our fears were set at rest as a restaurant car was hooked onto the back of our train. Though it was a long and rough journey through the corridor (French railways are hardly as smooth as the GWR) to the restaurant car, we were soon enjoying a very excellent feed of many courses. This put us on much better terms with ourselves and the rest of the journey passed pleasantly enough, enlivened by occasional conversations with two English people in the next compartment who had been on a hiking expedition.

When we came into Dunkirk it was a very moist looking night or rather early morning (12.45 a.m.). Profiting by our experience on the outward trip we lost no time in getting over the Customs formalities and making our way onto the boat (the same S.S. Picard), finding a sheltered spot and providing ourselves with deck chairs and blankets. It was just as well we came by an earlier train than was absolutely necessary, for before the boat started, a fresh mob arrived and it became uncomfortably crowded. Among them were two German girls both looking very cold and weary. We found them deck chairs and I volunteered to get them blankets but on application to the Stewards found that there were no more to be obtained. One of them succeeded in getting a berth below. The other one began to be ill directly as the boat got out of Dunkirk and was soon in such a pitiful condition that I was compelled to wrap her up in my blanket (N.B. get two blankets next time).

It was bitterly cold and I was glad to seek refuge in the hot, oily atmosphere of the engine room once or twice and keep myself alive with an occasional Guinness and a sandwich until the floor of the canteen got into such a state that it nearly induced sea sickness to enter it. In the meantime Jack had rolled himself in his blanket and remained oblivious of the regurgitation that was going on around him.

The male half of the pair we had met in the train was left forlorn as he had had to tuck his wife away in a safe place she having become "*hors de combat*". When the watery dawn at last appeared the ship presented a most horrible appearance. There was hardly a clean spot on it upon which one could walk. The lady of the train had once more come into sight looking like nothing on earth. I offered to get her a cup of tea. Her reply was "My dear man, I don't think I shall ever want to eat or drink anything again".

Everyone began to cheer up when the smooth waters of the Thames were entered. At Tilbury we got off the boat as quickly as possible and passed through our last Customs House. Leaving our bicycles to look after themselves, we got into the waiting breakfast train and the journey to St. Pancras was occupied in disposing of the 3/6 breakfast provided by the LMS Railway Company in the company with two quaint old spinsters, who had been spending a weekend in Paris. As we expected our bicycles had not come on the same train as we had and we had half an hour to wait before they turned up.

I had never found any difficulty in keeping to the right of the road on the Continent but continuing the practice nearly ended my career under a taxi coming out of St. Pancras. I arrived home about 9.45 a.m. having covered *39 miles* since leaving Gengenbach yesterday morning.

1931 SUMMER TOUR – MERLIN I

WEDNESDAY 19TH AUGUST

A sleepy soaker of a day

HAMMERSMITH – WINDSOR – MAIDENHEAD – HENLEY-ON-THAMES – DORCHESTER-ON-THAMES – ABINGDON – DUCKLINGTON – BURFORD – PIFF'S ELM – LEDBURY – HEREFORD – WHITNEY-ON-WYE

I made up my mind to start my tour at midnight but went to sleep and did not get off until 1 a.m. going through a sleepy Richmond and Twickenham, across the Staines road at Bedfont soon after which it began to rain. Thinking it could not be much, I put off caping until I was thoroughly wet. The rain, gentle at first, kept on increasing in volume so that by the time Windsor and Maidenhead were behind me it was a steady downpour. My last sight of a human being for many miles was when I got off to exchange notes on the weather with the policeman at the corner of Oxford road in Henley.

In spite of wind and rain in my face Bix Hill seemed exceptionally easy in the dark but the run down from the golf links was not as fast as usual. The village of Benson was passed, with an old man in a nightshirt standing at a cottage door with a candle in his hand surveying the dismal outlook. This was about 4.45 a.m. There was still no sign of dawn except for a slight decrease in the intensity of the darkness.

The rain was coming down as though it would go on for weeks. At

Dorchester I stopped for a few minutes to ring out my plus four knees and empty the water out of my shoes. The darkness had now thinned considerably and at Abingdon (5.45 a.m.) I turned out my light and got under the shelter of the Market Hall to eat some very dry ham sandwiches with which I had provided myself.

From Abingdon to Witney my recollection is very hazy. I remember gazing longingly at the 'Rose Revived' hoping to see some signs of life and hope of a cup of tea but in vain. At least three times I dropped into a half sleep and charged the hedge on the opposite side of the road and the desire to lay down somewhere by the roadside and have forty winks was strong. As I felt it would hardly do to fall asleep on the main road I woke myself up thoroughly by running a few hundred yards through Ducklington.

I had intended having breakfast at the 'Puesdown Inn' but at Burford (8 a.m.) the thought of the beloved 'Swan' was too much for me and I turned down the High Street and was soon enjoying dry stockings and borrowed shoes and a wash in hot water followed by the usual 'Swan' breakfast. It was 11 o'clock before I could tear myself away from the 'Swan' and by then I was completely dry even to cape and shoes. It was quite nice to be dry for a few minutes, but the rain continued unabated and was particularly venomous and stinging over Puesdown to Cheltenham.

Between Cheltenham and Tewskesbury I had my midday bread, cheese and beer at the 'Old Swan' at Piff's Elm, and a few miles beyond Tewkesbury on the Ledbury road got about an hour's sleep in a fairly dry spot by the roadside. This and the cooling rain made me full of beans and I only walked a few hundred yards of Hollybush Hill because I have always done so. The 'Old Trumpet Inn' about five miles beyond Ledbury provided me with an excellent tea and a cloud burst just beyond Hereford gave me an excuse to enter the 'Bay Horse' and have a Bass.

At Willersley Cross I found that if I proceeded straight to the 'Stowe Inn' I should just fall short of 150 miles, so instead of turning left I went straight ahead to Eardisley as I could not possibly get wetter than I already was. Turning again I arrived at the 'Stowe Inn' in another cloud burst, very wet and very sleepy but not too sleepy to dispose of the hot supper that was awaiting me.

A good lady staying in the house tried to engage me in conversation after supper but I was too sleepy to know what she was talking about and went to bed at 9.45 p.m. the rain and wind having made the *152 miles* I covered somewhat strenuous.

THURSDAY 20TH AUGUST

Sad news from the Cambrian Arms

WHITNEY-ON-WYE – CLIFFORD – HAY-ON-WYE – CRICKHOWELL – TALGARTH – CLYRO – WHITNEY-ON-WYE

It was still raining, with an increased wind when I got up so I made up my mind to have a run round during the morning and return to the 'Stowe' for lunch.

There is a wooded tump[13] at the back of the 'Stowe' marked on the map as 'the Knapp' which I had not explored. I made first of all for Bredwardine via Letton. From here the road goes steadily up, it seemed for many miles, with the wind and rain against me, eventually bringing me down with a rush to Clifford not far from the Whitney toll bridge.

The rain did at last cease about 1 o'clock and after lunch I set out through Hay and Three Cocks for Llangorse Lake via Talgarth. This lake though of large extent is of a most tame description, what might be described as a large puddle, so I struggled on through Cathedine up to Bwlch intent on running down to Crickhowell for tea at the 'Cambrian Arms', where I had happy memories of the hospitality of the Wynters, the family who ran it. Alas! When I got there I found the name of Griffiths over the door, learning that Mr Wynter had died in the spring and Mrs Wynter and Maisie, a charming damsel, had departed into the unknown. The tea I had there was a good one and the price reasonable but it lacked the pleasure of conversation with old friends.

I returned to the 'Stowe' by the beautiful road that runs up through the Black Mountains past Tretower and Cwmdu and down with a rush into uninteresting Talgarth, over Glasbury Bridge and through Clyro. Having regard to yesterday's run the *66 miles* covered today over arduous country was very good.

---

13 A hillock or mound

FRIDAY 21ST AUGUST

A cosy stopping place

WHITNEY-ON-WYE – GRAFTON – MONMOUTH – TINTERN – CHEPSTOW

I left the 'Stowe' about 10 a.m. making good time with the breeze astern to Hereford via Willersley Cross and Bridge Sollers. It was harder work when I turned south on the Monmouth road, and as a precaution I had early bread and cheese at the 'Angel' at Grafton just a few miles beyond Hereford. There is plenty of hard work on this road through St. Leonards and Welsh Newton but I arrived at Monmouth much too early to think of tea so went on along the bank of the Wye through Redbrook and Llandogo to Tintern. Here rain started so I made for the 'Wye Cottage' for tea, a very satisfactory one.

At Chepstow as it was not yet 6 o'clock I deposited my heavy luggage at the 'Bridge Inn' and made for Beachley to see how the ferry was running, as it was my intention to cross the Severn in the morning. I found the tide dead low and was informed that the 5 o'clock ferry was still cruising around as there was not sufficient water for it to approach the landing stage. However, I was assured that there would be plenty of water for the 10 o'clock boat to run tomorrow.

Supper at the 'Bridge Inn' was of its usual good quality and made me wish that this cosy stopping place was near enough to London for weekend tours.

Distance covered: 53 miles

SATURDAY 22ND AUGUST

Beloved Lacock

CHEPSTOW – IRON ACTON – CASTLE COMBE – LACOCK – MARLBOROUGH

I was down at Beachley Ferry at 10 o'clock sharp and there was quite a crowd including two cars waiting to cross. Thanks to the good Severn mud, getting them on to the boat was a ticklish business but we got off promptly to time.

I had to make for Marlborough were I had arranged to meet Frank. From Aust, my way was via Olveston, Tockington, Chipping Sodbury and Iron Acton where I took light refreshment at the 'Crown' before going onto

Castle Combe. For once I found this lovely village practically untenanted by the trippers who generally infest it and was able to do some photography without any cars and charabancs in it. One car in front of the market hall was very kindly removed by its owners to allow me a clear field.

I decided on the 'Castle Inn' as a suitable place for lunch and they apologised for being only able to put cold victuals[14] before me. However, everything was first rate and the evident desire to please decided me that the 'Castle Inn' is probably a good place to stay at. From Castle Combe I proceeded by familiar roads via Yatton Keynell, Biddlestone and Corston to Lacock not liking to pass through the beloved village without paying my respects to Miss Jenkins at the 'Corner House'. The consequence was that I was persuaded to stay to tea. This did not worry me much as I had bags of time and Miss Jenkins' teas are too good to miss.

It was about 5.30 p.m. when I left Lacock climbing to the top of Bowden Hill and dropping down into Calne from whence the Bath road via Beckhampton and Fyfield landed me at Marlborough just after 8 o'clock. It was my job to find quarters in Marlborough for the Sissons" and myself and I made first for the 'Green Dragon'. This was full up and I was sent onto the 'Crown' where the requisite accommodation was booked.

Having done my duty I went on as far as Savernake where I met Frank and Fon riding furiously, and we all scorched into Marlborough arriving at 8.45 p.m. a good quarter of an hour before schedule.

Distance covered: 61 miles

SUNDAY 23RD AUGUST

Two crowns

MARLBOROUGH – ALDBOURNE – LAMBOURN – CHOLSEY – STOKE ROW

We left the 'Crown' about 10.30 a.m. in a light drizzle not regarding our put up as anything to make a song about. As the tandemists were feeling full of beans we took the Swindon road as far as Ogbourne St. George where a steep and rough road runs up to Aldbourne.

At Aldbourne we decided to sample Mrs Barnes for 'elevens'. The tea and cake was of moderate quality but the crockery did not display that energy in the washing thereof to satisfy fastidious Fon. It is curious that I

---

14 An old word for 'provisions'

had observed the same thing at the 'Crown' when Jack and I stayed there in the spring, so it must be a failing peculiar to Aldbourne. We loitered so long in Aldbourne that by the time we had descended Baydon Hill to Lambourn it was time for lunch. Yet another 'Crown' supplied us with this, which was fairly good and at a fairly good price.

From Lambourn we made for Wantage over Crow Down and Hackpen Hill going on via Harwell to Aston Tirrold with the intention of finding the road marked on Bartholomew's map to Cholsey Ferry, which had so far eluded Jack and I. We scouted up and down from Aston Tirrold to Upton and at last found a muddy track which we were informed by a local boy would take us to Cholsey. So we essayed it. However, any resemblance to a road disappeared after the first few hundred yards and it degenerated into a mere track, even this being invisible at times, necessitating following the hedge and for a considerable distance riding over the stubble in a newly cut cornfield. Fon who was as usual riding without stockings got her legs considerably damaged in the process and had to have recourse to the iodine bottle.

We did eventually arrive at Cholsey only to learn that the ferry had ceased business some two years ago. This left nothing for it but to make for the next ferry at Moulsford. We had arranged to meet Jack at the 'Bricklayer's Arms' at 5 o'clock but it was quite apparent that we should be very late for this appointment. Once across Moulsford Ferry a rapid glance at the map showed a fairly direct route to our goal through Checkendon and Stoke Row, albeit mostly uphill and somewhat rough. It was only about five miles and we did not waste much time over it but even so it was 10 minutes past six and Jack had had his tea and given us up.

We had quite an excellent tea, the jam being especially good. As I had to find somewhere to stay the night and there was a bedroom going I booked it, accompanying Frank and Fon as far as Sonning on their way home, and returning to the 'Bricklayer's Arms' for the evening. I found the company in the bar parlour highly entertaining and after a good cold supper went to bed about 11.

Distance covered: 59 miles

MONDAY 24TH AUGUST
A rather inhospitable town
STOKE ROW – NEWBURY – HIGHCLERE – ANDOVER – SALISBURY – SHAFTESBURY

I made up my mind to make for the west after having breakfast surrounded by dogs, cats, pigs and poultry. I found I got on better with less company so expelled them all except a few of the best behaved of the cats.

This is a somewhat confusing part of the country and I must have gone several miles out of my way to Pangbourne via Whitchurch from whence, wishing to keep off the Bath road, I took a winding and devious course through Sulham, Tidmarsh, Bradfield, Chapel Row and Cold Ash, to Newbury. Here I started on the road to Winchester but changed my mind and took the Andover road having my midday refreshment at the 'Crown', Highclere. This is not too easy a stretch and rain starting just before the climb to Hurstbourne Tarrant did not make things any easier.

When I got into Andover it was in a state of carnival and not having a false nose or anything of that sort I felt decidedly out of place. Not only was I held up for about half an hour in the rain waiting for the procession to pass but was also milked of my small change by various damsels collecting for the local hospital. From Andover to Salisbury might be a speedway with a strong wind behind but I have never had that luck on it. Toiling up those long slopes in steady rain in a clammy cape was anything but a joy.

Just outside Salisbury I met a young tandem pair who wanted to stay the night near Salisbury so I conducted them to 'The Coach and Horses', having tea with them there before proceeding on my way. I had hoped to get to Sherborne or even Crewkerne before nightfall, but in the face of the rain and wind it was obvious that this was out of the question, and it was already getting dusk by the time I reached the inhospitable town of Shaftesbury.

After being turned down at all the C.T.C. appointments, I at last found bed and board of a sort at a barber's named Mitchell. The best I could get for supper was two boiled eggs and I was warned not to play too heavily on the bread and butter as butter was scarce. My hopes of an early start tomorrow were dashed as it was found impossible to give me breakfast before 9 o'clock and I found I had to share a bedroom with another man, a cyclist of sorts.

Distance covered: 84 miles

TUESDAY 25TH AUGUST

Inhabited by ghosts

SHAFTESBURY – SHERBORNE – CREWKERNE – WINDWHISTLE – CHARD – WHIMPLE – DAWLISH

The west wind was blowing strongly this morning though the rain had ceased.

Even the breakfast was none too punctual so that it was well past 10 o'clock before I got a start. However the Exeter road from Shaftesbury to Crewkerne is more downhill than up and Henstridge, Milborne Port, Sherborne and Yeovil were very soon left behind.

Consideration whether I should make north towards Bridgwater from Yeovil was decided in the negative and I continued westward through West Coker to Crewkerne. At Crewkerne the toil begins and reaching the top of Windwhistle perspiring freely, thoughts of lunch assailed me. The 'Windwhistle Inn' did not look too promising. I was therefore all the more satisfied to find there was a hot lunch going, which fortified me for the further toil to come.

It was market day in Chard, which justified strolling up the steep High Street of that town before tackling Yarcombe Hill of which I rode all but a few hundred yards, doing the usual giddy rush down to Honiton. Rather a long-drawn-out tea at a very pleasant little house (the 'Wayside Café') at Whimple made it approaching 6 o'clock when I was within a few miles of Exeter, and I did not feel like the somewhat strenuous 45 miles that remained to Holsworthy, which I had hoped to reach today. As a result I turned left before entering Exeter, crossing the Exe above the estuary to Exminster and proceeded on the very familiar stretch through Kenton and Starcross to Dawlish. It is always a job to find a billet in a seaside town, but after sundry enquires I found very satisfactory quarters at Montpellier House (Mrs Baker) at the end of the Lawn and more satisfactory still was a hot dinner just ready to which I did full justice.

Dawlish, after having known it so well up to the commencement of the War, since when I have become the sole survivor of my family circle and so many old friends resident in the town have passed over, seems inhabited by ghosts, but the town itself remains unaltered over the past 40 years. In the 'Teignmouth Inn' where I called for a Bass, I met an aged hackney coachman with whom I spent upwards of half an hour discussing the characteristics of dead and gone inhabitants including 'Monkey Davis' who died in 1898.

Distance covered: 78 miles

WEDNESDAY 26TH AUGUST

A breakfast fit for a king

DAWLISH – EXETER – COPPLESTONE – HATHERLEIGH – HOLSWORTHY – BUDE – STRATTON – HOLSWORTHY

The breakfast I had at the 'Montpellier House' deserves special mention! Starting with porridge and Devonshire cream it went on with fish, fried in a particular way they understand in Dawlish. Before I had congratulated myself on finding a variant to the usual eggs and bacon, those also appeared as a third course! Needless to say I did not feel it necessary to go far with the bread and butter and marmalade after this.

Having sundry calls to pay on old friends, it was 10.30 before I left by the Exeter road, this time having to go into the city to get the Crediton road via Newton St. Cyres. The wind was at last behind me and I got to the 'Cross Inn' at Copplestone in time to get some bread, cheese and a beer before closing time.

No map was required to find the road to North Tawton and on through Sampford Courtenay and Exbourne to Hatherleigh, where the picturesque old bridge has been destroyed to make way for a wide, gaunt stone structure quite ruining the aspect of this one time quaint and old worldly town. I well remember the first time I did the 13 miles from Hatherleigh to Holsworthy just 10 years ago. E.B.P. and I had been struggling against a poisonous headwind from Crewkerne and both of us having done very little riding during the year were so baked that only a dose of Guinness at the 'Bridge Inn' at Hatherleigh and the 'Golden Inn' at Highampton enabled us to struggle in to Holsworthy just after 11 p.m. This was the only occasion that I remember when I had the wallops[15] so completely that I could not sleep. This time the only effect of the continual climb was to give me a huge appetite and the 'South Western Hotel' at Holsworthy is the finest place in England to cure that complaint.

Resisting Gladys Jollow's suggestion that I should start off with a steak

---

15 "Wallop" is an old term for alcoholic drinks, especially beer

or a few chops, I waded into the famous Holsworthy ham followed with apple tart and various kinds of stewed fruit (there were six varieties on the table) with plenty of cream of course, sampled the various kinds of cake and finished off with bread and butter and jam. To shake this down a run over to Bude seemed highly necessary. Here I met two young campers, last seen at the 'Burford Inn' in June and after half an hour's talk with them and a Bass at the 'King's Arms' at Stratton I had a good appetite for cold chicken and ham for my supper.

However this day of overfeeding was not to finish without disaster for after a hot bath before going to bed, being in an unfamiliar and sloppy pair of borrowed slippers, I slipped on the stairs leading down from the bathroom and made a bad hash of my right elbow. As it refused to stop bleeding, first aid had to be requisitioned from a commercial traveller selling chemist's sundries who was staying in the house.

Distance covered: 74 miles

THURSDAY 27TH AUGUST

A pestilential wind

HOLSWORTHY – HATHERLEIGH – OKEHAMPTON – TEDBURN ST MARY – EXETER – AXMINSTER

Another wonderful breakfast, liver and bacon this time (it is a good job I do not set high living above all else otherwise I should be always touring in Devonshire).

The wind which had blown me from Exeter yesterday was now a pestilential nuisance. It was more or less counteracted by the down grade to Hatherleigh. Here at the 'Bridge Inn' a young tandem pair from Putney who had been blown across from Crediton that morning with a fixed 65" gear were disposed to scout the idea that touring in Devon was hard work. If they carried on their idea of making for Clovelly and returning via Bideford, Barnstaple and Taunton they have probably altered their views by now.

From Hatherleigh to Okehampton was one long grind on bottom gear in the teeth of a biting blast. There is a sharp and twisting run down into Okehampton after which it again continually rises for nearly seven miles with a few abrupt drops, which only mean another climb of a steeper grade.

At Okehampton I got some bread, cheese and beer at the 'Exeter Inn' to fortify me for the struggle to Sticklepath and from there to Whiddon Down after which, though it is mostly downhill, the wind compelled pedalling all the way. Cheriton Bishop not providing a tea place I went on to Tedburn St. Mary where the 'King's Arms' did me satisfactorily as to eggs and otherwise and I got into Exeter about 5.45 p.m.

After an hour in Exeter dusk was approaching when Honiton came into sight, but Honiton is not a town I love so I decided on making for Axminster, one of the most difficult places to put up at. After making the round and getting the usual "full up" excuses I risked a non-C.T.C. house, the 'Western Hotel' which gave me quite satisfactory bed and board but at a price which is rather more than I care to pay; therefore the landlord's request that I should recommend it for the handbook was turned down. *Distance covered: 69 miles*

FRIDAY 28TH AUGUST

Bicycle blown away!

AXMINSTER – WINTERBOURNE ABBAS – WEYMOUTH – OWERMOIGNE – WAREHAM – WIMBORNE

When I left Axminster the east wind was if anything, stronger and more bitter than it was yesterday and I had one of the most strenuous roads in the south of England to negotiate if I was going to keep my appointment to meet Jack at Winchester tomorrow. Through Charmouth, up Chideock Hill into Bridport and from there to Winterbourne Abbas was practically one continuous grind on bottom gear, and I called to mind scampering over the same road on the hottest day of last year with Parnell riding a fixed 75" gear which necessitated three stops for 'pints' before we got to Dorchester. This time it was nearly 2 o'clock before I got to the 'Coach and Horse' at Winterbourne Abbas, a distance of 23 miles covered in just 4 hours!

I took the right hand road for Weymouth via Winterbourne Monkton and Chalbury. If I had expected to escape the wind this way I was sadly mistaken for as I got nearer the coast it increased. At Weymouth I turned up a street off the Front to get some cigarettes and promptly had my bicycle blown out of my hand. The tide was out about half a mile which did not make Weymouth look too attractive and I made my way out at the east end on the Wareham road still with plenty of wind in my face.

At Owermoigne I found a tea house and was glad to get inside out of the wind for a bit and listen to it howling outside without feeling it. Continuing on through Wool into Wareham the thoughts of facing dead into the gale with some hefty hills intervening put me off making for Swanage; indeed the luxury of turning my back to the blast induced me to think of Wimborne as a fitting stopping place for the night.

From Lytchett Minster I found bye roads, which if more strenuous, were certainly pleasanter than the main road. The 'Crown Tap' provided me with a good cold supper before I went to bed feeling that the *60 miles* I had covered was quite sufficient under the prevailing conditions.

SATURDAY 29TH AUGUST

Plenty of time to spare

WIMBORNE – BLANDFORD – SOUTH DAMERHAM – LYNDHURST – ROMSEY – WINCHESTER

To make straight for Winchester would have meant a very short journey for me so I had to plan out how to lengthen it. I started by making for Blandford via Tarrant Keyneston, and with the gale astern this did not take much time. From there, after loafing for about half an hour I took the Salisbury road thinking I should get the wind once more behind me. However it seemed to have veered round several points and I had about 13 miles of arduous and uninteresting road before turning right through some very beautiful villages, notably Martin and South Damerham where I took refuge from a heavy storm and at the same time stoked up with bread and cheese at the 'Fox and Hounds'.

To go direct to Winchester from Fordingbridge was out of the question at that early hour, so I climbed up Godshill on the Cadman road and, by various steep and rough forest tracks which showed up the New Forest at its best, finally reached that village of refreshment houses,[16] one of which provided a satisfactory tea. I still had plenty of time to dispose of, as Jack who had first a wedding at attend was hardly likely to turn up at Winchester until late.

The Ringwood road was a seething mass of motors making for Bournemouth, so I took the Lyndhurst road, which as far as that town was

---

16 Fordingbridge

quite deserted but from Lyndhurst to Totton it was once more hell. Having plenty of time I made for Romsey and on to Winchester via Ampfield and Hursley in company with three young speed merchants, one of whom required some nursing up hill.

Though I had followed a most tortuous route from Wimborne and made 76 *miles* of it, it was barely 8 o'clock when I arrived at the 'New Inn' in Stapleton Gardens, and as Jack did not turn up until past 10 o'clock, having come as far as Woking by train, I had a couple of hours for strolling around the town.

SUNDAY 30TH AUGUST

Bank Holiday madness
WINCHESTER – PRESTON CANDOVER – FRENSHAM POND – CHOBHAM

We got away from Winchester before 10 o'clock, taking the Petersfield road as far as Cheriton Bishop and then making northwards to New Alresford, still continuing in that direction on the Basingstoke road to Chilton Candover and Preston Candover where the 'Purefoy Arms' gave us an excellent lunch.

Our next movements required some consideration. Basingstoke is a place to avoid on Sundays so we decided on finding our way by bye roads towards, but not into Farnham. Various stony tracks brought us eventually out onto the main road to Froyle, and after a mile or two we turned right at Bentley and made for Frensham Pond, which Jack had not visited before, nor had I been near it for at least 20 years. We did not see much of it for the shore was about six deep in cars, and it had all the aspect of Southend on a Bank Holiday.

We made all speed away through Churt up to Ridgeway Farm where we had tea. Soon after we restarted, a drizzle commenced which soon developed into a good steady rain. We made through Puttenham and over the Hogs Back through Normandy, Pirbright for Chobham, Jack having a return half ticket from Woking to Waterloo which came in handy.

I had written to the 'Old King's Head' to secure me a room for the night and supply us with supper. The latter was of excellent quality. Just after Jack had departed for Woking to catch his train a young tandem pair arrived very wet and with a sick back tyre. I was able to supply them with repairing material as they had used up all theirs on the way, and it was past

11 o'clock before they got off on their way to Fulham, anticipating further tyre trouble on the way.

Distance covered: 62 miles

MONDAY 31ST AUGUST

Beautiful Cowdray Park

CHOBHAM — GUILDFORD — PETWORTH — AMBERLEY — BIGNOR — COWDRAY PARK — PETWORTH

I decided to finish up this varied 14 days' tour in Sussex so took the road to Guildford via Knaphill and Worplesdon and then the usual road to Petworth through Godalming, Milford, Witley, Chiddingfold and Northchapel. I just got to the 'Wheatsheaf' in time for lunch and made arrangements to return there for the night before taking the road via Fittleworth to Pulborough, before stopping for tea at the 'Cricketers' at Amberley. When I got there it took some time to find the landlady to supply me with the tea but it was excellent when it arrived.

From the 'Cricketers' I made my way up Bury Hill and had some idea of having a look at the Roman Pavement at Bignor. However when I arrived there it was too late to obtain admittance so took various rough tracks which eventually brought me out at the foot of Duncton Hill.

After a Bass at the 'Cricketers' I decided that it was too early to turn in to the 'Wheatsheaf' so went along the Midhurst road to Cowdray Park, looking very beautiful in the evening sun. There was a full house at the 'Wheatsheaf' but no cyclists and was nearly persuaded by the huntsman of the local hunt to turn out at 5 a.m. tomorrow morning for cub hunting but on consideration decided against it.

Distance covered: 60 miles

TUESDAY 1ST SEPTEMBER

The same old fogies

PETWORTH — KIRDFORD — BUCKS GREEN — GUILDFORD — HATCHFORD — COBHAM — HAMMERSMITH

I had to return today but did not care to take the direct road and instead of forking left outside Petworth went straight on for Kirdford. Here at the

'Half Moon' I felt bound to stop for a space. Finding the same old fogies in the bar parlour who were there when last I visited it with E.B.P. three years ago, I stopped there so long that it was lunch time when I reached Bucks Green, so I got some cold ham and beer at the 'Queen's Arms' after passing through Wisborough Green and Billingshurst.

I went on via Alford Crossways and Bramley into Guildford, down the main road to Ripley and via Ockham to the 'Black Swan' at Hatchford for tea, finally getting home by way of Cobham and Molesey and just making 60 miles of it.

This had been a curious fortnight's tour of over a thousand miles, the first time I had ever tried to do that distance in 14 days. Given fine weather and a little less strenuous country it would have been easy enough, but with Wales, Devon and Cornwall and a finish up against a north easterly gale and scarcely a day without rain it is not to be wondered at that I began to feel a little wilted at the end of it.

1931 A QUICK SEPTEMBER TOUR – MERLIN 1

THURSDAY 3RD SEPTEMBER

After the last trip, Merlin 1 required sundry renovations and adjustments so I brought it back from Goswell Road today and took the opportunity of making a call at Nassau Road.

Distance covered: 9 miles

FRIDAY 4TH SEPTEMBER

A petrified poodle

HAMMERSMITH – HORTON – HENLEY-ON-THAMES – DORCHESTER-ON-THAMES – NEWBRIDGE – BURFORD

Once more I set out on the beaten track to the West. It had been arranged that I should accompany Frank and Fon Sissons on a week's tour. They altered their first plan to take the train to Oxford. I arrived at Burford tonight and I was not to expect them until midday tomorrow.

There was a good steady rain when I started at 12 o'clock. This was varied by cloudbursts, one of which drove me into the 'Five Bells' at Horton for an early lunch of poached eggs on toast. Among the renovations to the machine were new blocks to the back brakes. I had no occasion to use them until the descent of White Hill into Henley. They then let off such a shriek that an old lady with a small poodle on a string at the bottom of the hill seemed convinced that I had done it on purpose to frighten her dog.

On examination the new blocks appeared to be made of soft rubber and totally unfit for use on steel rims. I took the precautions of investing in a pair of 'Fibrax' blocks in Henley but it was raining much too hard to permit playing about with brakes for the time being. At Dorchester I had tea at the 'Fleur de Lis' and after a call at the 'Rose Revived' Newbridge arrived at the 'Swan' in a half drowned state about 8.30 p.m.

Distance covered: 76 miles

SATURDAY 5TH SEPTEMBER

A terrific tea, as usual

BURFORD – PUESDOWN – CHELTENHAM – TEWKESBURY

I had the morning (a nice wet one) to spend in Burford and the rain was much too fierce to make much wandering pleasant.

Frank and Fon turned up for lunch about 1.45 p.m. having ridden against the wind and rain from Tring where they had spent the night so they were therefore glad of some grub. It was about 3.45 p.m. when we got on our way having made up our minds to have tea at the 'Puesdown Inn'. Up from Northleach against that rain and wind it was a fierce struggle and the tandem, having already had a good stretch of it, felt a bit wilted. At the 'Puesdown Inn' we found the cloisters inhabited by a gipsy party who looked as though they might be snappers up of unconsidered trifles. We therefore deemed it necessary to find a safe place for our machines before seeking tea. We stowed them in a fowl house which seemed a fairly safe place. Tea, as usual at the 'Puesdown Inn' was everything that could be desired and we were delighted to find when we turned out again, the rain had ceased.

We had still the wind to contend with but this did not matter. Another map was required and it was perilously near 8 o'clock (closing time) when we reached Cheltenham. We tried four or five shops before getting a map of a kind which would do at a pinch. We then made for Tewkesbury where we put up for the night at the 'Shakespeare Hotel', which gave us a satisfactory supper and accommodation.

Distance covered: 31 miles

SUNDAY 6TH SEPTEMBER

Strange bedfellows

TEWKESBURY – LEDBURY – HEREFORD – LLANFIHANGEL-NANT-MELAN – WHITNEY-ON-WYE

After the last two days' rain this morning's sunshine was most welcome. We left soon after 10 o'clock being well supplied with cards for distribution among our friends by Mr Franklin of the 'Shakespeare Hotel'.

Taking the Hereford road we did not dismount until the steep bit of Hollybush Hill, though Fon was agog to pinch some of the tempting-looking apples overhanging this orchard-bordered road. At Ledbury we stopped at the only refreshment shop for tea and cake but it was too draughty to be comfortable and we soon rattled on though Stoke Edith, Trumpet, Tarrington and Lugwardine to Hereford. To get lunch in sleepy Hereford on a Sunday seemed a hopeless proposition but we referred the matter to the police and were directed to the 'Coach and Horses', which provided an excellent feed of pork.

After this, the sun being hot, it seemed rather doubtful if we should want to go on to Rhayader today, which had been our intention. By grossly understating the distance off our chosen route I persuaded the cavalcade to make for the 'Stowe Inn' for tea. The result was that any intention of reaching Rhayader today was abandoned and we thought the 'Red Lion' at Llanfihangel-nant-Melan would be quite far enough after we had booked up for a night at the 'Stowe' on the way home. I don't think I have ever covered the strenuous eight miles from the 'Stowe' to Kington as on this occasion behind that tandem, and the journey up into the Radnor Forest was done in record time. So fast was the pace that Fon failed to see the tramlines in the great city of New Radnor.

At the 'Red Lion' Mr Williams was in a position to put us up but not all in the house. I was given the choice of sleeping "with Miss Jones or with the postman". I decided that the latter was likely to prove the quieter bedfellow. On our return from a stroll before supper we found a gaunt bespectacled man sitting in front of the fire wearing the North Road badge. After a time he asked me if we had not met at Burford some years ago when he was there with the North Riders. I asked him if Charlie Sewell was there whereupon he announced he was Charles Sewell and it appeared he was motor cycling with his wife. It was about 11 o'clock before I got away from listening about his doughty deeds in the past and made my way to the postman's for the night.

Distance covered: 65 miles

MONDAY 7TH SEPTEMBER
Tea courtesy of a witch
WHITNEY-ON-WYE – RHAYADER – CWMYSTWYTH – DEVIL'S BRIDGE

A most unusual phenomenon for the Radnor Forest – the sun was shining when we turned out in the morning. We had the usual breakfast of highly flavoured bacon and eggs and as is usual at the 'Red Lion' there was a cake on the table as an additional fill up if the eggs and bacon were not sufficient.

We now met Sewell's wife, a hard featured young woman with a Hall's distempered face[17] and a rat-trap mouth accentuated by her lips being painted vermilion, which quite justified Fon in dubbing her the 'Letter Box'.

The escape of gas from Sewell still continued and one mournful tale of an insult he had received from two girls of the Rosslyn Club, while on his motorcycle, tickled us immensely especially as Fon was once a shining light of that dissolute organisation.

We got on the road soon after 10 o'clock going straight on, on the way to Rhayader and I got somewhat left on the stretch from the top down to Penybont. There were not quite so many flocks of sheep as usual on this road and it was barely 11.30 a.m. when we got into the uninteresting town of Rhayader. After 'elevenses' at the 'Kimberley Temperance Hotel' (late Webbers) we decided that a picnic lunch was not only desirable but highly necessary as there were not any tuck shops on the road to Devil's Bridge we proposed taking. We invaded the principal general store and after Fon had negotiated the purchase of at least half its stock she handed me back 5½[18] change out of sixpence. There seemed enough grub for even three hungry cyclists but she was still rather disgruntled because she could not get any cream and the tomatoes were not the native article.

We took the road to the Elan Valley and our rejoicings for the brilliant sunshine were counteracted by the paucity of water coming over the dams.

---

17 Hall's Distemper was a famous home decorating paint created in the 1890s as an alternative to wallpaper
18 Five pence and a halfpenny

It is only when it has been raining for several days that they can be seen at their best.

We outspanned for our picnic on a knoll overlooking Craig Goch[19] after having been held up several times by flocks of sheep and when we arrived there we congratulated ourselves that there was no one else in sight. However, before we had got half way through that 4/6½ worth of provisions, three charabancs and five cars had unloaded beneath us.

After leaving Craig Goch the welcome sign *'Unfit for Motor Traffic'* was soon reached and the River Ystwyth crossed. There is nothing particularly difficult about this road except for the number of streams running across it which mostly have to be ridden through. In negotiating one of these rather carelessly I got well drenched in the legs, and no doubt when there has been a spell of wet weather they are really difficult to navigate.

At one deepish stream where there is a footbridge, our passage across was disputed by two cows. Unfortunately, none of us thought to bring our cameras to bear on this interesting situation. At the hamlet of Cwmystwyth we found a cottage that gave us tea. The proprietress, a stuffy looking old dame in a high sugarloaf hat embroidered with fantastic designs, looked a typical witch. Sitting each side of a huge fire upon which was an immense kettle were two cats like evil spirits in attendance, making a perfect picture of a practitioner in the black arts. It is occasions like this that make one realise that photography, which is incapable of recording a scene like this in colour, is still in its infancy.

Shortly after we had got on our way we found a disused tin mine, and Frank and I in company with four other cyclists made an attempt to explore it by the aid of our electric lamps. Curiously enough the lamps seemed totally ineffective and after I had bumped my head, I decided it was not good enough and retreated back to the open air. Frank eventually came out again but did not seem to have found much there except water. We were not to get to Devil's Bridge entirely without mishap. The back tyre of the tandem first required attention and after that had been repaired my rear brake with its shrieking blocks gibbered to pieces. However I succeeded in getting to our destination on the front brake and was glad I had brought those spare blocks with me from Henley.

We got satisfactorily housed at the Post Office at Devil's Bridge and after supper fared forth down to the hotel in quest of beer not having had any all

---

19 A masonry dam in the Elan Valley, completed in 1904 to supply Birmingham with water

day. In this we were sadly disappointed for when we got there (about 9.30 p.m.), we found the bar closed and so, after writing sundry postcards we were compelled to go beer-less to bed.

Distance covered: 42 miles

TUESDAY 8TH AND WEDNESDAY 9TH SEPTEMBER

Lucky to be alive

DEVIL'S BRIDGE – EISTEDDFA GURIG – PLYNLIMON – TALYBONT – BORTH – MACHYNLLETH

Another brilliant morning. The first thing that engaged our attention after breakfast was my back brake blocks. With the aid of tools borrowed from a friendly motorist, my jellied ones were extracted and the spare 'Fibrax' ones inserted, Frank being chief engineer on the job.

Yesterday's route not having provided sufficient thrills, it was thought something more adventurous should be attempted. Bartholomew showed a path up Plynlimon from the south side, but no sign of a track of any description down the other side, towards Machynlleth, so it was decided that we should try and force one for ourselves.

When we got down to the view from the road in front of the 'Hafod Hotel', it looked so enticing that a photograph was deemed imperative. Unfortunately the sun refused to shine in the required direction, and we, in company with many others made up our minds to wait until it did.

About 11.15 a.m. Frank and I adjourned to the 'Hafod Hotel' bar each for a Bass (and inferior Bass at that) for which we were rooked 9d, leaving Fon in charge of the cameras, with instructions to let fly if the sun came through during our absence. However it did not actually come through until we had finished our drinks, and she was relieved of the responsibility. As yesterday, provisions for a picnic were a necessity. The Post Office, where we had spent the night, is a general store, and Fon had laid out the sum of 5/- or a little less in obtaining everything essential.

We arrived at Eisteddfa Gurig where the path to the top starts about 12.30 p.m. and as there is a tea shop there, we thought it advisable to have some tea and cake before tackling the rough stuff. It was as well we did for this was the last drink we were destined to have until the next day was well advanced. We made enquiries as to taking the bicycles up to the top, and the idea was treated with a certain amount of scorn by the woolly headed girl at the tea shop, and our suggestion of going down the other side was received with even more derision. This naturally put our backs up.

After passing through one or two gates the real climb began. There is no beaten track and the only guide to the pathway consists of posts at intervals of two or three hundred yards. It was tough work, especially for the tandem, but Fon harnessing herself to the front of it by a strap and pulling like a horse while Frank pushed and steered their pace, was quite fast enough to take most of the wind out of me with my lighter mount.

About 2 o'clock, when we were about half way up, we decided to have our picnic, and to tell the truth I was glad of the halt to recover some of my lost wind. It was thoroughly enjoyable as picnics with fellow cyclist always are, and there was a small residue consisting of two large oranges, a piece of bread and some cheese and butter which Fon carefully preserved. Tins etc. were buried and I used my last match to burn much of the refuse as could be disposed of in that way, before we continued on our way.

We had met three people coming down, a parson who did not speak, and two hikers who grinned when they saw our machines and informed us that the gradient down the other side was about 1 in 2 mostly. It was just past 3 o'clock when we reached the summit and after a short pause to admire the view which is prodigious, the next thing was to investigate as to the possibilities of descending the other side. The first look I had at it satisfied me that it was impossible; it would have been difficult, unencumbered, but hopeless with bicycles and one of them a tandem, with at least 40lbs of luggage on it. The face of the mountain went sheer down to the shore of a small lake and the gradient could have been nowhere less than 1 in 2 as the hikers had told us.

However the other two were by no means to be discouraged and decided on making the attempt at a spot where they thought it possible. Their plan was put into operation without delay. The tandem was divested of its luggage and a long strap attached to the rear carrier. It was then heaved over the side, Frank supporting the front, while Fon hung onto the strap behind digging her heels into the hillside and gradually letting out the strap while Frank eased the machine down. A drop of about 800 feet had to be negotiated in this fashion and it took them nearly two hours to do it.

In the meantime I being a very poor mountaineer could do nothing but remain at the top to see what happened, and I did not feel very confident of getting down without a broken neck or at least a broken leg or arm or two, let alone of carrying the machine down. On the other hand to let two people for whom I had more than a passing regard go on into the unknown with always the chance of a broken limb or at least a sprained ankle by themselves was unthinkable. With three, even if one of them is aged and infirm there is always the chance of obtaining assistance in case of such a mishap, which was then the one danger I had in mind.

However when they returned Frank solved my difficulty by packing my mount on his back and scrambling down, so burdened, at such speed that he had some time to wait before Fon joined him with their luggage. My lot did weigh more than about 14lbs while the two bags off the tandem must have scaled at least 20lbs each, and by all the rules of the game I ought to have carried one of them, but Fon overruled my somewhat diffident request to be allowed to do so, saying I was not to worry about her, as she was "as strong as little elephant". In view of subsequent events she can be acquitted of having made a vain boast.

We both came to grief more than once on the way down but with only trivial damage such as a few scratches and bruises. We thought that having overcome this obstacle our troubles were at an end and that we had only to follow the river which ran out of the far end of the lake and make a speedy return to civilisation. But so far from our troubles being at an end they were only just beginning. There was a notice board on the lake denoting it as a reservoir for the Aberystwyth Water Works so it seemed reasonable to suppose there must be some easier way of getting to it than by that by which we had come.

The surrounding of the lake upon which we turned our backs about 6.15 p.m. were marshy but as we proceeded along the margin of the river we were soon travelling through what can only be described as bog, making our way by a series of hops from root to root of the reeds and even the roots began to sink unless speedily vacated. The appearance of a broken down, uninhabited hut about a mile on the way satisfied me that we were on the right track or rather going in the right direction, for there was no sign of anything like a pathway. One or two more deserted and ruined huts were passed which appeared to have been unused for years or perhaps centuries.

In the meantime Fon was having a busy time, having frequently to leave her proper job of helping Frank with the tandem to come and give a mighty heave to get me out of a bog hole or up a boggy slope.

About 7.30 p.m. a new problem presented itself. The river which we had been following, hoping it would lead our faltering footsteps to the haunts of man, split into three separate streams. The obvious thing to do was to follow the middle one, but this of course made it necessary to cross the one upon the banks of which we were. This stream was about 25 feet across and its greatest depth did not appear to be more than about 18 inches. Some large stones in the water offered the prospect of a dry crossing to the young and active and the tandem was safely got across on these. This method of crossing did not appeal to me, and being already thoroughly wet in the feet and legs, I deemed it safer to wade it. Hoisting my bicycle onto my shoulder I stepped into the water finding it somewhat deeper than it looked and very cold.

My next step was an ill-advised one, for it was onto a large flat stone which, tipping up, precipitated my bicycle with me on top of it into the stream. It was lucky the bicycle was underneath for had I gone over the other way my immersion would have been total. As it was, though one of the pedals removed most of the skin from my right hip bone, only one half of me got wet. The bicycle went completely under including of course my bag containing my camera and all my spare clothing. Of course I scrambled out with the property as speedily as possible not feeling too well pleased.

This incident produced a temporary depression to come over the spirits of Fon, the lion hearted. Had she sat down on her haunches and laughed at the ludicrous spectacle which I must have presented it would have quite excusable though somewhat surprising and I should have felt slightly sorry for myself. As it was I had to treat it as a matter of course and pretend that I rather enjoyed the experience.

The fact of being somewhat damp was of minor importance beside the next problem that loomed ahead. It was now rapidly becoming dusk – we were in the midst of an apparently limitless bog which stretched for miles behind and before us. It was obvious that all hope of reaching civilisation before darkness was completely out of the question and that we should have to spend a night out under the stars. This would have been a small matter under ordinary circumstances for luckily the sky was gloriously clear and the possibilities of rain remote, but the problem was to find anywhere solid enough to rest without sinking into the bog. In the meantime there was nothing for it but to keep moving on in the dark.

When we started on this tour we were not prepared for much night riding and had only brought small electric lamps. Mine, having been dowsed in the water emitted only a feeble glimmer. About 9.45 p.m. Fon was a short distance ahead, carrying the lamp off the tandem when suddenly she disappeared, rather to the alarm of Frank and myself. However she soon reappeared having made a fortunate discovery. This was a kind of semi-circular shelf of solid ground in the side of the hill, with a low bank at the back of it. There was room for ourselves and our machines and it took no debate for us to decide to make it our quarters for the night.

Our preparations for rest did not take long. I took off my wet shirt and was just wringing out a flannel one I had in my bag to put on, when I was stopped by Fon. She insisted on my borrowing a dry one of Frank's. I also borrowed a dry pair of stockings from Frank and took off my shoes, putting them with other wet things out to dry. Fon had a thick woollen bathing costume in her bag. This she made me put round my neck. My macintosh cape was of course soaked, so it was deemed necessary that I should have one of theirs, while they both got into one, and when they got both their heads out of one hole they looked like the Siamese twins!

Before we finally settled down for the night Fon doled out to Frank and I part of the provisions saved from the picnic, refusing to eat anything herself. We were all fairly weary and must have slept about 2½ hours; at any rate it was about 2.15 a.m. when we all woke up feeling very cold and no doubt Frank and Fon were very cramped in their one cape.

After this I do not think anyone slept for more than a few minutes at a time. When I did doze off it always ended in the same way. I would dream we had just been investigating one of the ruined huts we had seen yesterday and just as we were satisfied it was uninhabited, a woman would issue forth carrying a tea tray fully equipped, and just as I was anticipating the hot tea I would wake up with a groan on realising the actual position.

That night seemed interminable. Time after time my repeater was struck by request only to find that what seemed like hours since last its chimes were heard, was in reality only a quarter of an hour. We told silly stories, sang songs, recited Shakespeare and talked about eatables. When I started moaning out Omar Khayyam, Fon who had no acquaintance with the Persian philosopher and poet, thought that I was becoming delirious! A competition to see who could keep longest without their teeth chattering proved too difficult. There was always a great commotion every time Frank and Fon wanted to turn over in their tight fitting joint overcoat and I was expecting to hear it split at any moment. There was no turning over for me as my right side was much too sore for me to want to lay on it. In consequence I was getting extremely stiff and rather worried about the difficulty I had in wagging my toes!

A GOLDEN AGE OF CYCLING

At last some signs of dawn began to appear and Frank got on his feet and did a war dance for about twenty minutes. When it got a little more light I reached out for one of my stockings which I had put out to dry. It stood up like a clothes prop, and then I understood why I had found it so difficult to waggle my toes. I had had nothing to cover my feet and the hoar frost settling on my stockings (or rather Frank's spare stockings which I had borrowed) had frozen them stiff. Everything that I had put out to dry was in the same hard, frozen condition, the worst case being my shoes which were as hard as wood. It took nearly half-an-hour's work to get them soft enough to put on, this delaying our start until about 6.30 a.m. the sun not having yet appeared over the hills.

Before we moved off Fon divided the remainder of the rations between Frank and I. No arguments would induce her to eat anything herself. When we went to our bicycles we found them frozen stiff and covered in hoar frost. It took quite an effort to get them on the move. We then found that had we gone on another fifty yards in the direction we were travelling last night we should have stood an excellent chance of all going over the top into the river about thirty or forty feet below. Bog in its natural state is difficult to traverse with bicycles but it is ever so much worse when it is semi frozen, and the reeds heavy with hoar frost. The wet half of me was stiff and creaking and my frozen feet were most painful.

About 7.30 a.m. I felt unable to go further and had an irresistible desire to sit down in the bog, and it was only a well-deserved scolding from Fon that got me on the move again. In the meantime Frank was trudging on with the tandem with grim determination.

The sun had now scaled the hills. This warmth was gratefully received, the only drawback being that the hoar frost melting under his rays wetted the parts of us which had not been wet before. About 8 o'clock we came upon evidence of the handiwork of man. It appeared to be some kind of drainage works, but at any rate there was a slab of solid concrete upon which we could rest without fear of sinking. Frank and I took advantage of it while Fon, still full of beans, went off on a scouting mission on her own.

She had scrambled to the top of a boggy hill about a quarter of a mile away when she suddenly became excited. Frank and I went up to where she was standing. She was sure she had seen smoke rising from the chimney of a small house standing by a lake about two miles away. I was quite prepared to find it was only a wreath of mist rising from the bog but after a few minutes the mist rolled away and we actually saw what she has seen. Reference to the map showed this house marked as 'The Angler's Retreat'. We hoped it would prove an inn, but at any rate whatever its inhabitants were, they could hardly refuse refreshment to folk in our plight.

Needless to say, stiff joints, frozen feet and such-like disabilities were forgotten and a bee-line made for that refuge with all speed. Such obstacles as bog holes, rivers of water and rivers of mud, did not deter us. When we were within about a mile we heard the welcome sound of a cock-crow. No music could have been sweeter for since we had left the summit of Plynlimon, yesterday afternoon, except for a few sheep we had seen or heard no living thing. There had been no sound of animal, bird or even insect life, in the place where we had spent the night, nothing but the sound of the river running below us.

We found our way into a cultivated enclosure with the house, a tumble-down- looking structure, below us. Frank undertook the job of ambassador to parley with the inhabitants, Fon and I remaining with the cycles on the path above. We had now nothing to worry about for leading away from the house was a well-defined track which must lead somewhere, but all the same it appeared that Frank was going to converse with the rough looking customer who came to the door, for ever, so that we got tired of waiting and came down to join in their deliberation.

It appeared that the house belonged to one of the local gentry who used it as a shelter for himself and his friends when they came to fish in the lake. The caretaker, who appeared to be in mortal fear of this terrible person, could not see his way to allowing us to enter the house, but if we liked, his old woman would bring us out some tea, and bread and butter and cheese, if that would be any good to us.

Needless to say this offer was accepted with alacrity, and in due course the good woman came out of the front door bearing the fully equipped tea tray which I had seen in my dreams so many times during the night, the only difference being that the tea was in a jug and not in a pot. I fully expected to wake up as usual and find it was not there, but nothing of the sort happened this time.

The savour of that feed was only equalled by a feast three of us had from a tin of sardines in another place in the hungry days of the winter of 1917. Fon, now absolved from the responsibility of getting us out of the mess in which we had involved her, did ample justice to it, after having fasted from 2 o'clock yesterday afternoon and displayed enough energy in the meantime for at least three ordinary people.

The caretaker seemed rather nervous about our taking the track which we had seen which led out to a road to Talybont about nine miles away, for fear that we might meet his terrible master, but we were not in a mood to worry about a thing like that and decided to go that way. The parting gift to Fon was a spring of white heather, "For luck," he said, "For pluck," said Frank and I both at once.

When we had got about a mile on the way Fon called a halt, opened her bag on the tandem and sat down by the side of a stream. Frank and I left her to it and in about ten minutes there emerged a brand new Fon who, so far from having spent a particularly uncomfortable night out in a bog under the stars, with no sustenance but some bread and cheese and tea for about twenty hours, might have stepped straight out of a seaside hotel after a good breakfast.

The road to Talybont was rough but being downhill all the way presented no difficulties and we arrived in that one-horse town about 10.45 a.m. revelling in the luxury of seeing people and dogs walking about again and even seeing motors and hearing the 'toots' of their horns.

Fon, who had now assumed undisputed command of the expedition, decreed that the first thing to be done was to find a shop where Frank and I could be fitted out with new stockings and me with dry shoes of some description. As in many country towns there was a general store probably kept by Mr Jones, which can supply everything in some form. Stockings were obtained at an expense that was by no means ruinous and a variety of other things were purchased, including a needle and thread for the repair of my bag, which had become unstuck during the night's adventure. Mr Jones, however, was a failure when it came to the question of shoes, not having anything large enough for my hooves.

There was another shop, which fitted me out with canvas shoes of the right size, and the next business was to find somewhere to don our new garments and also to obtain something to eat. It was not my first visit to Talybont and I had often admired the sign of the 'White Lion', though I had never been in that hotel. We made our way there, negotiated for the use of the bathrooms in which to change our things and found they could supply us with some eggs and bacon. We occupied the bathroom for about ten minutes.

The eggs and bacon were of the most meagre description, the tea was of the washy kind and we were charged 9/- and particularly requested to recommend the hotel to our friends! Needless to say we have advertised it freely but hardly in the way the proprietor intended. After this 'banquet' and the expert repair of my bag by Frank, it was decreed that we should make for the coast at Borth and seek repose in the sun on the beach or elsewhere.

Borth is the usual kind of sordid Welsh seaside resort but its beach is all that we desired. After some more light refreshment we sought the beach, and after parking the cycles Frank and Fon were making up for lost sleep in about five minutes. I spent the afternoon spreading out my wet goods to dry in the sun, effecting repairs to damaged mudguards and writing postcards, including a somewhat alarming one to Jack, who had warned me that if I went a touring with these people I must expect adventures.

We adjourned to tea at the 'Friendship Inn' about 4.30 p.m. just missing 'Wayfarer' who had been there just previously. It was quite a satisfying tea and after it we decided to make for Machynlleth for the night taking the coast road north and through the Artist's Valley.

At Machynlleth the commanding officer ordered that we must go somewhere where we could get hot baths before going to bed in blankets with double whiskies. This was to counteract any chance of chill resulting from our last night's adventure. "Orders is orders" but in a place like Machynlleth it was rather difficult to see how these particular ones could be carried out. Yesterday having been a cheap day we were not going to care much about expense, but the two large A.A. Hotels did not look particularly inviting. I remembered some years ago having had a very good tea at the 'White Horse' so we thought we would try that first. Here we were received with the greatest hospitability and when the landlady heard something of our story we were invited to ask for anything we wanted.

All wet stuff that had not dried on the beach at Borth was taken away and put before the kitchen fire. The latter was stoked up for our hot baths and after an excellent supper we did not delay in having our baths and getting between the blankets with "the something hot". Thus ended an adventure which though amusing to look back upon might have been a very unpleasant matter and we might even have been added to the list of people who have mysteriously disappeared from time to time.

There were so many things that might have happened and caused disaster. My fear all along was of disablement of one of the party. In that case one of us must have gone for help without any idea of where to look for it, and if and when it was found, the task of finding the other two would have been almost insurmountable even if they had not sunk in the bog in the meantime. Then supposing one of the drenching storms common to Wales had come up, it would have been impossible to move in the bog and the prospects of being added to the 'missing' list would have practically amounted to a certainty. Again a dense mist is always possible among any mountains, particularly boggy ones, so taken on the whole we could count ourselves extremely fortunate in coming out of it, not only alive but with no damage.

Distance covered 8/9/31: about 16 miles
Distance covered 9/9/31: 28 miles.

THURSDAY 10TH SEPTEMBER
Disappointment at Dinas Mawddwy
MACHYNLLETH – CEMMAES – DINAS MAWDDWY – LLANFAIR CAEREINON – MONTGOMERY

The good people at the 'White Horse' were determined we should have our sleep and when I finally struggled down about 9.30 a.m. feeling a bit stiff in the joints but otherwise quite fit, there was still no sign of my companions in crime. However, by the time I had had a stroll down the High Street and obtained the morning paper they had made their appearance and breakfast got under way about 10 o'clock, and soon after 11 o'clock we took leave of the 'White Horse'. The hospitable treatment we had received at this inn was above all criticism and removed for a time the impression which we had obtained of North Welsh innkeepers at the 'White Lion' Talybont.

Yesterday during the afternoon period of rest I had sent a postcard to Mr Maddox at Montgomery to expect us and that was to be our last day among the rocky mountain.

The 'Buckley Arms' at Dinas Mawddwy commended itself to me as a place where one could expect a good lunch at a price and we were most anxious to do ourselves well. Accordingly we made our way down the main road through Penegoes, turning left at Cemmaes Road Station for Mallwyd, taking things quietly so as to get our stiff joints in working order. Though we stopped for refreshments at the 'Penrhos Inn' Cemmaes we got into Dinas Mawddwy before 1 o'clock making at once for the 'Buckley Arms' where we were informed lunch would be ready at 1.30 p.m.

Full of anticipation of a really good tuck in we set out for a stroll up the Dolgellau road to get our appetites up to concert pitch. Our feelings can only be compared to those of 'Three Men in a Boat' prior to the incident of the famous pineapple when we returned for lunch. We were shown into a baronial hall glittering with plate and polished glass. The first course was some thin soup of a dubious nature. This was followed by either some cold salt beef cut off a very aged cow or ham from a consumptive pig (I am not sure which) and tongue from some kind of elderly animal. At any rate, hungry as we were, it took some getting down. A small slab of cold plum tart (tinned or bottled fruit) completed this banquet and we were glad to escape on payment of 11/6 for this wonderful blow-out.

True to its reputation Dinas Mawddwy treated us to tears as we left it and a pelting rain followed us as far as Cann Office, so that the views on this glorious stretch of road were lost to us. At Cann Office the rain had not entirely ceased but it was gentle enough to permit the removal of capes, a great relief as the temperature was by no means low.

At Llanfair Caereinon tea became a pressing need and we did very well at Mr Williams'. By the time this important event was finished the rain had died out for good. The direct road to Welshpool did not appeal to the commanding officer so she took us a short cut over many rough and troublesome hills, which eventually landed us at Berriew from whence it is only a few miles through Garthmyl to Montgomery.

At the 'Old Bell', Mr Maddox was able to put us up and once more the little room in the turret was to be my quarters for the night. More importantly there still was a very excellent piece of Welsh mutton for our consideration which somewhat made up for our disappointment at Dinas Mawddwy.

The rain had come on again so we were not able to do much wandering before going early to bed to clear off some more arrears of sleep.

FRIDAY IITH SEPTEMBER

A day of many mountains.

MONTGOMERY – BISHOP'S CASTLE – CLUN – KNIGHTON – PRESTEIGNE – WHITNEY-ON-WYE

Admiration of the latest Maddox baby and a visit to the castle ruins (where Fon got her unprotected legs stung by the special brand of nettle which grows in that spot), writing and posting many postcards, and a visit by Frank to the local agricultural implement and cycle accessories dealer made it nearly 11 o'clock before we got away from Montgomery.

A GOLDEN AGE OF CYCLING

Yesterday's rain had passed off and we saw the beautiful stretch of road from Bluebell to Bishop's Castle under the best conditions. The tandem dashing down the precipitous descent from the 'pulpit' end of Bishop's Castle left me with a lot of arrears to make up, but the pace was necessarily much slower on the strenuous road to Clun.

On arrival at this busy town we made straight for the 'Buffalo' and enquired for lunch. Mrs Lewis was much distressed to have to inform us that she had been eaten out of house and home. But if we did not mind waiting twenty minutes or so she could cook us some steaks. As it was only just 1 o'clock this suited us very well and, dumping our machines, we went for a stroll to spin out the requisite time.

When we returned everything was ready for us. Five steaks cooked to a turn with vegetables in like case. This was followed by a pudding of unknown composition which was delicious and we only wished we could have shown the lot to the 'Buckley Arms' as a sample of how things should be done. This fortified us and though feeling somewhat heavy, the notorious 'New Invention' road from Clun to Knighton held no terrors for us. Riding what we could we walked the steepest part of the two peaks, letting fly down the downgrades so that we accomplished this fierce seven miles well under the hour.

At Knighton, Fon's search for souvenirs of Wales, which we were leaving today, proved unfruitful and we adjourned to the 'George and Dragon' for a satisfactory tea. It was required as we had quite a lot more collar work to do to make the 'Stowe Inn' which was our chosen refuge for the night.

Between Knighton and Presteigne is Cwm Whitton Hill, marked on Bartholomew as 1208 feet. This was ascended at a steady 12 mph – quite fast enough to deprive me of all the wind I ever possessed. On the other side it runs down 378 feet at Norton in about 2½ miles. The tandem very soon whizzed out of sight down this declivity. The driver of a car which had drawn up by the side of the road, told me he had been doing 55 mph down the hill and they had passed him as though he was standing still! I rode as fast as I could possibly go and after six miles I at last found them waiting for me on the railway bridge at the entrance to Presteigne.

After this the road via Titley to Kington is plain sailing but we still had one more 'big push' to do to Eardisley. This however did not take long and we rolled into the 'Stowe Inn' just at the right time for supper of real 'Stowe Inn' quality.

Distance covered: 44 miles

1931 A QUICK SEPTEMBER TOUR

SATURDAY 12TH SEPTEMBER

Return to the Royal City

WHITNEY-ON-WYE — LEOMINSTER — BROMYARD — WORCESTER — PERSHORE — CHIPPING NORTON — GREAT TEW

We were aware that our scheduled trip for today to Great Tew was rather a handful and the weather was none too promising. We therefore made an early start just before 10 o'clock turning left at Willersley Cross and then right for Leominster through Dilwyn.

The state of the weather did not warrant our making the detour to visit the black and white picturesque village of Weobley. At Leominster a bakers shop supplied us with 'elevenses' and just as we were entering, a tandem pair I had met before somewhere were just leaving.

From Leominster the Bromyard road via Docklow and Bredenbury was very tough and coming down into Bromyard we met a heavy storm, which stung my eyeballs until they felt nearly raw so that we felt that a hot lunch was suitable to the occasion. The 'Falcon' did us quite well in this respect, but it was still raining steadily when we once more got on our way. It was not until we were within a few miles of Worcester that the rain abated sufficiently to allow us to remove our capes.

Since my last visit to the Royal City it has scrapped its trams but even without these encumbrances it is a dismal horror to get through. We spent about half an hour there, Fon having some shopping to do which resulted in my bag having to accommodate some large sticks of Worcester rock.

We were now in the Worcestershire lowlands and made short work of Whittington and Stoulton to Pershore. Tea was now a crying need and the 'Chequers' appealed to us as a suitable feeding station. Very welcome was the sight of a fire in the bar parlour and the tea was of excellent quality.

From Pershore through Evesham to Broadway is easy going, which was as well as time was getting on and we yet had a considerable distance to go. From Broadway we made for Moreton-in-Marsh from whence to Chipping Norton is exceptionally heavy going.

Darkness was now upon us and we were equipped with nothing better than feeble electric lamps. With this poor lighting power, the seven miles from Chipping Norton to Great Tew seemed interminable, especially when we had turned off the Banbury road. It was very nearly 10 o'clock when we at last reached harbour finding Jack awaiting us expecting to find us all with

239

hacking coughs and crippled with rheumatism after the Plynlimon episode. He had to be regaled with all the details while we were despatching the usual excellent supper provided by Mr Matthews.

Distance covered: 86 miles, mostly wet ones

SUNDAY 13TH SEPTEMBER

A fitting end to a short but rather eventful tour

GREAT TEW – AYLESBURY – IVINGHOE – ELSTREE – EDGWARE – HAMMERSMITH

Frank and Fon were anxious to get home as soon as possible but it is not easy to leave Great Tew in a hurry, especially on a fine morning such as this was. It was accordingly about 11.30 a.m. before we got under way, I having a naked cauliflower attached to my bag which flopped continuously.

We took the most direct road to Bicester and doing without 'elevenses', made on for Aylesbury where an indifferent lunch at the 'Tank Restaurant' did not take us long. Just beyond Tring, Jack and I parted with Frank and Fon after arranging for a meeting on Tuesday at home.

Jack and I made a detour for tea at 'The Bell' at Ivinghoe. I parted from him at Elstree and came home via Edgware and Wealdstone. The day had been as fine as yesterday was wet, a fitting end to a short but rather eventful tour.

Distance covered: 84 miles

1931 HAVE YOURSELF A MERRY CYCLING CHRISTMAS – MERLIN I

SATURDAY 26TH DECEMBER
The balloon retrieval expedition
DORKING – GODALMING – SHALFORD – HINDHEAD

I was under contract to re-join the other cyclists at 'Hindhead Nurseries', rather a cross-country trip from Halstead. Fortified with a supply of turkey and ham sandwiches I started off about 11 o'clock. In an effort to avoid Westerham Hill I got involved in Titsey which is rather worse and got through Limpsfield and Oxted to Godstone, from whence it was plain sailing to Redhill and Reigate and from there through Betchworth and Buckland to Dorking. Outside Dorking I sat down in a warm sun and demolished my sandwiches, washing them down with a Bass at the 'Punch Bowl Inn'.

Dorking to Godalming looks an awkward bit of cross country on the map, but via Westcott, Wotton, Gomshall, Shere and Albury turning left at Shalford I was surprised to find it took me less than an hour, being only 12 rather strenuous miles. There was therefore no particular hurry up the part of Hindhead leading to Thursley, and when I arrived at the Nurseries about 4 o'clock, I found Jack there disconsolate with no sign of Frank and Fon who should have been there to lunch. This was rather disconcerting and we were rather worried about them. However they turned up about 4.30 p.m. having had a very late Christmas night or an early Boxing morning involving a walk home from Kennington to Regent's Park.

We had rather a scratchy tea, Fon having to forage around for it as the place was so full up that everything was at sixes and sevens. After tea we got the "use" of a small room and after blowing up a few balloons, sat down in front of the fire. It being mild and moonlit, a stroll under the stars culminated in one of the balloons taking flight. Fon, as usual, full of beans, scaled the roof of an outhouse and by calculations based on the strength and direction of the wind, located the place where the missing aerostat should have taken refuge.

To reach the spot it was necessary to make an adventurous expedition into the cow yard. Fon has a decided objection to horned beasts and therefore it is another feather in her cap that she cast all misgivings aside and, making her way unfalteringly to the place she had located from the roof, there found the fugitive in an outhouse. Now comes the tragic part of the story. While returning triumphantly with the spoils of the chase it managed to touch a holly bush with the usual result.

Supper of cold turkey was also rather a scrawny affair and nothing at all like what we had hoped for. With the crowd who were there, 45 at least, sleeping arrangements became a problem. Mr Barnare appeared to be verging on insanity trying to work out arrangements. Eventually as far as our party was concerned, Jack, Frank and I were delegated to a caravan about 200 yards from the house, while Fon had a bed in the house in a large room with several other girls.

The other people were put out in a cottage nearby, a railway carriage of six compartments, and in various parts of the house, wherever there was room. We retired to our caravan about 1 a.m. and found it eminently comfortable, complete with three camp beds and an oil stove, but the night was so warm that we had all the windows and the door wide open. Under the circumstances, it is not surprising that we slept like tops.

Distance covered: 47 miles

SUNDAY 27TH DECEMBER

No ordinary girl

HINDHEAD – THURSLEY – RIPLEY – HAMMERSMITH

We woke up in our al fresco sleeping chamber, to a glorious morning. Tucking my pyjamas into my stockings to make plus fours I climbed out and had ten minutes run around a field about 7.45 a.m. Jack, when he was at last persuaded to wake up volunteered to go over to the house and get a teapot and some tea which we could make with water boiled over our oil stove. Seeing that he does not drink tea himself, this was rather sporting of him but doubtless he was sufficiently rewarded in seeing the pleasure with which Frank and I drank ours!

When we got to the house for breakfast we found Fon rather distraught. She had had by no means a comfortable time amid the noisy house party and only a negligible quantity of sleep. This was rather distressing considering that she had had only the minimum of rest on the preceding night. And of course she had to do most of the foraging around before we could get any breakfast. It would therefore have been quite excusable if she had sat down somewhere after breakfast and gone to sleep. However Fon is no ordinary girl and five minutes after we had set out on a hiking expedition she was full of beans as ever.

Frank and Jack stalked on ahead finding the way, while she and I were rushing about like four year olds, playing hockey with a stone, a fir cone or a marble for a ball. By the time we reached the top of Stony Jump we must have expended at least four times as much energy as Frank and Jack had.

On the return journey we found an old bicycle wheel, which was requisitioned as a loop. After everyone had had a go at driving it, it assumed all sorts of curious shapes and it finally reached Ridgeway Farm looking like nothing on earth, its final adventures being used as a cricket ball in opposition to a small tree as the bat.

It was too early for lunch so we decided to take the short cut to the 'local' at Thursley and have one. On the way down, Fon certainly appeared to be feeling the effects of the strenuous life. After we had finished our drinks, fully restored, she had an idea of getting back first ahead of Frank and Jack. By dint of fast walking and an occasional sprint when they were hidden by a bend of the road, we soon dropped them out of sight.

Unfortunately when we got in the rough we took a wrong path along which we had gone nearly a mile before we realised it. There was nothing for it but to sprint back to the point where we had gone astray. I was puffing like a grampus[20] by the time we had found the proper way and there was still much rough stuff to be negotiated, which was mostly taken at a trot. We were somewhat puzzled that we had not caught up the other two and when we got back at last found them calmly sitting waiting for us. It was not an occasion to stand upon scruples, so I started at once to lie bravely, stating that we had been back long since and as they did not turn up we had been out looking for them.

Fon, not being a disciple of pragmatism looked somewhat appalled at my display of mendacity, which was received in stony silence. It afterward transpired that Frank and Jack had also something to conceal. More cold turkey etc. (one soon gets tired of cold turkey) made up our lunch and after it we left the Commander-in-Chief asleep in an armchair in front of the fire for an hour before thinking of making a start on the homeward journey just after 4 o'clock.

As we proposed having tea at 'Warner's' at Ripley, there was no time to lose, so that the pace was quite lively in spite of sundry lamp troubles. I was just boasting of the reliability of the 'Hooded Terror' when its bulb went 'plut' and was only extracted with the greatest of difficulty for the insertion of a new one.

The tandem and I turned into 'Warner's' thinking Jack was close behind but he had stopped some distance down the road to tend his lamp. Consequently he went on a considerable distance (either because he did not know where 'Warner's' was or to put on an extra mile or two) and had to return. The roads for the rest of the way were fairly clear and we got home about 9.30 p.m. and thus ending the Christmas festivities for 1931.

It had been a marvellous time as far as weather was concerned, far superior to any Easter we have had of recent years. However, we felt that we had been rather let down at Hindhead Nurseries. Goodness knows it had been popular enough before without being made into a Youth Hostel and this has probably been our last visit, at any rate as an all-night stopping place.

The trip home only amounted to 36 miles.

---

20 A member of the dolphin family of cetaceans

1931 HAVE YOURSELF A MERRY CYCLING CHRISTMAS

CYCLING STATISTICS FOR 1931 BY MILES AND NUMBER OF RIDES PER MONTH

MONTH	NUMBER OF RIDES			MILES RIDDEN				AVERAGE MILES PER RIDE			
	ALL DAY	TOURING WEEKENDS	OTHER RIDES	ALL DAYS	TOURING WEEKENDS	OTHER RIDES	TOTAL	ALL DAYS	TOURING WEEKENDS	OTHER RIDES	ALL RIDES
Jan	3	-	6	234	-	244	478	78.00	-	40.66	53.11
Feb	2	4	5	141	263	137	541	70.50	65.75	27.40	48.27
Mar	3	8	4	210	596	149	955	70.00	74.50	37.25	63.66
Apr	1	13	7	60	792	262	1114	60.00	60.92	37.42	53.04
May	2	12	7	165	847	218	1230	82.50	70.58	31.14	58.57
June	1	12	7	91	874	221	1186	91.00	72.82	36.83	62.42
July	2	16	7	182	769	197	1148	91.00	48.09	26.71	45.92
Aug	-	22	3	-	1669	104	1773	-	71.31	34.66	70.92
Sept	2	13	6	175	783	173	1131	87.50	60.23	28.82	53.85
Oct	-	15	8	-	866	241	1107	-	57.73	30.12	48.13
Nov	3	5	8	189	346	280	815	63.00	69.20	35.00	50.93
Dec	2	7	7	151	428	244	823	75.50	61.14	34.85	51.43
Totals	21	127	75	1598	8233	2470	12301	76.09	64.82	34.73	55.41

The problem picture of the year. Part of what Bartholomew marks as a "road" from Aston Tirrold to Cholsey Ferry.

What is the lady doing?

1932 AN EASTER TOUR –
MERLIN I

WEDNESDAY 23RD MARCH

Good sustenance and mileage

HAMMERSMITH – GUILDFORD – FARNHAM – BENTLEY – SALISBURY – WINCHESTER – HURSLEY – ROMSEY – WIMBORNE

Arrangements were made that Jack should meet me in Salisbury by the first train arriving Friday morning. Having banking and other business to do first I made a late start about 10.45 a.m., and as the New Forest was my destination I decided on the most direct road especially as there was a steady wind against me. Consequently I took the main road to Guildford and over the Hogs Back to Farnham arriving there at about 1 p.m.. I had two meat pies and a pint of Courage at the 'Star' at Bentley.

The long rise from Alton to Four Marks was arduous owing to the wind and I arrived in Winchester at 4.45 p.m. before turning left on the Romsey road. For some reason I was feeling very sluggish so at 4.30 p.m. I turned into the 'King's Arms' at Hursley for an excellent tea after which complete recovery ensued.

I proceeded to cycle through Romsey and Cadnam and though it was rather early I tried to put up at the 'Stoney Cross' but was turned down. The same fate befell me at the 'Kettle', Picket Post and the night being fine, rather than put up at Ringwood, I decided to push on to Wimborne. Here my confidence in the 'Crown Tap' was not misplaced, and I had a first rate dish of ham and eggs followed by hot cake before going to roost hoping that the sun which had shone throughout the day would continue over the Easter Holidays and with a mileage of *101 miles* to my credit.

THURSDAY 24TH MARCH

The miraculous ascent of the piano organ

WIMBORNE – BLANDFORD – SHAFTESBURY – MERE – FOVANT – COMPTON CHAMBERLAYNE – DINTON – WILTON – SALISBURY

It was a bleak misty looking morning but with no sign of rain. I made first of all for Blandford via Sturminster Marshall and Charlton Marshall. I wanted to get to Mere without having to climb into Shaftesbury but my only map of the district was a quarter inch one, the scale being too small to enable me to find a satisfactory route.

Accordingly, I made for Shaftesbury up and down many tedious hills with little of the picturesque to make amends for the hard labour involved. Iwerne Minster attracted me off the main road but it is spoilt by new red brick buildings. Melbury Hill is a long plug and as usual there is a precipitous descent before the final climb into Shaftesbury. From Shaftesbury, the seven miles to Mere via Motcombe is mainly downhill.

I called at the 'Walnut Tree' for bread, cheese and beer and much chat with the people there who are friends of the Sissons[1]. The main road from Mere to Hindon was a mass of motor traffic going in both directions so I was glad to get on the quieter way to Tisbury and Fovant. This road goes up and out of Hindon like the side of a house and my bottom gear was inadequate to tackle it. About half way up an old Italian was struggling with a piano organ, his only means of progress being to tack across, getting up about a yard at a time, but with me pushing behind we managed to make a straight job of it and soon got it to the top. I left him amid a shower of thanks but it puzzles me as to how he got it down the other side, which was equally steep, and over the succession of hills to the next town, Tisbury, which has a most precipitous High Street.

From Tisbury I found bye-ways to Fovant and turned in at the 'Cross

---

1 The owners of the Walnut Tree Inn in Mere near Shaftsbury were obviously friends of the Sissons. The Walnut Tree was pulled down in 1938.

Keys' for tea afterwards, taking a leisurely tour of many spots familiar in my Army days, including the village of Compton Chamberlayne which I had not visited since those days. I even went a long way out of my way to visit the 'Wyndham Arms' at Dinton where I once spent a riotous Sunday evening with a party of men due to leave for France the next day, nearly all of whom were swallowed up in the holocaust of the Somme within a few weeks of their landing.

I eventually made for Salisbury via Barford St. Martin and Wilton, and after wandering around to get a new cable release for my camera which I eventually obtained from Fowler Smith, the C.T.C. Consul, I put up as usual at the 'Coach and Horses' where a telegram was awaiting me from Jack saying he was arriving at 12.20 p.m. tomorrow.

Distance covered: 59 miles

GOOD FRIDAY 25TH MARCH

An old acquaintance

SALISBURY – WILTON – WARMINSTER – LEIGH-ON-MENDIP – WELLS

In spite of a gloomy weather forecast it was a bright sunny morning. After strolling round the cathedral I took a short run down the Stonehenge road and then met Jack's train, going back to the 'Coach and Horses' for lunch. We set off about two o'clock taking the westward road and bearing right at Wilton. We were not eager for main roads and while consulting the maps at Wishford, Collett, an old acquaintance, turned up. He was making for Leigh-on-Mendip for tea and as it was the direction we wanted we submitted to his guidance.

The road we took through Wylye, Stockton, Tytherington and Sutton Veny, ran parallel with the main road and we eventually landed in Warminster going on through Frome to Leigh-on-Mendip (pronounced 'Lye'). Here we had a gorgeous tea leaving Collett there with two friends from London. We proposed stopping in Wells for the night and got there via Oakhill just as it was getting dark. Wells is notoriously difficult to get put up in so we were agreeably surprised to have an affirmative answer from our first attempt at the 'Angel Inn', which proved quite a good billet. Wells in the evening is as dead as mutton and after an eggs and bacon supper we went to bed early.

It had been bright and sunny all day but the sunset was ominous.

Distance covered: 53 miles

A GOLDEN AGE OF CYCLING

SATURDAY 26TH MARCH

A curious quest

WELLS – CHEDDAR – GLASTONBURY – ILCHESTER – MOSTERTON – BEAMINSTER

While we were having breakfast the rain started as if it meant it. We donned our capes and made for the cathedral making a complete survey of the interior of this wonderful old pile which occupied us until nearly 11 o'clock. Our next move was through Westbury and Rodney Stoke to Cheddar. We each invested one shilling in a personally conducted tour amid stalactites and stalagmites of Gough's Cave, which was very wonderful, but when you have seen it you have seen it. Rose Cottage supplied us with a good hot lunch and we made for Wedmore, Westhay and Meare to Glastonbury, up to 'mean' Street and then left on the Somerton road.

Leaving Somerton on our right we went onto Ilchester for a very good tea at the 'Dolphin' and then went on to Crewkerne, which was as usual full of corner boys[2]. Taking the Dorchester road we thought that we should have no difficulty in putting up at Mosterton. We tried the two pubs in that village and were turned down. We met a cyclist coming from the opposite direction who informed us he had raked Beaminster with the same result but we found one place the 'Red Lion' in the handbook which he had not visited. While in converse with him a tandem came along. We warned them that it was no good stopping but they apparently did not hear us and made for the house we had tried. Under the circumstances we thought we had better get to Beaminster first, so dashed on.

It is a toilsome bit of road and at one time the tandem was just behind us but it faded away. At Beaminster we made a dash for the 'Red Lion' with the usual result but a reference to someone nearby. Then began a curious progress, with each place we went to being unable or unwilling to take us in but knowing someone else who might. We tried at least 15 places. The tandem which turned up just afterwards was engaged in the same quest and for some time we were in opposition, which seemed to afford some amusement to the inhabitants who were following our doings with much interest. They were therefore rather disappointed when a coalition took place and we all started the hunt together. The issue was somewhat complicated by having a single girl to provide for, Miss Kymance of the Rosslyn Wheelers.

---

2 Disreputable youths who loiter on street corners

However, success was achieved, a room with two beds to accommodate Jack and I and the captain of the tandem, and a room for the 'crew' being obtained in the same house. Exhausted by our efforts but flushed with success we all adjourned for a sort of supper at the 'Red Lion' where we were exploited to the extent of 1/6d each for, in my case, bread and cheese and half a pint. However as we were garaging our cycles there, we made the best of it. Luckily the rain ceased about 4.30 p.m. otherwise this amusing experience would have been unpleasant!

Distance ridden: 52 miles

SUNDAY 27TH MARCH

Water, water, everywhere
BEAMINSTER – BRIDPORT – DORCHESTER – WAREHAM

Our unpromising 'put up' proved trumps for breakfast time, for in addition to the usual eggs and bacon there was a dish of liver of supreme excellence.

The rain was coming down in full swing when we retrieved our machines from the 'Red Lion' garage, and full storm outfits was the rig of the day. The Cook-Kymance combination proposed making for West Bay and the coast road to Abbotsbury and we accompanied them as far as Bridport. Here the rain ceased for a few minutes but no sooner had we shed our capes than it came on worse than ever.

We parted from the tandem and made for the Dorchester road with the howling gale in our faces. At the best of times this is a formidable stretch but today it was at its worst. It seemed to consist of nothing but toilsome uphill plugs with no compensating run down. For a few miles to Winterbourne Abbas it is a trifle easier but after that the long grinds begin again. It is sufficient to say that the 15 miles took us an hour and a quarter and we arrived in Dorchester tired, wet and hungry at 1.45 p.m. The 'Phoenix' provided us with a satisfactory lunch but it was marred by a charge of 6d each for two cups of inferior coffee. We proposed making for Swanage or as near thereto as the elements would allow us.

The rain continued unabated and there were plenty more slopes to negotiate at any rate as far as Owermoigne after which it is a trifle easier. After passing the unprepossessing village of Wool, the rain increased in intensity and at Wareham, though it was only about 5.30 p.m. we decided to try our luck. The 'Castle Inn' was full up but the proprietor sent us to an adjoining house (Mr Riggs) where we did excellently, a change of stockings and shoes for me (Jack had no change) being a real luxury. Jack removed his stockings and shoes at teatime and put them to dry in front of the fire, having to conceal his nude understanding beneath the table when anyone came in the room.

Except for a short walk after supper when the rain ceased for a few minutes we went out no more and retired very soon after 10 o'clock. It had been the worst possible Easter Sunday and the mileage only amounted to a paltry *38 miles.*

MONDAY 28TH MARCH

A welcome baked jam roll

WAREHAM – CREECH GRANGE – CORFE CASTLE – SWANAGE – STUDLAND – NOMANSLAND –SALISBURY

We hailed a sunshine morning with glee. Even a fine Easter Monday was something to be thankful for.

We succeeded in getting away before 10 o'clock heading in the direction of Swanage and turning right for Creech. Creech Grange[3] was looking very nice in a daffodil starred park but the sun declined to give us its aid for the purpose of photography.

We followed a rough road opposite the Grange, which went over the top of the Purbeck Hills and then petered out into a track, which necessitated the opening of several gates. At the top a small cloud burst drove us to the shelter of our capes and though we took them off again about half way down the other side we once more had to get into them at the bottom. The road we took brought us into Corfe. The Castle looked very impressive from both sides.

From Corfe to Swanage the wind at last began to get behind us. Finding Swanage, a seaside resort of the most ordinary type we soon cleared out in the direction of Studland bent on finding the new road to Bournemouth over the Sandbanks floating bridge. This road, overlooking Poole Harbour, is a very fine one but there is a toll for cyclists of 6d and we were unfortunate in just missing the 10 o'clock trip of the bridge. However we got across to the Poole side about 1.30 p.m. and made our

---

3 Elegant country house completed in 1559 for Sir Oliver Lawrence

way into the Westbourne end of Bournemouth where our first thought was for food.

'Dickenson's Commercial Hotel' looked promising and we did not grumble at being fed on sausages and chips followed by baked jam roll served by a sylphlike waiting maid of anything but reticent manner, named Phyllis. In fact we came to the conclusion that if at any time we were condemned to put up in Bournemouth we might do worse than 'Dickenson's'. When we did get clear of the maze of triangles, squares and streets known as Bournemouth, we found the road to Ringwood merry hell with a procession of cars nose to tail all engaged in trying to run one another down, and we were glad to side track from the Fordingbridge road out of Ringwood and plunge into the New Forest by many stony tracks. It is impossible to trace the tracks we took on the map but we came to a pub at Nomansland (its name I omitted to note) which gave us an ample and rapid tea.

It was now necessary to make all speed for Salisbury as Jack had to leave that city by train tonight. Just after we had lit up a heavy storm made us cape up but it ceased before we got into Salisbury where we made for the station. Enquiry removed Jack's anxiety as to trains and we had plenty of time for supper before he started. The 'Coach and Horses' had no food left and after a stroll round we supped off eggs, bacon and coffee at the 'Cadena Café' in the Market Place, first finding our way to the bathroom at the 'Coach and Horses' for a wash. After seeing Jack off at the station I returned to the 'Coach and Horses' and spent so much time in conversation with two cyclists who had toured in Germany and stayed at Gengenbach that it was long past midnight before we got to bed.

The weather had been a distinct improvement on the two preceding days and the *mileage was 63*.

TUESDAY 29TH MARCH

A breeze to Andover

SALISBURY – ANDOVER – BASINGSTOKE – CAMBERLEY – STAINES – HAMMERSMITH

Owing to the late retirement last night it was nearly 9 a.m. before I could get breakfast and 10 o'clock before I left the 'Coach and Horses', even then having to return after the first mile for my cape which I had left hanging to dry. My final start was not therefore made until about 10.15 a.m.

About two miles out of Salisbury the 'Hooded Terror'[4] was rattling so that I took it off the bracket and stowed it away. The wind behind made the long slopes easy and the 17 miles to Andover only took one hour, despite stopping to cape up when the rain started a few miles before Andover. An hour and ten minutes sufficed for the next stage of 18½ miles to Basingstoke, at 12.25 p.m., and by 1.30 p.m. when something to eat became desirable I was just outside Camberley with only 32 miles to do.

After half an hour's stop for two sandwiches and a Bass at the 'Ely Hotel' I continued on the main road, and reaching Staines at 3.50 p.m., I had a cup of tea and some biscuits. At Twickenham the rain started and I finally reached home just after 4.30 p.m., a fitting wind up to one of the wettest Easters of recent years.

Distance covered: 79 miles

---

4 The cover for the bag at the back of Charles' bike.

1932 A LONG WEEKEND – MERLIN I

FRIDAY 8TH APRIL

Tough going

HAMMERSMITH – WINDSOR – WALTHAM ST. LAWRENCE – HUNGERFORD – LECHLADE – FILKINS – BURFORD

Wanting hard work I set out for Burford in the teeth of a westerly gale. Taking the usual road to Windsor and after 45 minutes conversing with Cushing[5], I went on through Clewer, Waltham St. Lawrence and Twyford to Reading after filling up with bread and cheese at the 'Star' in Waltham St. Lawrence. A heavy storm in Reading drove me to a cape but it soon passed off. The gale was dead in my face down the Bath Road and the last five miles to Newbury had to be crawled on the bottom gear. Newbury to Hungerford was not quite so bad but I was glad of tea at the 'The Red Lion'. Conversation with Bert Hunt, the landlord, made it past 6 o'clock before I left.

As the sun went down, the breeze, though still strong enough, moderated a trifle and in spite of the long up through Chilton Foliat and Aldbourne to Liddington, it was comparatively simple going. The wind was now in

---

5 Likely to be Arthur Frederick Ernest Cushing, born 1904 and married Amy Wheeler in 1934.

my favour and I bowled down to Stratton St. Margaret up to Highworth (scarcely noticing the hill) and down to Lechlade over the Thames in fine style. At Filkins I somehow took the wrong turning in the dark and got to Kencot but regaining the Burford Road turned into the 'Swan' about 9.45 p.m. after a *very tough 96 miles.*

SATURDAY 9TH APRIL

A lordly resting place

BURFORD – CHIPPING NORTON – DEDDINGTON – STONY STRATFORD – NEWPORT PAGNELL – OLNEY – YARDLEY HASTINGS

After sitting up until nearly 1 a.m. talking, it was past nine before I got breakfast and 11.30 a.m. by the time I left the 'Swan'. I had a cross-country trip to do to meet Jack at Newport Pagnell tonight and it did not look very terrifying with the wind in its present quarter.

Shipton-under-Wychwood, Chipping Norton, Swerford over Iron Down and up to Steepness Hill to Deddington (where the 'King's Arms' gave a good cold lunch for 1/6d) was all easy and I was blown through Clifton, Aynho, Croughton and Tingewick into Buckingham. At Stony Stratford a cup of tea and some cake seemed advisable as Jack, owing to the wind was sure to be late and I got into Newport Pagnell through drab Wolverton just after 5 o'clock.

Having found a suitable place for tea I went slowly along the Stratford Road to meet Jack about three miles along it. We returned to the 'Crown' on London Road which did us excellently and decided to make for Yardley Hastings on the chance of getting put at the 'Rose and Crown' there. This took us through Olney and when we found the village it was so dark we had to enquire for the location of the 'Rose and Crown'. However when we found it we had a good enough welcome. There was a pleasant sitting room and a good supper of ham and eggs followed by fruit salad and cream, as much as could be expected in a small inn in an out of the way village. We also had the honour of sleeping in a lordly four-posted bed, the property of the Marquis of Northampton.

Distance covered: 69 miles

1932 A LONG WEEKEND

SUNDAY 10TH APRIL

A ferocious headwind

YARDLEY HASTINGS – BEDFORD – GIRTFORD BRIDGE – WELWYN – ELSTREE

Moist and cloudy daylight revealed Yardley Hastings as a pleasant, well-kept village of mixed thatch, tiles and slate but Jack was in a hurry to get away after breakfast and we gave it little attention.

Lord Northampton's Castle Ashby Estate dominates the district and we made off through the park to Castle Ashby village, which involved much opening of gates. We wandered round through many pleasant villages such as Easton Maudit, Grendon, Bozeat, Harrold and Pavenham and finally entered Bedford by the way of its suburb, Clapham. The district through which we had come certainly merits more leisurely consideration and I shall certainly visit it again later in the year. We turned north east out of Bedford towards St. Neots, and after getting off the track near Great Barford and Blunham, we finally arrived at Girtford Bridge on the Great North Road for lunch at 'Fuller's' – a great rallying place for the racing fraternity.

Turning for home down the Great North Road we had to dig into the breeze. Progress through Biggleswade down to Baldock on that bleak highway, was slow owing to the ferocious headwind. It was little better on through Stevenage and Knebworth. At Welwyn we had a good tea at the 'Rose and Crown' and after climbing up Digswell Hill took to the bye-roads through Roe Green, Shenley and Boreham Wood, to Elstree where after light refreshment at the 'Red Lion', Jack and I parted.

A drenching shower about a mile from home drove me into a cape but this was all the rain we had all day, the mileage being 82.

The 247 miles I had covered in three days is probably the most strenuous bit of riding I have done. First the drive westwards with 80 of 96 miles dead into the wind and then the final struggle from Girtford Bridge which kept every muscle taut the whole time.

1932 A HARD MAY WEEK – MERLIN I

SATURDAY 7TH MAY

A sprint finish

HAMMERSMITH – WINDSOR – HENLEY-ON-THAMES – EWELME – THAME – ABINGDON – NEWBRIDGE

Having telephoned the 'Rose Revived' at Newbridge last night, I found all O.K. for Jack and I for the week and arranged to meet Jack at Thame for tea at 5.30 p.m.

I took the Windsor, Maidenhead, Henley and Nettlebed road to Benson, having bread and cheese at the 'Traveller's Rest' at Henley and turning right to Ewelme where I loafed about for half an hour before going on through Britwell Salome to Watlington. From there, I got to Thame via Shirburn and Lewknor arriving about 4 o'clock. I put in half an hour with a pot of tea and some cakes and proceeded to Long Crendon to see what this straggling but picturesque village looked like in sunshine and in blossom time. When I got there a fine black cloud let fly and I was well doused before I could get into a cape.

Coming down to Thame again in a steady drencher I went on the Princes Risborough road to meet Jack, picking him up just before Longwick and soon afterwards we were able to uncape. Returning to Thame 'Walker's' gave us an indifferent tea. From Thame to Abingdon is a curly road and we made our way via Little Milton and Stadhampton. After another drenching storm we came out on the Dorchester–Abingdon road at Clifton Hampden. It was 8.45 p.m. when we went in Abingdon and we finished up the last eight miles at a sprint. However the supper we had at the 'Rose Revived' was worth it. My day's wanderings were just 100 miles.

SUNDAY 8TH MAY

A century exactly

NEWBRIDGE – LONGWORTH – BAULKING – KINGSTON LISLE – SPARSHOLT – WANTAGE – WEST HAGBOURNE – MOULSFORD – STOKE ROW – PEPPARD – MAIDENHEAD – WINDSOR – MARYLEBONE – HAMMERSMITH

A glorious morning made us linger at Newbridge, and Mr Matthews of Great Tew turned up just as we were about to start, he having been out with a cargo of pigeons.

This part of England wants a lot of beating in springtime. We wandered around to the charming village of Longworth and took in a bridle path to Hinton Waldrist then down to Stanford in the Vale. After about a mile of the White Horse Vale towards Wantage a sharp right to Uffington took us off the broad highway. We went out of our way to inspect the pleasant but scattered village of Baulking and then made for Kingston Lisle, turning aside once more to have a go at the 'Blowing Stone'[6]. From here, we went back to the Ridgeway turning left to explore Sparsholt and the 'Who'd Have Thought It' Inn, before returning to the Ridge of stupendous prospects, left with regret at the descent into Wantage.

Out of Wantage by the Reading Road we fared indifferently at the 'Hare', then down to Steventon in a vain quest of the picturesque and so onto Harwell. A bridge path which we expected would take us to West Hagbourne, brought us out at Harwell Church but a few twists and turns soon brought us into West Hagbourne. The cutting down of a tree has marred the beauty of this thatched village and we found another path in the direction of East Hagbourne. We were unable to track this path to its logical conclusion, having the choice of following through a 'kissing gate' into the church yard or through the vicarage gardens, so it became necessary to

---

6 A renowned perforated sandstone that can emit a booming sound if air is blown into it in the right way; the legend goes that King Alfred used this stone to summon his Saxon troops.

seek the road for a few hundred yards to get into the village. This would be a gem of English villages were it not for the telegraph and telephone wires which disfigure it in all directions.

We waited longingly for the sun to shine but gave it up making for Aston Tirrold and up to the Goring Road and a rough run down to the Moulsford Ferry. The ferryman had to be roused from his Sabbath repose to convey us and our cycles across in a rickety punt with about four inches of water in the bottom of it. We paid our 2d each devoutly thankful at having escaped a watery grave and took a deep breath for the toil ahead.

The three miles up to Woodcote would be simple with a smooth road but this seems to be composed of brickbats[7] set in Portland cement garnished with loose gravel. But we were hungry and anxious for tea so that it did not particularly worry us. After a smooth mile from Woodcote to Checkendon we again sought the rough through the woods surrounding Wyfold Court. We emerged at Stoke Row and dropped down the Peppard Road to the 'Bricklayer's Arms' where our hunger was appeased by an excellent tea.

The usual route from the 'Bricklayer's Arms' is via Caversham and Twyford but this time we turned left at the 'Unicorn' for Peppard and down the lane labelled *'Unfit for through traffic'* into Henley. Jack, feeling eager for work after the easy time we had been having, decided on the direct road to Maidenhead involving first the ascent of White Hill and then the shorter but fiercer lumps up to the Temple golf links. This bit of road generally takes it out of me but tonight it presented no difficulties. Turning right at the top of the hill out of Maidenhead we were soon into Windsor and by the usual way home. After supper, the spring fever in my blood induced me to go part of the way to Tottenham with Jack. I parted with him at the top of Baker Street but from there had to take a rather circuitous route to make the day's run up to *100 miles.*

TUESDAY 10TH MAY

Fon being unfit did not do the usual Edgware trip which consisted of Hanger Hill, Greenford, Ruislip, Northwood, Rickmansworth, Chorleywood, Chenies, Latimer and Flaunden. Tea was taken at Stagg Farm and home via Chipperfield, Kings Langley, Watford, Bushley and Wembley. No rain and *miles covered 50 miles.*

---

7 Fragments of building bricks

1932 A HARD MAY WEEK

WEDNESDAY 11TH MAY
Primroses aplenty
HAMMERSMITH – CROYDON – SANDERSTEAD – MAIDSTONE – LENHAM – CANTERBURY – SANDWICH – DEAL

Set off to Deal to visit Mr and Mrs Lawther.

Headed to Croydon by the usual Mitcham route turning by the 'Red Deer' through Sanderstead (much climbing), Westerham, Brasted, and Riverhead where I turned onto the Maidstone road through Ightham. Had ham sandwiches and a Bass at the 'White Horse' Maidstone and took the desolate main road via Harrietsham and Lenham, all nicely marked out with a black and white check border as far as Charing. Charing Hill does not seem to get any less steep, but I negotiated it safely on a 49" gear. Longbeach Woods just beyond Charing was wonderfully flowery with mainly primroses and bluebells but at Chilham, once a beauty spot, 'uglification' has set in with a vengeance.

Spent nearly two hours in Canterbury and had tea at the 'Falstaff' for which I was rooked 2/6d! The route from Canterbury to Sandwich is a pleasant enough road through Ash and to explore the ancient Cinque Port[8] of Sandwich. Arrived in Deal at 7 o'clock and put up at the 'Swan' before seeking out the Lawthers with whom I spent the rest of the evening, having ridden some *91 miles*.

THURSDAY 12TH MAY
The most beautiful town in the South
DEAL – DOVER – SANDGATE – HYTHE – ROMNEY – RYE

I spent the morning with Mr and Mrs Lawther in a walk along the front to Kingsdown, coming back by the bus.

The 'Swan' did me well on cold fowl and ham for lunch and I set off along the coast road about 2.30 p.m. The south west gale made it all a plug and the road to Dover is both ugly and strenuous. It is little better from Dover to Folkestone and though it runs down to Sandgate and out onto the flats of Romney Marsh the wind made it impossible to exceed 10 miles per

---

8 An association of five ports (Hastings, New Romney, Hythe, Dover and Sandwich), which dates back to around AD 1100.

hour. The 'Prince of Wales' just beyond Hythe with a C.T.C. sign attracted me for tea but I was charged 1/10d for a very moderate feed.

My intention had been to make for Hastings but I thought Rye would be enough. After passing through Dymchurch and Romney I had an idea of seeing what Appledore was like. It was nothing much and the track southward from there towards Rye was nothing but loose gravel which brought me over twice. At Rye I put up at the 'Warden' and spent the last hours of daylight in the choice spots of this, the most beautiful town in the South of England. Another dry day.

Distance covered: 42 miles

FRIDAY 13TH MAY

Abominable Croydon

RYE – HAWKHURST – PEMBURY – TONBRIDGE – HAYES COMMON – STAMFORD BROOK –HAMMERSMITH

A brilliant morning induced me to pay a visit to Bodiam Castle (via Udimore and Cripps Corner), but when I got there the sun retired for the day. Soon after leaving a desultory rain started in large stinging drops. The wind seemed to have veered round so that I still had it full in my face through Hawkshurst.

I joined the Hastings road at Flimwell and having regard to the weather, thought it best to take it as the shortest way home. Even so the wind and drizzle made it hard work, so just outside Pembury I stocked up with bread and cheese at the 'Blue Boys' in Kipping's Cross. When I got into Tonbridge the rain was heavy enough to justify a cape. However I took it off again before ascending River Hill. Sevenoaks up Polhill to Farnborough, where I took the Croydon road via West Wickham and Hayes Common, was all hard work. St. Mary's Cottage on Hayes Common gave me an excellent tea but Croydon in a state of grease and slime and tramlines was an abomination to get through so that it was nearly 7 o'clock when I got to Stamford Brook for an evening's Bridge.

Distance covered: 73 miles

SATURDAY 14TH MAY

Three Red Lions

HAMMERSMITH – WINDSOR – OAKLEY GREEN – WALTHAM ST. LAWRENCE – READING – THEALE – HUNGERFORD – LECHLADE – BURFORD

Deserted by everyone I had fixed up for Whitsun at Burford.

Feeling fresh enough after the last few days' strenuosity I made my mind to make a century of it by taking the Windsor–Waltham road to Reading and then the Bath road as far as Hungerford. Some early refreshments at the 'Red Lion' at Oakley Green kept me going to the 'Red Lion' at Theale which I left full of bread, cheese and beer about 2.30 p.m.

The going was good and on top gear I arrived at 'Red Lion' No.3 at Hungerford for a jaw with an entertaining landlord and a first class tea. Afterwards I thought of making my way by the bridle path through Littlecote Park to Ramsbury. The Park was looking a dream of daffodils and narcissus but after coming a cropper on the muddy track I returned to the road and took the old familiar way through Chilton Foliat, Aldbourne, Liddington, Stratton St. Margaret, Highworth and Lechlade. After half an hour at the 'Three Horseshoes' I arrived at the Burford 'Swan' about 8.30 p.m. with *102 easy and pleasant miles* to my credit.

SUNDAY 15TH MAY

A dream of loveliness

BURFORD – STOW-IN-THE-WOLD – EVESHAM – STANWAY – PUESDOWN – BURFORD

It was pouring with rain when we had breakfast but it had left off when I made for the Stow road about 11.45 a.m., riding all the tough bits to Stow for the good of my soul.

At the 'Coach and Horses' just before the Five Miles Drive I dined off bread and cheese and went on through Broadway (full of petrol as usual) to Evesham, being disappointed to find the apple trees in the Vale not yet in bloom. After an hour in Evesham I took the Winchcombe road via Sedgeberrow and Toddington to Stanway for the wonderful tea supplied by Mrs Stratford. The tea and cottage and its surroundings were a dream of loveliness with every imaginable spring flower and it was difficult to get away from it. Turning aside to see what Hailes Abbey might be and finding

6d admission to view the ruins, which from the road look worth the money at a more convenient time, we spotted an inviting looking road which Bartholomew[9] showed running over Sudeley Hill (986 feet) and then Roel Hill (834 feet). In spite of threatening rain this was too good to be missed as it was precisely in the direction I wanted to go.

Much of the hill necessitated some walking and unfortunately the views for many miles of fairly even road at the top was obscured by mist, but nevertheless it was magnificent and must be revisited. I came out on the Andoversford–Stow road and out across this through Hazleton to a point about a mile beyond the Puesdown Inn. As usual I did not pass the inn and after a pleasant half an hour there, dropped down through Northleach back to Burford, finding the 'Swan' occupied by a bright party of the Trent Valley C.C. from Nuneaton with whom the rest of the evening passed very pleasantly.

Except for about 10 minutes down into Northleach there had been no rain since the morning but a deluge descended about 10.30 and two of the Nuneaton party who had pitched a tent for the night on the Stow road returned to the 'Swan', soon after midnight in a half-drowned state, their tent having been washed away.

Distance covered: 60 miles

MONDAY 16TH MAY

A very wet adventurer

BURFORD – BAMPTON – KINGSTON BAGPUIZE – ABINGDON – GORING HEATH – FELTHAM – HAMMERSMITH

After seeing the Nuneatonians on their way I left the 'Swan' about 11.45 a.m. and made for Bampton via Brize Norton. Bampton was *en fete* for folk dancing and proposing to proceed via Buckland I found the road flooded in that direction as far as I could see. A party of five cyclists arrived and I induced one of them to try his luck. The other four jibbed and two of them took my guidance to Abingdon via Cote, Aston, Standlake and Kington Bagpuize. I went to the 'Blue Boar' to lunch with the four dry ones, and about 2 o'clock the adventurer turned up there – very wet.

From Abingdon I took the usual road to Goring Heath via Sutton Courtenay Bridge, Appleford and Wallingford. The 'King Charles' Head' was full up but I got an excellent tea at the 'Pack Saddle' about two miles on.

Distance covered: 84 miles

9 Bartholomew's "Half Inch to the Mile Map"

1932 THROUGHOUT THE NIGHT

SUNDAY 19TH JUNE

Heartily stuffed

HAMMERSMITH – WATFORD – FLAUNDEN – CHESHAM – GREAT HAMPDEN – TRING – EDGWARE – BAYSWATER – HAMMERSMITH

I departed early at 7 o'clock for Watford to meet Frank and Fon for a breakfast run. They turned up rather late as usual but were readily forgiven and we decided to make for Flaunden and try Stagg Farm for breakfast. When we got there old Mrs Major alarmed us by saying there was nothing to eat. This is an old joke of theirs as I should have remembered. We had a splendid feed of porridge, eggs and bacon supported by bread and butter and marmalade which tasted all the better for the ride we had to get to it, afterwards making for Chesham and from there to Missenden.

We did not want the main Risborough road so took the one by the station in the direction of Great Hampden. Hereabouts we found a suitable spot to picnic only 11 miles from our breakfast place. Fon as usual had provided the necessities of life with that unnerving skill which one has learnt to respect from her. There was a chicken (dissected), salad and bread and butter, not to mention sausages and the necessary condiments. There was also a tin of pineapple and a carton of cream, bananas and oranges.

In fact we all stuffed so heartily that there was nothing for it but to seek repose afterwards.

Thus we dozed for about an hour after which Fon picked marguerites and pink vetch while Frank and I disposed of the debris of our picnic. In the meantime two cheap motor and sidecar people had encamped lower down in our field. The lady (or as the case may be) effected alarm at our bonfire in which we burnt up the consumable debris while the 'gent' tried to get me into an argument as to the distance from High Wycombe, a subject in which I was not interested.

We went on towards Monks Risborough and came out on a promontory, which we thought was Coombe Hill not far from Tring. After admiring the view we went down a steep and rutty hill and found ourselves instead in Princes Risborough, on the wrong side of the Chilterns. There was no alternative but to climb them again which was a bit of a nuisance as the C.O. was looking distinctly fatigued[10]. We eventually reached Tring via Wendover and had tea at the 'George', leaving 20 miles back to Edgware of easy main road. I left Edgware for home in the thick of the weekend drivers on the arterial road so that it was a relief to get down to the comparative quietude of the Marylebone Road and Bayswater.

The day had been fine but with very little sun and distinctly chilly at night but the breakfast at Flaunden followed by the picnic lunch made it a memorable occasion and I think we all thoroughly enjoyed it. *My day's riding was 86 miles.*

TUESDAY 21ST AND WEDNESDAY 22ND JUNE

Phantom coffee stalls and falling asleep

EDGWARE – TRING – AYLESBURY – THAME – OXFORD – WITNEY – PUESDOWN – CHELTENHAM – GLOUCESTER – ROSS-ON-WYE – WHITCHURCH – REDBROOK – CHEPSTOW

I had decided on a night ride on the way to Barry starting from Edgware and, having had a pretty late night on Monday, I should have got some sleep in the afternoon. However, Tom Offord turned up at 2 o'clock and did not leave until after 4 o'clock so that was off.

I felt unaccountably sluggish on the way to Edgware but arrived

---

10 C.O. is the abbreviated form of Commanding Officer. Charles serviced in WW1 so would be familiar with army ranks.

punctually to time at 8 o'clock as usual. After supper and a hand of Bridge I got going at 11.40 p.m. Fon wanted me to take some provisions but as Offord had assured me there was an all-night coffee stall just the other side of Tring I only accepted two bananas. Naturally I took the arterial road via Boxmoor, Berkhampstead and Tring to Aylesbury finding no sign of the alleged coffee stall.

At Aylesbury I found it necessary to don not only a waistcoat but also a cape and sou'wester as protection against the hoar frost[11] and for warmth. On the Bucks–Oxon border between Aylesbury and Thame I was held up by a policeman on the lookout for poachers. A cigarette and about a 20 minute conversation ensued. 'Dawn's left hand'[12] was now in the sky, a brilliant three-quarter moon low in the west and the trees enveloped in dense frost fog.

At Thame (3.45 a.m.) dawn was advanced sufficiently to make a tolerable twilight and at 4 o'clock I was able to dispense with a lamp before coming into Wheatley. I had already eaten one of my precious bananas and just outside Oxford, consumed the other, trusting to find a coffee stall in such an important city. However, I was doomed to disappointment and Oxford at 4.30 a.m. on the longest day looked cold, grey and inhospitable. Even the G.W.R. Station refreshment room was closed.

Just beyond Botley two cold journeyman plumbers on the tramps[13] hailed me over for a match. As they only had one cigarette between them I supplied a few more, being overwhelmed by their grateful thanks.

The Evynham Toll Bridge keeper who turned out yawning to collect my ½d at 5 o'clock opined it was going to be a hot day. My cape was now stiff with hoar frost, the sun not yet having appeared. It was not until I reached Witney that it suddenly arose in a blaze of glory in a perfectly clear sky. The effect was magical. The mist was gone in a trice and in a few minutes I had about half a pint of water from the melted hoar frost in front of my cape. I took it off and stowed it away joyfully. There was only one fly in the ointment – hunger.

Sturt Farm, outside Burford, nearly tempted me to test its 6 o'clock breakfast service. I knew it was no good trying the 'Swan' at 6.30 a.m. and there was nothing for it but to dash onwards. Hunger is certainly conducive to speed. The 13, by no means easy, miles from Burford to the Puesdown

---

11 A grey-white crystalline deposit of frozen water vapour
12 An illusion of dawn occurring when light appears on the horizon before dawn begins
13 Homeless

Inn took me exactly 45 minutes. When I got there at 7.15 a.m. there was no sign of life. My heart fell and I feared to try the door. However I took my courage in both hands. The door came open and just inside was a smiling 'Fanny' who promised to give me breakfast with the utmost despatch. She was as good as her word and before 7.30 a.m. I was putting away a large dish of eggs and bacon. All feelings of lassitude I had had in the early morning were now gone.

I was in Cheltenham by 9.30 a.m. and after half an hour in that pleasant town came into busy Gloucester by 10.30 a.m. I had now the long pull up, through the Huntley Forest to Ross and arriving there at 12.30 p.m. I went down to Wilton Bridge as usual before seeking lunch. Going to the 'Swalia Hotel' for lunch I found old Mrs Pugh has passed over at the age of 80 and a niece reigning in her stead. After a moderate cold lunch I would have rested awhile, but the new proprietress was too talkative, so at 2.30 p.m. I went on my way taking the Walford and Kerne Bridge road to Whitchurch.

From the Kerne Bridge to the uplands I had my first walk for a few hundred yards of the steep part. I was now feeling very sleepy and turned in at the 'Bell' at Redbrook, three miles beyond Monmouth, for an early tea, promptly sat down on a hard chair and went to sleep having to be wakened to partake of it when it was ready.

As soon as I had finished I moved off again before slumber once more overtook me. Though my head was decidedly 'wonky' my legs were still working perfectly and in a tear up[14] with a local would-be speed merchant on the slope beyond Tintern, I was an easy winner and I arrived in Chepstow for the giddy dive down to the 'Bridge Inn' at 5.45 p.m. Here I sat down in an armchair in the front room overlooking the Wye, accepted Mrs Wilding's suggestion of a steak or two nice chops for supper and wrote two postcards and put stamps on them. I was just going to post them when I fell asleep again.

I was wakened just before 7.45 p.m. by having my two postcards twitched from my fingers. It was Mr Wilding who wanted to post them for me in time for the London mail. I had got to wake up enough to eat that promised supper. I had a quarter of an hour's stroll feeling very unsteady on my pins, came back and demolished two large chops with peas and potatoes, several jam tarts and some biscuits and cheese washed down with

---

14 Race

a pint of beer. I staggered off to bed in broad daylight at 9.30 p.m. and knew no more until ....zzzzz.

Distance *covered: 156 miles*

THURSDAY 23RD JUNE
CHEPSTOW – CAERWENT – NEWPORT – WENVOE – BARRY

I was awakened by someone knocking on my bedroom door with a cup of tea and some hot water at 8.30 a.m.

It was past midday when I left Chepstow by the very familiar road to Cardiff lingering on the way to inspect the Roman Wall at Caerwent and for lunch at the 'Royal Oak', about three miles from Newport. I tried a new route to Barry by lanes to Wenvoe, but it was not a success, involving walking many miles of newly tarred roads, so that I did not get to Barry with the normal welcome at 'Talland' until past 5 o'clock.

Distance covered: 40 miles

FRIDAY 24TH JUNE

After a morning around the docks and island I had an afternoon amble to Llantwit Major via Aberthaw and St. Athan, returning the same way.

Distance covered: 23 miles

SATURDAY 25TH JUNE

A famous doorway
BARRY – NEWPORT – CAERLEON – ABERGAVENNY – HEREFORD – EARDISLAND

I left Barry at 9.30 a.m. making straight through Cardiff to Newport and then to the left up a long tram lined hill. This eventually brought me to Caerleon, which seems to set too much store by its Roman remains so that what was prior to the excavations a pleasant enough little village is now mostly made up of tea shops and petrol pumps.

From Caerleon to Abergavenny, leaving the smoke of Pontypool on the left, is a pleasant road looking forward to the Black Mountains with the Sugarloaf always prominent. Abergavenny was very crowded (Saturday and Market Day).

By the map the Hereford road looks fairly strenuous, at any rate as far as Pontrilas but such was not the case. At St. Devereux I turned aside to visit Kilpeck Church. The famous doorway has been so much photographed that I refrained from using my camera on it but devoted one film to the interior giving a purely speculative exposure of 75 seconds.

I sought out the 'Coach and Horses' at Hereford and they evidently got mixed up with my request for 'tea with two eggs'. Instead I got a large dish of ham and eggs. However only having lunched on bread and cheese at the 'Goytre Inn' near Pontypool, I made no complaints especially as I was only charged 1/6d.

The Pembridge road from Hereford via Canon Pyon is an up and down stretch of typical Herefordshire and arrived at Eardisland, my destination, about 7.45 p.m. finding that sweet village bathed in golden sunshine. The 'White Swan' now kept by Mr and Mrs Miles, late of the 'Angel' at Kingsland, received me enthusiastically and I spent much time wandering round the more secret parts of Eardisland trespassing freely with an interlude of an excellent supper at 9 o'clock. *Distance covered: 82 miles*

SUNDAY 26TH JUNE

A heroic riding companion

EARDISLAND – LEOMINSTER – LEDBURY – EASTNOR – TEWKESBURY – BREDON – STANWAY – BURFORD

It was past 10 o'clock when I left Eardisland, it being necessary to make first for Leominster via Barons Cross and then on the Hereford road to Hope under Dinmore before turning left for Ledbury. I was joined by a hefty young farm labourer on a heavy Raleigh roadster on his way from Welshpool to his home at Dymock. He had been riding since 5 a.m. and the way he pushed uphill and downhill on a top gear in the nineties[15] was amazing. I parted from him at the 'Old Trumpet' and owing mainly to his heroic efforts found myself in sleepy Sunday Ledbury at 12.15 p.m.

I thought of trying the 'Somers Arms' at Eastnor for lunch but found it too 'motorsome' and to my great surprise getting to the top of Hollybush Hill without much effort, decided to make for Tewkesbury and the 'Shakespeare Hotel'. Here after a heavy feed of roast beef, I went to sleep with a cigarette and burnt a hole in my jacket. This warned me to get on

---

15 Ninety revolutions per minute.

with it and as I had bags of time, Bredon, with visions of tea at Stanway, attracted me. From Bredon via Kemerton, Overbury and Counderton brought me to Stanway at 4.30 p.m. and the usual big tea at Mr Stratford's followed.

As on my last visit to Stanway I took the road to Hailes Abbey and over Sudeley Hill down into Burford and into the 'Swan' about 8 o'clock, having made 76 *miles of it.*

MONDAY 27TH JUNE
Poor and expensive
BURFORD – KINGSTON BAGPUIZE – ABINGDON

Leaving Burford at 11 o'clock, I proceeded via Brize Norton, Bampton, Buckland, Kingston Bagpuize, Fyfield, Tubney Corner. I was through Abingdon before 1 o'clock and finally arrived at the 'Bell' at Sotwell for bread and cheese. Then via Wallingford, Streatley and Pangbourne to Reading and so home via the usual route stopping for a poor and expensive tea at the 'Red Lion' Oakley Green. Called in on Cushing and heard that owing to an affair of the heart he intends giving up cycling. *Distance covered: 86 miles*

1932 GOING FOR A DOUBLE CENTURY

SUNDAY 3RD JULY

Looking like a just landed salmon

HAMMERSMITH – COBHAM – SHERE – EWHURST – PETWORTH – WITLEY – CHERTSEY – STAMFORD BROOK – HAMMERSMITH

I was faced with the prospect of a stalemate with Jack sick and Frank and Fon entertaining relatives. However I fixed up for a day's run with Gordon, his stipulation being that it must not be less than 100 miles.

We got off about 9.40 a.m. and took the Oxshott road to Cobham across to Effingham and over White Down through Abinger Hammer and Gomshall to Shere. It was evident that Gordon, who had a slight cold, was feeling it, especially on the long slopes, but my suggestion of an early lunch at the 'White Horse' was turned down. About three miles of the long plug up to Ewhurst put paid to Gordon for the time being and he had a long walk. Running down to Ewhurst we had an excellent cold lunch at the 'Crown' and then went on to Rudgwick down to Wisborough Green (via Bucks Green), Kirdford and Ball's Cross to Petworth, the headwind and hills making Gordon groan a bit. It was easier on the Guildford road when we turned for the home run.

At 4.45 p.m. the 'Half Moon' at Northchapel was turned down for tea but the ascent of the slope which eventually runs down to Ramsnest was too much for Gordon – I heard a disturbance behind me and found him lying by the side of the road looking like a just landed salmon. However we got carefully to the 'Sun' at Witley for tea in the garden and this had its usual reviving effect.

On the easy road down to Guildford Gordon fairly made things hum and we could scarcely have been doing less than 'eighteens' over this stretch. Taking the Chertsey road in preference to the main road a good speed was still maintained. At Chertsey, a small brown Courage each had a further reviving effect and it was not until Walton was past that Gordon began to fly again.

Coming through the park it was only his superb grit which kept him going and he was very, very stiff when we got back to supper to which he did full justice, and I saw him back to Stamford Brook about 11 o'clock.

Distance covered: 105 miles

TUESDAY 5TH AND WEDNESDAY 6TH JULY

A proud day!

EDGWARE – TRING – OXFORD – WITNEY – BURFORD – ANDOVERSFORD – CHELTENHAM – ABINGDON – DORCHESTER-ON-THAMES – HENLEY-ON-THAMES – MAIDENHEAD – HAMMERSMITH

I had always had a desire to try and put 200 miles into 24 hours and now found myself getting old and still it unaccomplished. The short nights and apparently settled weather of the present period seemed to give me the opportunity.

A desultory rain all the morning and again in the evening rather looked as though it put the lid on it but I went over to Edgware in the evening fully equipped and fortified with an afternoon's sleep. My idea was to make for Gloucester via Aylesbury and Oxford and return through Abingdon and Henley way.

I left No.8 High Views Gardens at 11.40 p.m. Fon had lent me her Thermos flask full of hot coffee and thrust onto me a large parcel of grub with her usual forethought. It was raining gently but I did not cape up and the rain ceased entirely soon after I started.

It was a very dark night – no moon or stars until about 2 a.m. At Tring I decided to assume a waistcoat. While doing so under a street lamp I was pounced on by a hatless policeman who I had some difficulty in persuading that I was out riding for pleasure at that time of night and not on some nefarious pursuit. He was only partially satisfied when I showed him my C.T.C. membership card and I feel sure that if see him again in Tring at 1.30 a.m. I shall be arrested on sight.

I met no more policemen nor any kind of human being until Wheatley about 3.45 a.m. where a furniture van was just making an early start from one of the pubs. Oxford, with all its street lamps alight though it was nearly daylight (4.15), looked as though it had been smitten with the plague, without a soul stirring in it. Just beyond I met a real cyclist on a Grubb just going home to bed after night duty. We rode together for a couple of miles until he reached his home just outside Eynsham.

The night had been fairly mild but the interim between daylight and sunrise was bitterly cold, dense banks of mist hanging in the dips in the road and over the fields. About three miles from Witney (5 a.m.) I had my wayside early breakfast sitting on my cape by the side of the road and soon demolished practically the whole of Fon's parcel and washed it down with boiling hot coffee from the Thermos (thank-you Fon, ever so many times for that gorgeous feast!).

I was now fortified for some hours and Witney, Burford and Northleach soon slipped by. The rise up over Puesdown was scarcely noticeable, Andoversford was still sleeping and Cheltenham just waking into life when I rode through the town at 8.15 a.m. Another three miles towards Gloucester brought me to the 'Pheasant' at 8.30 o'clock precisely but the breakfast there was hardly up to the Puesdown standards. To complete the desired 200 miles (excluding the thirteen from Hammersmith to Edgware) did not necessitate going right into the city so I turned about 10 a.m. to commence the return journey.

The wind which, though not very strong, had been against me from the start, now made things easier. I had no reason for forcing the pace yet I found myself dropping down Burford High Street at 12.10 p.m. After a cold lunch I left the 'Swan' at 1.45 p.m. and took the Bampton road, then through Aston and Cote, Newbridge and Marcham to Abingdon for tea at the 'Fleur de Lis' Dorchester at 4.30p.m.

As usual after tea I felt very fit and rode the tough hills – Beggars Bush, Huntercombe and Nettlebed – hardly feeling them. From a motion of caution, I did walk a few hundred yards of White Hill out of Henley, but the other hills between Henley and Maidenhead came easy and, taking the

Windsor–Bedford road, reached home at 9.45 p.m. not tired, but very sleepy.

Distance covered: 214 miles but excluding last night's run to Edgware, 201, within the 24 hours. Actual time 22 hours and 5 minutes.

Stops – 1st breakfast: 30 mins, 2nd breakfast: 1 hour, Burford lunch: 1 hour 30 mins, Dorchester tea: 45 mins, making a total of 3 hours and 45 minutes.

Actual riding time (including incidental stops, arguing with policeman etc.) equates to 18 hours and 20 minutes, making an average of 12 miles per hour.

1932 SUMMER WEEKENDS AND TOURLETS

SATURDAY 9TH JULY

A dash before closing time

HAMMERSMITH – MOOR PARK – CHESHAM – TRING – BICESTER – GREAT TEW

I started for the weekend at Great Tew soon after 10 o'clock but called at 85 Wendell Road on the way and did not get away until past 12. It was intensely hot and the tarry roads melting in the sun made going hard. I had bread and cheese and a beer at the 'Green Man' at Moor Park and took it gently through Rickmansworth and into the shady Chess Valley to Chesham.

More hard labour followed over to Berkhamsted and along the main road to Tring where I had arranged to meet Frank and Fon for tea at the 'George'. I spent much time sitting in any shade that could be found. They turned up at 5.15 p.m. naturally rather weary with the hard going. We had a heavy tea at the 'George', Frank and I having 2½ eggs each, the odd one being skilfully cut in equal halves by Fon.

It was 6.30 p.m. when we got on our way feeling much better, that wonderful tandem pair who should have been dead out of form and dead slow, making me go all out. Aylesbury was soon passed and the monotonous 17 miles from there to Bicester where a short pause was made for a little shopping and some light refreshment.

It was now cool enough to be really pleasant riding and the last stage was most exhilarating. A stop about a mile from Great Tew for a little wind in the tandem's back tyre made it necessary for me to dash on to secure beer before 10 o'clock. Outside the 'Falkland' were Tom and Hilda who had wired from Corwen that they were joining us, both looking like Red Indians after a week in North Wales.

This rather complicated things for Mrs Matthews, who did not know how to put us all up, but Fon has a way a getting over difficulties and we were all made comfortable thanks to her suggestions. Supper and talk made it nearly midnight when we got to roost.

Distance covered: 79 miles

SUNDAY 10TH JULY

A troublesome tandem but a glorious day

GREAT TEW – ASKETT – AMERSHAM – EDGWARE – WATFORD – HAMMERSMITH

The feminine and infant members of the Great Tew establishment were out and about unreasonably early and even the males of the party were down by 8.30 o'clock, the morning being well worth it. We were almost in despair about Jack, who was due to arrive for breakfast, but he rolled up about 9.30 o'clock. The early rising gave us all fine appetites and the eggs and bacon were delicious.

As usual the fascinations of Tew kept us until midday before anyone thought of a move and then it was found both tandems wanted attention so that it was 1 o'clock when we got on our way. After a few miles the Sissons' tandem's back tyre went again and we all just struggled into a pub about three miles on our way, for a light refreshment in lieu of lunch. This seemed to suit us all very well, for in spite of the great heat and glaring sun, the pace was very bright. The extraordinary 'unfit' Sissons[16] had generally led uphill and none of us could get near them, though I was generally not far away.

We came down to Islip and turned left through Charlton-on-Otmoor and Murcot to Thame and via Long Crendon, then left at Longwick and finally to Askett where we were quite ready for tea at the 'Three Crowns'. This inn, Jack's discovery, provided us with a tea of extreme excellence.

16 It's likely here that Frank and Fon Sissons claimed to be 'unfit', but they were, in fact, the complete opposite.

Going onto the foot of Longdown, we walked the steep parts and coming down into Missenden our next stop was the 'Chequers' at Amersham for some lubricant in which Fon and Hilda did not participate. Up the hill from the 'Chequers' Fon had a go on Jack's Sunbeam but was not allowed to continue as the wonky back tyre of the tandem was not equal to Jack's weight. We waffled on through Rickmansworth to Watford, the only delays being for extraction of flies from eyes, until we got on to the steepest bit of Clay Hill, where Fon spotted a shop which had some lemons, as it appeared the whole party were coming back to No.8 High Views Gardens and the question of providing drink was acute.

We got 'home' to Edgware about 9.30 p.m. and Fon in some miraculous way found the means of feeding the multitude. We broke away soon after 11, I riding with Tom and Hilda as far as their flat and getting home about 12.15. This had been a glorious weekend, the blazing sun today having been tempered by a moderate breeze and everybody finished up happy.

Distance covered: 80 miles

SATURDAY 16TH JULY

To Edgware in the afternoon for the start of a night ride.

Distance covered: 15 miles

SUNDAY 17TH JULY

A great run, worthy of credit

EDGWARE – AYLESBURY – THAME – OXFORD – PUESDOWN – BURFORD – LONG HANBOROUGH – ASKETT – AMERSHAM – WATFORD – HAMMERSMITH

After a short sleep, refreshment, and packing provisions for an early breakfast on the road started off on the Watford bye-pass, Tring-wards, just after 1 a.m. all feeling rather slow and dopey. The first incident was the collapse of Jack's lamp outside the 'Spider's Web'. This was repaired by Tom, with a whittled down match stick. Jack was mounted on a new, wood-rimmed, lightweight, geared to 58". Tom had his special Sunbeam geared to 63", while Frank and I each had our ancient general utility mounts with 3 speed gears. It was therefore natural that the fixed and the variables more or less hunted together throughout the run.

We soon shook off our lethargy and by the time Berkhampsted was reached, we were going nicely, with Frank and I generally leading. Soon after leaving Aylesbury we were aware of other road farers behind us. They chased us for several miles and then streamed past us – all nine of them. Then the usual thing happened. When they had got past us they immediately spread themselves all over the road and slowed down to about 10 m.p.h., and after about a mile of this funeral business all stopped, still all over the road, presumably for refreshment, so that we had some difficulty in getting through them.

We stopped for our early breakfast between Thame and Wheatley but saw no more of them for which we were thankful. When the day finally dawned it was as usual very cold, and the sky being overcast, we did not reap any benefit from the sun when it rose.

Tom had some trouble with his saddle, but between Oxford and Witney it got more comfortable. In the meantime, Jack on his new lightweight was moving nicely, in spite of his low gear. Frank and I with our three speeds were of course at a considerable advantage and after slowing down two or three times to let the other two come up, thought it better to go on to Puesdown to see about breakfast, for which we were all quite ready.

We kept up a steady pace and were at Burford at 7.30, Northleach by 8 o'clock precisely and rolled up to the 'Puesdown Inn' where breakfast utensils were laid ready for us in the bar parlour, just after 8.15. Our first business was to get a wash and we were already indulging in a rest when Jack and Tom arrived just 25 minutes after us. By this time they had washed, breakfast was ready and the bacon and eggs were of very fine quality or they seemed so. At any rate we were all agreed that it was the finest breakfast we had had for months.

The question of the return journey was discussed at some length. We wanted to call in at the 'Swan' at Burford, so turned off about four miles past Northleach via Sherborne, Windrush and Little Barrington, but turning the wrong way came out on the main road again about three miles from Burford entering the town by Sheep Street.

Light refreshment at the 'Swan' occupied about an hour after which we made for Witney and turned off left on the Woodstock road with a view to making for Thame via Otmoor. At Long Hanborough we stocked up further on bread, cheese and tomatoes. On restarting just beyond Bladon, Frank and I came on a field which looked suitable for half an hour's kip. Jack and Tom were not inclined for it so decided to go on, leaving us to follow and at any rate meet them for tea at the 'Three Crowns' Askett.

We had about thirty minutes of the most refreshing slumber, which left us with a fair stretch to do to Askett and not too much time to do it in. However we arrived at the 'Three Crowns' very shortly after Jack and Tom and had a comfortable rest and a very enjoyable tea. The walk up Longdown and the run down to Missenden put us on good terms with ourselves, and there was no faltering on the main road stretch through Amersham to Rickmansworth.

Out of Watford we all decided to walk Clay Hill and at the top went on our respective ways. In many ways it had been a great run and my three fellow Ammerstots deserve great credit. Perhaps Frank's was the best performance notwithstanding that he had scarcely ridden a single, or done more than 70 miles at a stretch on the tandem for the last nine months, yet he made the pace the whole way and right up to the finish always left us all when it came to a slope.

Jack, though, on a new machine with only one small medium gear in place of the vast range to which he is accustomed on his 'Sunbeam' rode like a machine all the time and seemed quite fresh, though sleepy when I parted from him on Clay Hill. Tom could not get his saddle comfortable and there is nothing takes the steam out of you like saddle soreness. All the same he carried on most cheerfully, and so far from making any complaints, was even able to joke about his discomfort. The only credit that belongs to me is that I had the biggest mileage to wit, *176 miles.*

PS - Even this distinction is taken from me for I found that Jack registered 178 miles!

TUESDAY 9TH AUGUST

Full up with non-cyclists!

HAMMERSMITH – WINDSOR – MAIDENHEAD – DORCHESTER-ON-THAMES – ABINGDON – NEWBRIDGE – BURFORD

Determined to seize the chance of a four-day 'tourlet' over prepared ground. A call at Nassau Road caused a late start on the way to Burford and I had to take the shortest way with a quick 'semi' lunch at the 'Queens Arms' midway between Windsor and Maidenhead.

An early tea at the 'Fleur de Lis' gave me ample time for the remainder but just outside Abingdon my back tyre came to grief and caused some delay in repairs.

The day was so hot that two small Morlands were necessary at the 'Rose Revived' and I finally reached the Burford 'Swan' via Bampton and Brize Norton at 8 o'clock. The 'Swan' was full up with non-cyclists and I was put up at the 'Golden Ball'. The question arises whether this famous inn is at an end as the hub of the cycling world.

Distance covered: 76 miles

WEDNESDAY 10TH AUGUST

The Stowe standard

BURFORD – PUESDOWN – CHELTENHAM – TEWKESBURY – LEDBURY – HAYLEY – HEREFORD – WHITNEY-ON-WYE

My next stage was to the 'Stowe Inn'. A 9 o'clock breakfast made it 11 o'clock before I got on my way. After a small one at the 'Puesdown Inn' I made all speed through Andoversford and Cheltenham to Tewkesbury with the idea of a feed at the 'Shakespeare'. Alas this cyclists' inn has changed hands and all I got was some ham sandwiches. These carried me on to Ledbury where a ginger beer and a cake provided further power.

The road from Ledbury to Hereford provided a feast of nastiness for new tar frugally covered with chips, extended from Trumpet to about four miles beyond Tarrington. My tyres were coated so that it took twenty minutes to partially scrape them when the road did get fairly clear and there was still enough left to make them run like lead.

I got an excellent tea at a flowery cottage in Hagley before running into Hereford. The rest of the journey, broken for a drink at the 'Kites Nest Inn' was easy enough, the 'Stowe' being reached at 7.30 p.m. Supper was up to the 'Stowe' standard and after a stroll I went to bed at 11 o'clock. Another steaming hot day.

Distance covered: 74 miles

THURSDAY 11TH AUGUST

An absolute scorcher

WHITNEY-ON-WYE – LEOMINSTER – LEDBURY – TEWKESBURY – STANWAY – CHIPPING NORTON – GREAT TEW

A heavy mist proclaimed that the day was going to be a scorcher and I had a strenuous run to do to Great Tew. The easiest way would have been via Hereford–Ledbury but it was impossible to negotiate that tar again. Consequently I made through Dilwyn to Leominster and turned off at Hope under Dinmore to Ledbury even then having some miles of wet tar to do.

Some bread, cheese and beer in Ledbury gave me enough power to climb up over Holly Bush Hill on the Tewkesbury road but the heat was now intense and I had half an hour's rest in the shade after the big climb. At Tewkesbury two glasses of home-made lemonade went down well and the Stow road as far as Stanway was fairly easy. I drank at least ten cups of tea at Mr Stratford's and leaving just after 6 o'clock rode all the way up Stanway Hill to Ford. This road to Stow is about as formidable as any ten miles in England but by the wayside I found a plentiful supply of wild raspberries and strawberries, which were very refreshing.

After the finest run down from Stow on the Chipping Norton road, the hard work starts again and through Cornwell it was very rough. The thirst induced by the intense heat necessitated another one at the 'Blue Boar' Chipping Norton and I arrived at Great Tew just after 9 o'clock. Mr Matthews had provided a splendid hot supper and bed was very welcome after a most strenuous day of intense heat.

Distance covered: 90 miles

FRIDAY 12TH AUGUST
GREAT TEW – BICESTER – WADDESDON – AYLESBURY – TRING – BERKHAMPSTEAD – WATFORD – HAMMERSMITH

It was gratifying to find the sky overcast this morning and I felt that some cooling rain would be welcome but at any rate I made up my mind to take the shortest and easiest way home. Consequently I made my way through Sandford and Middle Barton to Bicester and took the monotonous 16 miles to Aylesbury and onto Tring with one stop for light refreshment at the 'Bell' Waddesdon.

The 'George' at Tring gave the usual excellent lunch and after it a comfortable sofa induced me to slumber for over an hour. A shower meanwhile had made the atmosphere more endurable. I continued on the main road to Berkhampstead[17], Boxmoor, and Kings Langley to Watford

---

17 The present spelling of 'Berkhamsted' was only adopted in 1937

and called in at the 'Lyonesse' for tea arriving home at 7 o'clock. My shortest ever trip from Great Tew.

Distance covered: 70 miles

SATURDAY 20TH AUGUST

Putting up at Pangbourne

HAMMERSMITH – EDGWARE – MOOR PARK – MARLOW – HENLEY-ON-THAMES – PANGBOURNE

To Edgware and then with Frank and Fon and Tom and Hilda via Stanmore, Moor Park, Harefield and Chalfont to Marlow. Here we found our usual tea place closed down and went to a swank pub for a moderate tea in the garden.

Then on through Medmenham to Henley up to Peppard through the woods around Wyfold Grange, and after much wandering on steep and rough roads, we found our way down to Whitchurch and Pangbourne. Putting up at Pangbourne was some job but Frank and Fon got a doss at a hotel where they paid through the nose and Tom and Hilda and I at a private house where we had a good cold supper and comfortable rooms.

A thunderstorm descended on us about 11 o'clock but the thunder did not keep me awake. The rest of the day had been hot and sultry but not as bad as yesterday.

Distance covered: 62 miles

SUNDAY 21ST AUGUST

Crashes, punctures and stings

PANGBOURNE – THATCHAM – INKPEN – PEWSEY – COMPTON BASSETT

We got away from Pangbourne about 10.30 and soon met disaster. We hit a patch of mud which caused me to crash down first and then Tom and Hilda followed suit. Frank and Fon safely got through but Fon (off the tandem), coming back to pick up the bits, also came a wallop. Further progress was painful to me for a time with a painful wrist and ankle and turning to Sulham way we struck some very rough country to Bucklebury and from there to Thatcham.

While having 'elevenses' a speedster rolled up with a puncture. Frank rendered first aid at tyre changing with great celerity and with a cup of tea inside him he was sent on his way rejoicing. At Newbury we turned south and at the village of Inkpen we had a curious feed of beer, cheese and biscuits and Smith's chips before beginning the arduous climb to the Beacon. Here it was decided to rest for a time and Hilda promptly sat on a bee which left its sting in her leg. However, after extraction and application of iodine she suffered little discomfort but went to sleep, with the three others.

On restarting, several miles of grass track had to be negotiated which rather rattled my bones trying to keep up with the more stable tandems. Re-joining the road I was left behind on the long descent to Ham. Then followed one of the hottest bits of riding I have done for some time, the seven miles to Pewsey being accomplished in 20 minutes.

A wash and an excellent tea at the 'Phoenix' restored me and here I parted from the rest, they going on their way to Mere while I decided to make for Compton Bassett. For 10 miles through Alton Priors and Allington I was running into a thunderstorm and just outside Cherhill caught it for about 10 minutes enough to drench me before I got my cape on. It soon passed and I got to Compton Bassett about 8.15 and put up at the beautiful 'White Horse'. I had to be content with boiled eggs, salad and bread and cheese for supper and spent some time afterwards seeing the fantastic formations of the surrounding trees by night in the company of the landlord and his sister before going to bed.

Distance covered: A strenuous 57 miles (as good as an ordinary 100).

MONDAY 22ND AUGUST

A drenching on the way home

COMPTON BASSETT – HUNGERFORD – NEWBURY – READING – OAKLEY GREEN – WINDSOR – HAMMERSMITH

Made an early start as I wanted to get home quickly. At Cherhill a driving rain started in my face which made matters difficult and the long Bath road a real job of work. I did not put on protection and was fairly drenched when I put in at the 'Red Lion' Hungerford for a drink. The rain had ceased by the time I got to Newbury and I had some inferior bread and cheese and some rank bad beer (Strange's Aldermaston) between Woolhampton and Theale. I took the usual Twyford to Windsor route from Reading with a hasty tea at Oakley Green and after visiting Cushing at Windsor I arrived home at 7 o'clock.

Distance covered: 87 miles

CYCLING STATISTICS FOR 1932 BY MILES AND NUMBER OF RIDES PER MONTH

MONTH	NUMBER OF RIDES			MILES RIDDEN				AVERAGE MILES PER RIDE			
	ALL DAY OUT AND HOME	TOURING WEEKENDS	OTHER RIDES	ALL DAY OUT AND HOME	TOURING WEEKENDS	OTHER RIDES	TOTAL	ALL DAY OUT AND HOME	TOURING WEEKENDS	OTHER RIDES	ALL RIDES
Jan	3	-	6	234	-	244	478	78.00	-	40.66	53.11
Feb	2	4	5	141	263	137	541	70.50	65.75	27.40	48.27
Mar	3	8	4	210	596	149	955	70.00	74.50	37.25	63.66
Apr	1	13	7	60	792	262	1114	60.00	60.92	37.42	53.04
May	2	12	7	165	847	218	1230	82.50	70.58	31.14	58.57
June	1	12	7	91	874	221	1186	91.00	72.82	36.83	62.42
July	2	16	7	182	769	197	1148	91.00	48.09	26.71	45.92
Aug	-	22	3	-	1669	104	1773	-	71.31	34.66	70.92
Sept	2	13	6	175	783	173	1131	87.50	60.23	28.82	53.85
Oct	-	15	8	-	866	241	1107	-	57.73	30.12	48.13
Nov	3	5	8	189	346	280	815	63.00	69.20	35.00	50.93
Dec	2	7	7	151	428	244	823	75.50	61.14	34.85	51.43
Totals	21	127	75	1598	8233	2470	12301	76.09	64.82	34.73	55.41

CYCLISTS' TOURING CLUB

HANDBOOK & GUIDE
1933

1933 SUMMER TRIP TO HO! – MERLIN I

SUNDAY 6TH AUGUST

Toiling under the boiling sun

SLOUGH – WINDSOR – BAGSHOT – STOCKBRIDGE – SALISBURY – SHAFTESBURY – SHILLINGSTONE

As arranged I turned up at Slough at 9.30 o'clock to start with Reynolds on a short tour to Westward Ho! It was nearly 10.30 a.m. when we got going through Windsor, Waltham and Sunningdale out on the main Salisbury road at Bagshot, in a very hot sun. Between Hook and Basingstoke we had a light lunch and then by-passed Basingstoke coming out some miles beyond that uninteresting town.

There was a question of whether we should make for Salisbury via Andover or Stockbridge. Reynolds decided for the latter though I warned him we should find it rather tough. We toiled up the long slopes on this trying stretch in the boiling sun and we were very glad of a drink of ginger beer at Stockbridge. Yet another drink was necessary before Salisbury was reached and it was as well we had it for Salisbury, reached at 6.10 p.m., drew an absolute blank for tea. We had to go onto Wilton, a P.R.H.A. House supplying the necessary nutrient.

After tea we had still a long road to cycle, some of it rather strenuous up through Barford St. Martin, Fovant and Swallowfield to Shaftesbury where we turned to the left just at the Salisbury end of that town. After some ten miles, we went through Child Okeford to Shillingstone where we had booked up for the night at the 'Old Ox'. It had been rather a strenuous first day out on a tour — *120 miles of stiffish roads.*

MONDAY 7TH AUGUST

A glowing piece of country

SHILLINGSTONE — MILTON ABBAS — WOOL — LULWORTH COVE — DORCHESTER

We made an early start through Okeford Fitzpaine up Woolland Hill, a glowing piece of country. After about half an hour's contemplation we turned left down to Milton Abbas spending some time in the ancient building used as a clubroom, recreation house and tea shop. After a light lunch at the 'Hambro Arms' we made for Milton Abbey and spent about half an hour there before making our way towards Lulworth Cove, stopping at Wool for tea at the 'Black Bear'.

Lulworth, once an unsophisticated spot, was littered with people, perhaps to be expected on a Bank Holiday. We stayed there for about an hour and left soon after 8 o'clock on the Dorchester road. After the first climb out this is a fast stretch and we almost indulged in a tear up.[1] Nevertheless, it was necessary to light up for safety's sake just inside Dorchester. We got a satisfactory 'put up' at the 'Central Temperance Hotel'.

Distance covered: 42 miles

TUESDAY 8TH AUGUST

Full to capacity

DORCHESTER — POWERSTOCK — WEST MILTON — BRIDPORT — LYME REGIS — BRANSCOMBE

Started out on the Bridport way and turned off by the old Roman road to Exeter just beyond the Wireless Station. It is difficult to see why this road has fallen into disuse for it is certainly straighter and with much easier gradients than the main road nearer the coast which is the generally

---

1 A race.

accepted route. It is overgrown in parts and the surface has been allowed to get in a complete state of disrepair.

We made rather further north than we should have done and got to Powerstock where lunch was getting urgent. The "local" 'Three Horseshoes' supplied some doubtful beer but was unable to supply anything to eat more sustaining than bread and butter. We accordingly, after a vain search for another pub which was reported to be in the vicinity, made for West Milton where the 'Red Lion' was able to give us some bread and cheese.

We reached Bridport through Bradpole and then took the arduous climb via Chideock to Charmouth and onto Lyme Regis, which had as many people to the square yard as it could comfortably hold. The 'Newhaven Inn' gave us a good tea at a window from which we could see some of the 'sights', which now add diversification to our pleasure resorts.

Our intended destination was Branscombe, a small village just round the corner of Bar Head on the coast. We therefore took the Roman road via Colyford; my chief bother was the sun low in the sky and directly ahead, having lost my green eye shade en-route. The road down to Branscombe was an apparently endless descent and when we did reach the Promised Land it appeared that at least 10,000 other folk, mostly with tents of every description, had got there first.

At 'Bank Cottage' we were informed there was not an inch of vacant room anywhere. However as a concession they could give us some blankets and things in a tool shed. This we thankfully accepted and it did not prove a too uncomfortable night's lodging. Before closing time we strolled down to the local pub which was full of summer freaks and doing a roaring trade.

Distance covered: 46 miles

WEDNESDAY 9TH AUGUST

Many-coloured pyjamas
BRANSCOMBE – SIDMOUTH – EXMOUTH – STARCROSS – DAWLISH – TEIGNMOUTH

Breakfast and letter writing on the beach meant that we whiled away all the morning. It was about 12.45 p.m. when we commenced the climb out of Branscombe towards Sidmouth and we were glad of a feed of fish and chips when we arrived there. Sidmouth is quite a pleasant little resort and it is easy to understand those who make it their annual holiday place year after year.

Exmouth was our next port of call, after a few more hills intervened our journey. Curiously enough I had never been in Exmouth before though I had seen it from the other side of the river. It does not impress us at all, the ideal resort! We made for the official G.W.R.[2] Ferry and just caught the boat. A scheme for dropping my cycle aboard from about fifteen feet was navigated and it was got on somehow just as the boat was moving off.

Starcross was looking much as it has looked for the last forty years, nor were any alternations apparent in the three miles of up and down road to Dawlish where tea was the first consideration. We made for the local café and left our machines there while strolling round the town and front. The Lyme Regis pyjamas were easily surpassed by those here and one pair of many colours absolutely took the bun. It was past 8 o'clock when we left Dawlish intending to make Teignmouth our resting place for the night. At the foot of Holcombe Down we turned down Smuggler's Lane and walked the remaining mile or so along the front.

Teignmouth was pretty full and we did not anticipate getting put up easily. However, a C.T.C. place sent us to the 'Jolly Sailor' which did us quite cheaply and satisfactorily.

Distance covered: 29 miles

THURSDAY 10TH AUGUST

A nocturnal visitor

TEIGNMOUTH – TORQUAY – PAIGNTON – BRIXHAM – POMEROY CASTLE – TOTNES – BUCKFASTLEIGH

We passed out over Shaldon Bridge and took the trying Torquay road which is somewhat better as to the surface than when I had traversed it about eight years ago.

Torquay like everywhere else this week was teeming with people in various stages of dress and undress. We did not stay there long but continued with the worst tram track in southern England to Paignton. At one place there is the notice "*Pedestrians are requested to walk tight to the*

---

2 Great Western Railway

walls", a direction which is likely to be misconstrued. We were glad to leave Paignton and its trams behind and with nothing appearing that might supply lunch except a 'Railway Hotel'. at Churston Ferrers we pushed on to Brixham, and it being too late for a licensed house, had some fish and chips at a restaurant.

Brixham, though full of visitors, has not yet become a popular seaside resort and its old fishing atmosphere remains in full force. Leaving Brixham by the road by which we had entered it we turned left just past Churston Ferrers for Stoke Gabriel and Berry Pomeroy. Examination of the ruins of Pomeroy Castle occupied us for about 1½ hours and it was past 6 o'clock before we thought of tea, too late for the lodge keeper at the Castle gate to entertain the idea. So we made for Totnes, full of traffic and had a satisfactory tea at 'Clarke's' before going onto Buckfastleigh, our chosen night quarters.

At Buckfastleigh we got a satisfactory put up though our bedroom left only a space of about nine inches to get around it. We had one disturbance during the night, a large Persian cat coming in through the window and having to be ejected.

Distance covered: 38 miles

FRIDAY IITH AUGUST

Incidents and thunderstorms

BUCKFASTLEIGH – HOLNE – DARTMEET – TAVISTOCK – LAUNCESTON – HOLSWORTHY

Our first thought this morning was to do Buckfast Abbey, the wonder building which has been in course of erection by the monks themselves for many years past is now nearly complete[3]. Early though we were, we were not in time to forestall charabancs and motors from all parts from the occupants of which the monks were doing their best to extract what toll they could in exchange for examples of their handicrafts, some of which appeared to come from Birmingham or possibly from Japan. Granted the Abbey is an amazing and beautiful structure but one feels some disgust of the commercialisation of a building primarily erected for the glory of God.

After many weeks of drought there were indications of a break today

---

3 Construction began in 1907 and was finally completed in 1938

as some rain fell while we were in the Abbey. We decided to plunge into Dartmoor by way of Holne, and achieving the top after a long climb it was apparent we were in for a thunderstorm and that we were meeting it. It was upon us before we could get our capes on and, shelter being absent, it had to be faced.

We were at the highest point of Holne Moor and the road ran steeply down, the gradient appearing to be about 1 in 12. The drenching rain made rim brakes almost inoperative. I soon decided to play for safety and found a place where I could conveniently run up a bank and stop, and then commenced a walk to the bottom. Reynolds went on and was soon out of sight. It took me about 15 minutes walking down, feeling perhaps I was being unduly cautious. Near the bottom I found his machine but no Reynolds. Then the owner of a car standing by informed me he had got him inside after he had come a cropper through his brakes not holding.

He seemed rather shaken up and was cut about a bit but with no bones broken and was most concerned about the buckled front wheel of his bicycle. The people in the car were quite prepared to take him and the cycle to the nearest place where both could receive some attention. This happened near Hexworthy; the next place on the map was Dartmeet and an inn was marked at Two Bridges about three miles on towards Princetown. The car went ahead and was soon out of sight.

The Dartmeet 'inn' proved to be a large AA Hotel and the only information I got there was that the car had been seen going down the hill on the main road (Ashburton to Princetown). I turned left as Two Bridges had been mentioned but about three miles on this road I met two cyclists who said they had seen a car with a cycle tied on the back going in the other direction. I therefore turned back to Dartmeet and again enquired at the hotel with a negative result.

After light refreshment I turned once more towards Two Bridges and after yet another blank I headed to Princetown. There I was advised to try Tavistock. This is a tough piece of road and further delay was caused by a punctured back tyre, which held up for the four miles descent into Tavistock. By the time I had made fruitless enquiries, had tea and mended the puncture, it was about 6.30 p.m.

I decided to make for Launceston and then on to Holsworthy if time permitted. The road through Milton Abbot to Launceston was surprisingly easy and I decided on the fourteen miles and fourteen hills route to Holsworthy. Visions of being welcomed at a favourite resort gave me ginger[4] and with one stop for a Bass at the 'Arscott Arms' I arrived at the 'South Western Hotel' at 10.30 p.m. ready for supper and bed. An eventful day of incidents and thunderstorms.

Distance covered: 60 miles

SATURDAY 12TH AUGUST

The glorious sands of Bude

HOLSWORTHY – BUDE – KILKHAMPTON – CLOVELLY – STRATTON – BUDE

It was not much use trying to make further efforts to find Reynolds. My back tyre appeared to have a slow puncture so a spare tube seemed desirable. I accordingly made first of all to Bude to get one and then on the road nearest to the coast to Kilkhampton where the 'London Inn' gave me light refreshment. And so on the Bideford road. After lunch of sandwiches and beer at the 'West Country Inn' (now a curious place where you may only drink if you eat as well), I went on and turned down to Clovelly, garaging my cycle at the top.

Clovelly was, as anticipated, full of people so I took to the beach and wrote some letters and paddled my travel-worn feet in the watery brine. An early tea was taken at 'Shackson's' and I returned to Bude via Stratton. There is now a new road which gives a rapid coast down to Stratton of about three miles. The sands of Bude were very attractive and after a drink of draught Worthington's at the 'King's Arms' Stratton, I returned to my base having made a round of *59 miles.*

SUNDAY 13TH AUGUST

A swarm of man-eating flies!

BUDE – GREAT TORRINGTON – SOUTH MOLTON – BAMPTON – TAUNTON

It was time to think of returning home and I decided on the North Devon way first making over Holsworthy Beacon to Stubbs Cross. Here I carelessly took the road to Black Torrington instead of Great Torrington and had got about four miles on the way before discovering my error. However I found a cross road which took me in the right direction.

---

4 A 19th century expression meaning to incite enthusiasm or excitement

After getting steadily up a considerable height I was hurled down to a bridge over the Torridge, meeting on the way a swarm of man-eating flies who drew my blood five times before I beat them off. Great Torrington seems to consist mainly of one dilapidated street which runs steeply uphill for about half a mile, a most dismal town. I found a pub which supplied some bread and cheese and a pint and then took the road to South Molton.

Great Torrington to South Molton is not a road I shall willingly seek out again on a hot August day. It is only 16 miles but it took me nearly 2½ hours. The surface is good but the gradients are terrifying. About midway is the descent to Umberleigh and after a climb of (it seems) some miles it is not quite so bad.

It was 4.30 p.m. and I was rather hungry and extremely thirsty. South Molton showed nothing in the shape of a tea shop and I was relived to find a little pub by the wayside about a mile on with a welcome tea sign. I knew the road onto Bampton and regarded it as a hilly one but it was a billiard table compared with what I had just come over.

I had to make up for lost time and soon got through Bampton and onto Wiveliscombe. There seemed no other alternative but to make for Taunton for the night and there I arrived just as a thunderstorm commenced. Two C.T.C. places turned me down but I eventually found sanctuary at the 'Saracen's Head' in the High Street after a *strenuous 75 miles.*

MONDAY 14TH AUGUST

Through the Mendips

TAUNTON – GLASTONBURY – WELLS – TROWBRIDGE – LACOCK – HUNGERFORD

I got away from Taunton just after 10 o'clock on the fast stretch to Glastonbury over Sedgemoor via East and West Lyng, Burrow Bridge, Othery and Street.

At the 'Coxley Pound Inn', where I stopped for bread and cheese, a heavy thunderstorm came on which kept me here for an hour. The accompanying rain had not ceased when I got to Wells and I did not linger there but continued on the ascent of the Mendips through Chewton Mendip to Farrington Gurney. Here I turned right for Radstock climbing out of that uninteresting town up Frome Hill via Norton St. Philip and Farleigh Hungerford to Trowbridge then onto Melksham and via Beanacre to Lacock. Here I had hoped to stay the night but was frustrated as Miss Jenkins was in hospital with phlebitis.

The 'Red Lion' gave me tea, after which I climbed Bowden Hill and dropped down to Calne and sped along the Bath road through Marlborough to Hungerford, where the 'Red Lion' gave me supper and bed.

Distance covered: 92 miles

TUESDAY 15TH AUGUST

Home, and news of Reynolds

HUNGERFORD – WALTHAM ST LAWRENCE – WINDSOR – STANWELL MOOR – UXBRIDGE –HAMMERSMITH

There is nothing to be said about a run down the Bath road from Hungerford through Newbury, Thatcham, Woolhampton and Theale to Reading and thence via Waltham St. Lawrence (lunch at the 'Star') to Windsor. Tea was taken at Stanwell Moor, then a visit to Arthur Cushing and a fruitless call at the Carfax pub for news of Reynolds and so home via Uxbridge and Ruislip – *76 miles*.

I found a letter at home from Reynolds to say he had been taken to Ashburton and had come back by train from there on Saturday after medical attention, mostly cuts, and no broken bones

1933 A SCOTTISH TOUR
WITH MISS WILLSON

FRIDAY 8TH SEPTEMBER

To Euston Station via the Arterial road with Ron White to catch the 11 o'clock train to Edinburgh.

Distance covered: 22 miles

SATURDAY 9TH SEPTEMBER

The first camp
EDINBURGH – QUEENSFERRY – KINROSS – LOCH LEVEN

Met Doris Willson on arrival at Edinburgh at 7.45 a.m. and spent the morning in the exploration of Edinburgh including the Castle. After lunch, we made for Queensferry via the ferry under the shadow of the Forth Bridge and via Crossgates and Cowdenbeath to Kinross. Our first camp was on the shores of Loch Leven.

Distance covered: 31 miles

1933 – A SCOTTISH TOUR WITH MISS WILLSON

SUNDAY 10TH SEPTEMBER

The Fair Maid's House

LOCH LEVEN – GLENFARG – PERTH – DUNKELD – BUTTERSTONE LOCH

Awoke to a misty morning and it was 10 o'clock when we left after the tents and I had dried out. We made for Milnathort, Glenfarg and Bridge of Earn[5] arriving at Perth. I sought out the Fair Maid's House[6] then via Bankfoot and Dunkeld where we turned right to what appeared our attractive camping spot by the Loch of the Butterstone. There we found an ideal site by the Loch side.

Distance covered: 36 miles

MONDAY 11TH SEPTEMBER

Easier than expected across the Grampians

BUTTERSTONE LOCH – PITLOCHRY – BLAIR ATHOLL – DALWHINNIE – LOCH ERICHT

After a little necessary washing by Doris, in a bright sun we left the Butterstone Camp at 11.30 a.m. getting back to the main road to Pitlochry where we lunched before doing the Pass of Killiecrankie. From there to Blair Atholl where we had a picnic tea in a field after having some difficulty in purchasing some milk and water, the local Post Office finally obliging.

We had now to cross the Grampians and anticipated some hard work. However the gradient was easy all the way and before we began to feel the steep ascent we had reached the top of the Pass and were speeding downhill towards Dalwhinnie. At Dalwhinnie we turned left and found a camping spot by the side of Loch Ericht, a wild and barren place, before obtaining milk and eggs from a small cottage nearby.

Distance covered: 49 miles

---

5 A small town deriving its name from its famous sandstone bridge across the River Earn, remains of which survived into the 1970s

6 Dating back to c.1475, the Fair Maid's House is the oldest secular building in Perth; it is now used as the headquarters of the Royal Scottish Geographical Society

TUESDAY 12TH SEPTEMBER

Permission granted

LOCH ERICHT – DALWHINNIE – NEWTONMORE – KINGUSSIE – AVIEMORE – LOCH PITYOULISH

A damp, misty morning made our surroundings appear wilder than ever and it was late in the morning before our tents were dry enough to pack. We went back to Dalwhinnie and made our first stop at Newtonmore, obtaining an excellent lunch at a C.T.C. house.

Then we made our way to Kingussie and Aviemore with designs on camping by Loch Pityoulish reached by a detour to the right. It was an ideal camping spot but alas we were duly warned against camping here. However we managed to meet the Lady Reuter of the Estate who readily gave us permission and referred us to her head keeper for milk and eggs. After tea and supper we took a long walk and was entertained by Doris with various tales of hospital life.

Distance covered: 31 miles

WEDNESDAY 13TH SEPTEMBER

Curious lights in the sky

LOCH PITYOULISH – CARRBRIDGE – BOAT OF GARTEN – DAVIOT

From Pityoulish we regained the main road via Boat of Garten[7], which was much more picturesque than Carrbridge (where we had a light lunch), where the ruins of the old bridge are worth seeing. The road through Tomatin was very wild and we camped just beyond Daviot, having tea in camp. After tea we went for a long walk under the stars and were puzzled by curious lights in the sky, probably the Aurora Borealis. It had been a rather blowy day with some rain.

Distance covered: 28 miles

---

7 A small village deriving its name from the old ferry over the River Spey

THURSDAY 14TH SEPTEMBER

A lost watch
DAVIOT – INVERNESS – GARVE

We had not too far to go for Inverness and as we were getting away from civilisation did ourselves well for lunch at 'Burnetts'. Unfortunately I left my watch in the bathroom there; though I telephoned from a village five miles on there was no trace of it so we proceeded over Beauly Bridge, Muir of Ord and Moy Bridge to Garve where we encamped in a rickyard[8] adjoining a farm. Wind still very high.
Distance covered: 53 miles

FRIDAY 15TH SEPTEMBER

Pancakes by the loch
GARVE – ACHNASHEEN – GLEN CARRON – LOCH DOULE

Still windy and we headed west through Achanalt, Achnasheen (lunch and tea taken at the 'Achnasheen Hotel') Balnacra, Glen Carron and camp to Loch Doule. Scottish pancakes were made whilst we waited and eggs, milk and blackcurrant jam secured. A most picturesque camping site.
Distance covered: 32 miles

SATURDAY 16TH SEPTEMBER

The 'Misty Isle'
LOCH DOULE – STROMEFERRY – KYLE OF LOCHALSH – BROADFORD

We awoke to a bright morning, which showed up the beauty of the surrounding countryside. We left the site at 11.30 a.m. and headed along the shores of Loch Carron detouring to Stromeferry where we did not have long to wait for a passage to the other side.

The road across to Lochalsh is rugged and very steep. On arrival at the Kyle of Lochalsh, letters were the main consideration and then lunch. Afterwards Doris scented the ferry just going over to Skye and we all

---

8 A place where haystacks are stored

chased after her just getting the boat. Skye, the 'misty isle', greeted us with sunshine. Through the small village of Broadford we finally found a cheery campsite about eight miles on with the usual useful nearby cottage for supplies of eggs and milk.

Distance covered: 38 miles

SUNDAY 17TH SEPTEMBER

Blustery Skye

BROADFORD – SLIGACHAN – BROADFORD

A howling gale nearly blew our tents away in the night but the sun in the morning was brilliant and, though there was a nip in the air, we all took advantage of the proximity of the sea to get rid of some of our travel strains.

We had camped on the corner of an inlet and after we had packed our belongings we took the road that skirted this inlet. The strong wind was mostly behind us, but when we did face it on one of the twists in the road there was no doubt of its power. At about 1 o'clock we found ourselves at the 'Sligachan Hotel' and as it was beginning to rain we entered that palatial hostelry and asked for lunch, expecting to be stung. However our expectations were not realised, the charge for the excellent feed we had being most reasonable.

Time would not allow our continuing the exploration of the glorious Isle of Skye and we had to turn back. The rain and the wind were terrific and many times we were in danger of being blown over the precipices on the off side of the road. It was getting dark when we got back to Broadford and we decided to put up if possible instead of camping. We at length found it difficult to sleep in a bed after getting used to a sleeping bag and the hard ground.

Distance covered: 26 miles

MONDAY 18TH SEPTEMBER

A misbehaving tyre

BROADFORD – KYLELEALIN – KYLE OF LOCHALSH – DORNIE – GLEN SHIEL – TOMDOUN

We had to make for the mainland once more. Skye gave us a brilliant send off from Kyleakin to Kyle of Lochalsh in bright sunshine. From there we made for the Dornie Ferry at the head of Loch Duich. On the other side we had lunch at the only refreshment house and it was not cheap.

Eilean Donan Castle nearby is a picturesque feature of Dornie. The next five miles was mostly a walk and I realised I had left my map of Skye and Inverness at the refreshment house. However a passing motorist promised to ask the folk at the bottom to send it to me at our next stop for letters. This road skirting Loch Duich was the most beautiful we had struck and onwards through Glen Shiel was very fine. Doris, wanting a drink, fell down a water hole but was safely rescued.

At the beginning of Glen Cluanie we took the left hand fork, which took us with much hard labour up to 1424 feet. The run down was fast and rough and my sprite tyres twice required attention. Darkness was coming on so Doris and Ron left me with a third puncture while they went on to find a camping spot. My tyre only lasted about a mile and I went on in the dark bumping over stones with a front tyre nearly devoid of air after it had been pumped up every quarter mile.

I found the other two at Tomdoun, a weird spot but we succeeded in pitching our tents on a disused road, having some difficulty in getting our skewers in the ground.

Distance covered: 49 miles

TUESDAY 19TH SEPTEMBER

Gorgeous blackberries
TOMDOUN — INVERGARRY — FORT WILLIAM

We went on through Glen Garry to Invergarry and crossed over the Caledonian Canal at Loch Oich and skirted pass Loch Lochy. Here we found the most gorgeous blackberries and we over saturated ourselves. We had to leave the canal to pass over Spean Bridge and then made for Fort William. Shopping in Fort William delayed us and then we lost Doris. She was, however, found again having only gone into a shop to buy bread while we were not looking!

A good camping spot became a problem and the one we chose though picturesque swarmed with midges that nearly ate us alive, a gentle rain having livened them up.

Distance covered: 40 miles

WEDNESDAY 20TH SEPTEMBER

Doris descending at full pelt

FORT WILLIAM – ONICH – BALLACHULISH – PASS OF GLENCOE – BRIDGE OF ORCHY

The road now ran for some miles besides Loch Linnhe and through Onich, and a ferry across the top of Loch Leven brought us to Ballachulish – a drab slate quarrying village. We had lunch at a refreshment house by the station before tackling the Pass of Glencoe.

It was fitting that this glorious and tragic pass should be done in stormy weather. It rained relentlessly all the way up (all ridden) and, after stopping for a short time at the top, the weather drove us into capes again as soon as we had started down the other side. For many miles of steep down grade the surface was vile. Doris recklessly went full pelt regardless of the bones of 'Augusta' (her Ellis cycle). I followed her as closely as possible but Ron was more careful and soon dropped a long way behind.

After about ten miles of this rough stuff the road improved and we began to look for a camping site. A farm close by the picturesque Bridge of Orchy attracted us and we *'came to Leros'* as usual[9]. It was a pleasant spot with a roaring torrent on one side of us and a broad shallow river at the end of the field where we camped. There were no eggs at the farm and I went to the village shop and paid ½ for six articles, thereby drawing down the wrath of Doris on my head. We seemed to have brought some of the midges with us from our last camp and had a rather itchy night. *Distance covered: 24 miles*

THURSDAY 21ST SEPTEMBER

Poor Doris!

BRIDGE OF ORCHY – TYNDRUM – GLEN DOCHART – LOCHEARNHEAD – STRATHYRE – CALLANDER

The usual mist soon gave way to sunshine. As Ron and I were attending to the washing up Doris wandered away and thought she would like to cross the river but about half way across she slipped and suffered total immersion. She divested herself of her clothes and donned her bathing costume getting additional warmth from my sleeping bag draped round her neck. Ron found

9 It's possible that Charles is referring to the Greek Island of Leros here, a famous sanctuary of Artemis.

a line upon which to hang her wet clothes but after two hours her clothes were only partially dried and she had to wear them still damp.

This incident shortened the day's run and we decided to cut out the Trossachs, our routes being through Tyndrum, Crianlarich, Glen Dochart, Killin Junction, Lochearnhead and Strathyre along Loch Lubnaig and the Pass of Leny. About a mile from Callander, Ron ran into my back wheel and shed three spokes so we had to camp there and then, striking quite a pleasant spot but the good lady at the farm was very anxious to know where Doris came in the scheme of things.

Distance covered: 40 miles

FRIDAY 22ND SEPTEMBER

In search of spokes
CALLANDER – DUNBLANE – STIRLING – DOUNE – FALKIRK – LINLITHGOW

The first thing after breakfast was for Ron to go into Callander in search of spokes while Doris and I struck the tents and packed up. He was lucky and we got on our way by midday. We went on through Callander via Doune and Dunblane to Stirling and spent the afternoon in Stirling Castle but apart from the view we were not much impressed. Had tea in Stirling and continued via Fallin, Airth, Grangemouth and Falkirk and camped at a farm just short of Linlithgow surrounded by all kinds of farmyard animals. Duck eggs were a compensation.

Distance covered: 39 miles

SATURDAY 23RD SEPTEMBER

Joining the hustle and bustle
LINLITHGOW – PHILPSTOUN – KIRKLISTON – EDINBURGH

We left the farmyard camp to the great regret of the cows, calves, sheep, pigs, turkeys, geese, ducks and hens en route for Edinburgh via Linlithgow, Philpstoun, Kirkliston and Corstorphine. At Edinburgh our first thought was to find somewhere to stop for the night. Doris decided that the cheapest place would be best and in due course we found it at Barlows, 21 Broughton Place which did us famously.

Although we had to take train home tomorrow Doris had made up our minds to make the most of the little time left to us by exploring the city. In the evening we strolled the floodlit gardens of Princes Street and joined in the hustle and bustle of the packed streets. Before going to bed Ron informed us of the result of his camping audit, which cost us £1.4.5[10] for the fortnight's camping feed. A sobering thought.

Distance covered: 19 miles

SUNDAY 24TH SEPTEMBER

We left Edinburgh homeward bound on the 'Royal Scot' in the pouring rain, sad to see 'Auld Reekie'[11] fade away in the smoke. A wonderful and glorious tour in the most exhilarating countryside I have ever seen. Although the tracks and gradients were testing, Scotland was a cycling paradise and I vow to return once north of the border. Tiring journey home but finally arrived with all cycles and persons in one piece. Bade farewell to Ron and Doris and duly arrived back home to letters and the luxury of a real bed without the accustomed noise of various farmyard animals.

Distance cycled: 14 miles

EPILOGUE

This last passage brings to an end Charles' recording of his adventures in the golden age of cycling. We may never be sure why Charles stopped writing his accounts of cycling around the country, but it may have something to do with his companion on this last trip to the romantic, bonnie shores of Scotland. Rather than cycle alone Charles would require a bicycle 'made for two' in the future as his 'Daisy' (in this case Doris) gave him her answer true.

Charles James Pope married Doris Willson in November 1933 at Stokenchurch Methodist Church, Buckinghamshire, thus ending his bachelor days at the ripe old age of 54. I wonder if they had the reception at 'The Swan' Burford! The happy couple went on to adopt three children and continued to live in Oxfordshire.

---

10 One pound, four shillings and five pence
11 An old nickname for Edinburgh, on account of the Old Town's pungent mix of sewage and smoke

POSTSCRIPT

Charles' disaffection with the motor car proved to be, sadly, well placed as he was to lose his life on the road whilst cycling. It is believed that Charles was killed by a driver of an unknown vehicle whilst returning from watching his sons perform at the Long Crendon School Sports Day. Charles was a governor at the school.

Details of his death were recorded in the Oxford Mail on the 26th May 1951, the day after the accident. A lorry driver found Charles lying in the road at around 4 p.m. Unfortunately, at the same time, his youngest son, Michael Pope passed the scene on the double decker school bus and realised it was his father who was receiving treatment at the roadside.

Charles' untimely death had a huge impact upon his family and left his widow, Doris, to bring up their three children alone.

ACKNOWLEDGEMENTS

Although I have adored finding, researching and publishing my previous books, I felt more closely connected to Charles as an author as we share a common passion, cycling. Whether Charles began cycling as a means to escape his experiences and memories of the Great War or it was the allure of adventure on the open roads we will never know. However, I am extremely grateful that Charles recorded his cycling exploits in such well observed detail that it transports you back to the 'Golden Age of Cycling'.

I am indebted to Michael Pope for entrusting me with publishing his father's diaries. Michael has been extremely supportive and helpful throughout the publishing process and I know that he is very proud to see his father's treasured diaries in print.

I cannot praise Blink Publishing, 535 and Joel Simons enough for having the insight and passion to transform the diaries into this wonderful book. They have made the publishing process such an enjoyable experience – from the design of the cover to the format of the contents – everything is what I dearly hoped it would be.

Although a creature rarely seen outside the world of publishing, an agent is the unsung catalyst that makes the whole book process work. I am extremely fortunate to have the best of agents, Gordon Wise of

ACKNOWLEDGEMENTS

Curtis Brown and without Gordon neither I nor Charles would be in this privileged position.

There is a cast of supportive persons who have greatly assisted me with this project. I would like to thank John Brownfield Pope and Shayne Brownfield Pope for their help in providing the background to the Pope family and businesses; Liz Wood and the staff of Modern Records Centre, University of Warwick for allowing me to explore the Cyclist's Touring Club archive; Niall Harman of Curtis Brown for all his valuable assistance and expertise; Nathan Joyce for his editing prowess; Amanda Robb for her timely roadside assistance; Timothy Xu of the Oxfordshire History Centre and of course my most supportive partner Joan Bower who has lived through another publishing adventure with me.

I hope Charles' cycling adventures have inspired you to take to the roads and cycle paths and discover the hidden gems this wonderful country has to offer, not forgetting to have the odd Bass along the way. Cheers and happy cycling!

Shaun Sewell
Northumberland
April 2018